CRITICAL ISSUES
IN AGING POLICY

SOME OTHER VOLUMES IN THE
SAGE FOCUS EDITIONS

CRITICAL ISSUES IN AGING POLICY

Linking Research and Values

Edited by
Edgar F. Borgatta
Rhonda J.V. Montgomery

SAGE PUBLICATIONS
The Publishers of Professional Social Science
Newbury Park   Beverly Hills   London   New Delhi

For information address:

SAGE Publications, Inc.
2111 West Hillcrest Drive
Newbury Park, California 91320

SAGE Publications Inc.
275 South Beverly Drive
Beverly Hills
California 90212

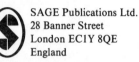

SAGE Publications Ltd.
28 Banner Street
London EC1Y 8QE
England

SAGE PUBLICATIONS India Pvt. Ltd.
M-32 Market
Greater Kailash I
New Delhi 110 048 India

Printed in the United States of America

Library of Congress Cataloging-in-Publication Data

Critical issues in aging policy.

(Sage focus editions ; v. 86)
1. Aged--Government policy--United States.
I. Borgatta, Edgar F., 1924-   . II. Montgomery,
Rhonda J. V.
HQ1064.U5C75   1987   305.2'6'0973   87-4813
ISBN 0-8039-2895-5
ISBN 0-8039-2896-3 (pbk.)

Contents

1

Aging Policy
and Societal Values

EDGAR F. BORGATTA and RHONDA J. V. MONTGOMERY

The field of aging research has probably been stimulated more from the applied needs of practicing professions and concerned individuals than some other areas of research in the social sciences. In fact, some academic areas still resist the notion that the field of aging deserves specialized attention. So, in departments of economics, sociology, anthropology, and psychology, courses specifically directed to older adults and the later aging processes are often in competition with a wide variety of other specialized courses and may not be part of the regular curriculum. There are obvious exceptions, such as special courses on memory in psychology; but, in general, psychology, for example, has not moved to give the kind of emphasis to the older ages that it has to childhood or adolescence.

The stimulus from the practicing professions and interested individuals may have created a situation in which assumptions and hypotheses have been based on generalizations from few cases. After a flurry of attention to the growing field of aging, recently some corrective has been applied. For example, George Maddox is quoted as saying "the good news is that some of the bad news has been wrong." The same report indicated that "one speaker after another echoed his view that we need no longer fear hurtling through the years toward an inevitable, feeble grayness" (*APA Monitor,* July 1985). But, the more telling question that needs to be answered is how and why the "bad news" was given credibility by researchers in the first place. Post hoc it is not possible to answer such a question with any finality, but it can be repeated that social scientists did not spur the research interests. Policymakers, including agencies created by them such as the Administration on Aging and the National Institute on Aging, have generated interest with funds but with no specific agenda. Many of us are willing to accept a problem as plausibly stated if there is money to support the research.

Although this may be too cynical a view of the process, the influence of policymakers on the definition and study of aging policy is unmistakable and to a large degree has resulted in a narrow view of policy analysis. Policy has been bounded by our culture and debated within the confines of the values that currently prevail. Attention has been directed toward little problems that require fine tuning the existing systems while issues resulting from major uncontrolled, worldwide changes have been largely ignored. As social scientists have been occupied with the design and evaluation of programs that will serve as Band-Aids to immediate problems, the more basic issues and questions concerning values and social systems go unexplored.

The World Context

In our consideration of policy we hedge in a way that is common in American society: by dealing with many of the issues that are the subject matter of legislation and of the practicing professions. We do obviously go beyond the narrow meaning of policy in the chapters in this volume, but we do not take the broadest view. The broadest view requires us to consider a world perspective and our place in the world. We will note below some demographic facts about the United States, but let us first give attention to the world perspective.

The postponement of death, or as otherwise stated, the increase in life expectancy is a worldwide phenomenon, although changes in death rates on which computation of life expectancy depends have not been uniform in different nations and cultures. The major changes in death rates can be noted in different terms: by the persons affected, by the mechanisms involved, or by the disease processes. The most dramatic shifts seen as critical have been those in the reduction of infant and child mortality. Similarly, there have been major reductions of maternal deaths. The mechanisms involved have generally been described as changes in sanitation and hygiene. The diseases controlled have been infections and communicable diseases. These mechanisms, while having some costs in economic terms and of culture change are generally available in a worldwide sense, and so population shifts have been worldwide rather than restricted to any group of nations. While the death rates in underdeveloped countries may not approach those of the more favored nations, the changes in death rates have had massive impacts in changes in population size.

If one looks at the changes in population that are projected, the changes in terms of older persons are completely overshadowed by what is projected to happen to the world population as a whole. The change process has been named the "demographic transition," and not all nations appear to undergo the transition in the same way. However, the process is simple to understand and describe. As death rates are reduced, particularly with reduction of infant and child mortality, the population begins to increase rapidly because of the excess births over deaths.

If there is a notion that the population increase is to be controlled, the control is seen to occur with the decrease of birth rates. In some nations the demographic transition has occurred quickly, as in the case of Japan. China, with its new and forcefully stated policy of one child families, will obviously move to the stage of low fertility and low death rates, the end stage of the demographic transition. However, much of the world will not follow the example of the quickly industrializing Japan or of the planned control of China, and we have already seen great increases in population sizes in other areas. This is reflected most importantly in the underdeveloped nations, and is expected to be most dramatically visible there in the next 40 years. Consider that the population of the "more developed regions" was estimated to be about 945 million in 1960, and in 1980 was about 1.135 billion, or an increase of about 20 percent. By contrast, the population of the "less developed regions" was estimated to be about 2.045 billion in 1960, and in 1980 was about 3.315 billion—a much greater increase of about 60 percent. More directly to the point, we have recently seen the problems of starvation in Africa. That region went from 275 million to 475 million in the same period—an increase of over 70 percent—and the projected increase to year 2025 is to 1.640 billion. The population of the more developed regions is expected to be 1.395 billion and of the less developed regions 6.780 billion. If there are potential pressures on food and other resources today, the world situation is likely to be even more difficult with regard to availability and use of resources then. If we are to be realistic in planning our resource uses we will need to take the world situation more into account (United Nations, 1985).

Possibly it is an issue that we wish to avoid, but how much more valuable is a human life in the United States than one in Africa? We may be able to avoid such questions for the time being, but it may not be possible to do so in the future. Therefore it is necessary for some attention to be addressed to this world perspective as we look at our national perspective. However, as will be clear in the chapter on health and health care, the world implications of what we feel is a baseline level of care and support are not easily masked. We spend billions of dollars each year to provide dialysis therapy for kidney failure to virtually all possible cases in the United States. This is a state-ment of social value for those within the nation. Similarly, it is becoming more universal that all older persons in the condition of needing nursing home care can obtain it. Such trends may appear to reflect a humanitarian and desirable policy direction, but the trends also quickly bring us to the question, At what point is it appropriate to sustain life, and even more radically, are there points at which even positive action toward termination—euthanasia—may become viable? Even to raise such questions is considered improper and immoral by some; but they are being raised, and the world context suggests that they will need to be examined even more in the future.

Defining Aging Policy

While we have suggested the broad world perspective for policy consideration above, it is appropriate to move to more immediate con-siderations at this point. In the United States the basis for concern with aging policy has been the demographic trends viewed in historical perspective and the projections for future growth of the elderly popula-tion. Even within this national context a broad perspective of policy is desirable. To a large degree however, concern with aging policy has been limited by a narrow perspective that views aging policy as an arena for study and manipulation apart from broader policy issues that involve basic social systems. Unfortunately, this perspective has lead to narrow discussions of aging policy that fail to acknowledge or ques-tion the values that are defining policy. Here we opt to analyze aging policy as an element of larger public policy and a product of societal values that are sometimes in conflict and always subject to change. This broadened perspective adds clarity to our understanding of the issues and leads to recognition of a larger number of options for future change. In the next two sections we provide major examples of analyses to illustrate this broad approach.

Economic Support Systems and Aging

Concern with public policy in a society that has so many sources of values, as does the United States, requires tact and delicacy. The role of the social scientist in public policy analysis can be precarious, particularly when one goes beyond simply describing the situation as it is. But even describing the situation becomes a delicate matter when one compares statements of policy with the implementation of policy.

It does not take great wisdom to recognize that the more general the statement of a value, the easier it is to state in a platitudinous way so that very few people are likely to disagree with it. Few would disagree, for example, with a statement such as "Life should be highly valued in society." But, with more specific statements of that particular value, some massive disagreements exist in American society today. The diversity of positions is such that any representation of there being only two sides to the issue is generally naive and an oversimplification. So, any attempt to suggest what the dominant themes for this society are is fraught with difficulty and not likely to be successful. Still, is there no underlying agreement about what the proper values in society should be? Surely this is not the case and, if nothing else, it needs to be observed that behavior is relatively narrowly bound in terms of what is tolerable and what is not. Possibly some reasonable thread can be outlined.

If the task is not impossible, let us emphasize that it still will be difficult. We may look at one such attempt as the jumping off point for the comments that will be made here. It does not require cynicism to suggest that a presidential commission is influential only to the extent that the president is willing to recognize its work after the fact. If there has been a change in presidents, the amount of recognition a presidential commission will get is likely to be diminished. Still, ordinarily such groups are brought together in a fashion that is presumed to maximize objectivity, goodwill, and other positive qualities. A presidential commission that has not received a great deal of attention is the one for

A National Agenda for the Eighties (1980). Here the report from this presidential commission will be used as a reference point with regard to some values seen to govern policy. The presentation of these values, however, has to be seen in a utopian context. If the values were in place, obviously, they would not need to be proposed as an agenda for the eighties. On the other hand, one may quickly ask whether or not these values could have been the agenda for the seventies, or the sixties, or for any other period. The answer probably is that the specifics that are written into the agenda are timely and would have seemed inappropriate (or radical) in some earlier periods.

The values that are suggested as those to which the nation should strive in the eighties are "a guaranteed minimum income, a coherent urban policy, an effective educational system, universal health insurance, and the advancement of civil rights" (President's Commission, 1980: 58). Such lists exist in myriad places in our philosophical and historical writings about injustice and the good life, and so there is nothing new in the basic identification. What is new in the treatment by the presidential commission is the explicit attention to the failings of the current system historically. The failings, if they can be summarized briefly, result from the fact that the system is an accumulation of politically acceptable approaches to particular problems, an uncoordinated collection. The commission states:

> Analyzing the American welfare system requires the skills of an archeologist, the ability to sift patiently through layer upon layer of government programs. Sorting out the layers, one finds at least five distinct types of welfare programs. They vary by the era of their creation, and by whether they offer the poor money, advice, or a particular commodity. These types of programs include *aid to the poor,* which are programs that offer money and advice, such as Aid to Families with Dependent Children (AFDC) program; *social insurance programs,* like Social Security, that provide money as a right; *government aid to purchase essential commodities,* as in food stamps; government provision of minimum standards, such as minimum wages; and *government provision of opportunity,* such as vocational rehabilitation (1980: 72-73).

What is of particular interest with regard to the presidential commission's report is the fact that the recommendation it makes is relatively radical.

After reviewing these various reform proposals, the commission recommends that Congress legislate a minimum security income for all Americans. The income guarantee should be related to the poverty level—within a possible range, as determined by Congress, of from two-thirds to three-quarters of that amount—and the tax on earnings should be relatively low—perhaps 50 percent. The new program would replace the current AFDC, food stamp, and general assistance programs. It would provide the sort of permanent, effective reform that would obviate the need for new crash programs, such as the recently proposed "energy stamps."

The minimum security income would not serve as a substitute or replacement for all existing or proposed welfare programs. Because we recognize the importance of the gains made in the past decade, the Supplemental Security Income program would remain in place for the elderly and disabled—groups that require a higher guarantee because they are not expected to work (1980: 75).

Several things should be recognized in the proposal. First, the way in which the income guarantee is to be implemented is not mentioned in the proposal. From the prior discussion, one would assume that the method of implementation would be through a negative income tax. If this is the case, then the proposal is really not very different from many others that have been made in the past. Second, the need for politically acceptable and timely approaches to particular problems is emphasized by the commission itself immediately by placing a footnote on the reference to energy stamps, which are seen to require some thought since Congress will not be able to act immediately on more general welfare reform. An additional recognition of special problems is further given in the support for continuation of the Supplemental Security Income (SSI) program, which is directed to the elderly and the disabled. It becomes obvious that in attempting to be practical, compromises are involved, and that building in exceptions may soon vitiate the entire proposed change.

From the point of view of the external observer, obviously, one question that remains is whether or not the alternative of the negative income tax is the only one available for the income guarantee. That this is not the only alternative is easy to document by the general literature in economics when one refers to the particular area of welfare reform. There have been a number of presentations of "universal" or "entitlement" alternatives such as presented in the discussions by

Garfinkel (1978) and Theobald (1976). These proposals most generally are associated with a credit income tax system rather than a negative income tax, and the tax credits would be available to all persons. The reason that appears to be the most prominent for why people do not look at the universal proposals is the immediate implication that if such a system existed, an overwhelming response of people would be to stop working. Again, from the point of view of an outside observer, this suggests that the belief that people are intrinsically lazy and inclined to malinger is stronger than the belief that everyone should have a minimum income. More to the point, the values are combined in some statements into the more complex form: Everyone is entitled to a minimum income, but only if they are not lazy and do not malinger. A relatively recent statement of this type has, in fact, been phrased as saying that the "truly needy" in society will get attention. Historically, this latter position is that of "charity," and as such it should be bountifully clear that it is *not* compatible with a notion of a "right" to a minimum income.

The reason the credit income tax system must be considered as an alternative is that it may alleviate some of the consequences that the negative income tax does not. The most immediate and most important of these problems is the one that is generally associated with issues of marginal taxation. If a credit income tax system is utilized, then there is no special penalty of high tax rates that apply to the earnings of persons who are in the lowest income brackets. That is, income would continue to be taxed as it has been, and this system would be applied to all persons. The contrast is the welfare person who may be taxed at a marginal rate of 100 percent or 50 percent for each dollar earned. The ramifications of this difference are not elaborated here, but what is immediately obvious is that the credit income tax system will not remove the motivation to work for additional income. To the contrary, it will increase the motivation to work because the potential penalization from taxation will be reduced. Thus, contrary to the value expressed that such a system may tend to encourage laziness and malingering, it probably would motivate people to work, especially those in the lowest income brackets.

The president's commission notes by way of example that a minimum security income guarantee would replace such current programs as AFDC, food stamps, and general assistance programs. Additionally, no crash programs such as responses to energy shortage would need to be taken into account. It is not known why the president's commission would select these examples, or why it would stop at these. Certainly additional consequences will arise from such a change, and they should be considered. There is the possibility that people who might have been expected to be liberal in examining such alternatives would have to reexamine their usual positions. For example, one relatively obvious possible ramification is that unemployment insurance would become unnecessary if its objective is to provide a minimum income. The purpose of unemployment insurance, under the circumstances of a universal minimum income system, could be to maintain a *level* of income. Such insurance might then be desirable, but would it be necessary? Another economic consequence to consider is whether, under such a system, the legislation of minimum wages is desirable or necessary. These questions are not answered here, but they are raised to show that what might be considered liberal under one system may look quite different under another.

It is appropriate now to turn to the relevance of the minimum security income for the elderly. The president's commission suggests that to recognize the gains made in the past, the Supplemental Security Income program should remain in place to provide a higher guarantee for the elderly who are not expected to work. At minimum this is a bad phrasing of the suggestion, since the idea of a minimum security income is that it should provide a minimum for everyone. If it does not, then anyone with a problem becomes a special case, and special programs would continue to be needed. This points to a policy question that is a very important consideration in how resources are allocated. Should the elderly be treated as different from any other age group? This is not the same question as some people seem to imply in their definition of the elderly, namely: Should the frail and disabled elderly be treated differently from the well in younger ages? It should be noted that if one is speaking about the well elderly in a system that has a minimum security income guarantee, then the options available to the elderly are really no different from those that are available to any other age group. Indeed, under such a system, the definitions of retirement and participation in the labor force might have quite different meanings than they do under the current system. It is not necessary to assume that people would not save in order to provide for their retirement years, but at the same time it raises the question of the place of accumulation of wealth, insurance, and other such matters with regard to planning for the future.

One of the suggestions associated with the proposals for guaranteed minimum security incomes is that it would eliminate the need for many special services, particularly those that are associated with maintaining minimum standards of living. Duplication and overlapping efforts could presumably be minimized. One of the consequences is a possible saving in the structure of government by way of simplification and elimination of government agencies and corresponding employees.

This points to the notion that welfare programs have two constituencies—those who are the beneficiaries or clients of the program, and those who are the administrators of the program. When the world of political realities is brought to bear, it is frequently noted that great resistance to welfare reform is found in the ranks of those who administer programs. Policymakers receive advice and are responsive to many types of demands that are placed on society, and it is not suggested that any change in society can be effected without some dislocation. Fortunately, the comments here are not directed to the pragmatic implementation of a proposal but to the analysis of some of the issues involved and the context in which a more general view of policy can be placed.

The issue of whether or not older persons should be treated the same as young persons is immediately involved in looking at SSI but also at social security more generally. It is now clear to most persons that the social security system is a tax transfer system, and *not an insurance system.* The President's Commission on Pension Policy, which was almost as ignored as the first president's commission we have discussed above, gives some recognition to this problem. The President's Commission on Pension Policy makes recommendations that can be tied directly to the issues of a guaranteed minimum security income. For example, if the social security system is a tax transfer system, then as has been noted elsewhere (Borgatta and Loeb, 1981), it immediately raises the question of why there should be differential benefits on the basis of the taxes originally paid. This is an important issue and one that is vital to the consideration of *costs,* both of the social security system and also the possible costs of a guaranteed minimum security income system. Phrased most simply, if everyone were at a minimum level, the social security system would not be under threat of bankruptcy. Such a statement may appear harsh for those who have believed the myth of insurance, but an objective analysis of what is going on seems to require naming the processes for what they are and trying to describe them objectively. It is not a trivial question to raise: Should persons who pay more taxes get more benefits? It is not the purpose here to answer the question of whether they *should,* but to note that society does operate in this way at many turns. For example, those who are socioeconomically most favored are also those who historically have gotten the most benefit out of certain governmentally supported systems, such as education. In the example of education, however, the benefit is received through taking advantage of available resources and not through a direct return, as is the case in social security. Among its recommendations the President's Commission on Pension Policy suggests bolstering *individual* private pension programs and moving them in the direction of individual accounts. An actual move in this direction has occurred with the establishment of the generalization of IRAs, although these are with minor exception available only to those who have earned income. The direction of this thrust, however, is extremely important since it raises many questions about the values involved in such savings. For example, and this has been raised as an issue under other circumstances, it raises the question of how vesting has operated in the past. In the past, industrial organizations and unions have controlled such benefits through vesting and individuals have not owned the benefits as a matter of wages.

The question of cost is not trivial, and no practical answer is provided here for what a minimum security income system would cost. However, some indications exist that can be discussed reasonably. For example, we do have some baseline types of information, such as the guidelines published in the April 9 *Federal Register* which indicate that for 1982 the poverty income for a non-farm family of one person is $4,680, for two persons is $6,220, and for four persons is $9,300. Estimates of the numbers and proportions of persons who are below the poverty line are also available. What these estimates are, of course, depends upon the frame of reference that is utilized. For example, while an estimate for 1979 indicates that 11.1 percent of the nation's population was below the poverty line, taking non-cash benefits into account would reduce that percentage substantially. With regard to the elderly, 14.7 percent in poverty in 1979 presumably would be cut by 69.5 percent to approximately 4.5 percent (*Older American Reports,* April 23, 1982; p. 8). The issue here is not the appropriateness of this analysis or the exact percentage, or whether these are the latest figures. The point is that the percentage is relatively small in any case, so that if there is a concept of additional cost of something like a guaranteed minimum income system, it only involves the additional expenditure for that relatively small percentage that needs to be raised above the minimum. That cost, however, can be balanced against additional savings that might be possible by transformation of the social security system in the direction indicated earlier, that is, into an equal benefits-oriented system.

It is clear from this discussion of economic support programs that when aging policy is discussed from the vantage point of broader public policy, the issues to be addressed are not restricted to alternatives defined by prevailing systems and values, but include basic values that, if questioned, might lead to changes that may even be radical. The importance and benefits of approaching issues in aging policy from a more broadly based perspective is further illustrated in the following discussion of family responsibility.

Family Responsibility and Aging Policy

The relationship between public policy and the role of the family in providing care for the elderly is a second broad policy area that begs attention from social scientists. Over the past decade a large literature has developed that describes patterns of family assistance to older persons and documents the prevalence of family members as the primary caregivers (Horowitz, 1985; Shanas, 1979). This recognition of the family as the primary source of long-term care services has led to questions about the ability of the family as an institution to provide these services, and has prompted analysts and policymakers to advocate programs and policies aimed at supporting the family in its efforts (Horowitz, 1985; Sussman, 1979; Whitfield, 1981; Callahan et al., 1980).

This growing interest in the family as a primary source of services has prompted a number of social scientists to look at public policy for the aged and its impacts on the family. These analysts have raised questions about apparent value dilemmas. For example, Achenbaum (1983), in his analysis of federal policy for the elderly, argues that the value dilemma is whether or not the individual or the family unit should be the focus. In agreement with numerous other scholars Achenbaum concludes that governmental policy in the United States has never simultaneously taken the needs of the individual and the family into consideration. Legislation has been directed to the individual elderly person despite wide acclaim for the support of the family.

A second approach to analyzing public policy as it relates to the family's role in long-term care has been to conceptualize the dilemma as one of achieving a balance of responsibility between the family and the state. Litwak and Figueria (1968) maintain that caregiving functions must be shared since families and bureaucracies are differentially effective in performing certain types of tasks. Maroney (1980) analyzes the relationship between the family and the state in terms of level of transfer of responsibility, and is concerned about whether the transfer is supportive or substitutive. Nelson (1982) suggests that policies and programs may complement the family role, support the family role, or substitute for the family role. He argues that services should substitute or replace nonviable families and should facilitate and complement the effort of the modified extended family. The underlying assumption of these analysts is that both the family and the state have responsibility for the provision of care to dependent elders. The dilemma that faces policymakers is that of appropriately balancing the responsibility.

Unfortunately, whether the value dilemma has been viewed as that of individual needs versus family needs or as that of balancing family and state responsibilities, previous analyses have been limited by their implicit acceptance of the underlying value imposed by current and proposed policies. These analyses do not question whether the family members should be responsible for the care of older physically dependent persons. Should individuals be held responsible for the care of relatives based upon their status as spouse or child? Rephrased from the perspective of the dependent elder, the question is, Should an individual's right to public dependency be determined by the presence or absence of a spouse or relative?

If the analysis of policy as it relates to the family begins by exploring this underlying value, a more basic dilemma can be identified, as well as options for policy change that are not limited to the redistribution of responsibility. However, to address this value, analysts must be able to look beyond the existing structure and be able to question personal value systems.

Just as policymakers impose their own values on legislation, social scientists tend to impose their values on the study of policy. For example, researchers and analysts have been quick to use the fact that the family is the major source of care for the elderly as evidence that most families *choose* to care for older members (Noelker, 1984). This "choice" has in turn been interpreted as public support for the idea that families should be responsible for elders (Maroney, 1980). This interpretation is very comfortable since it does not require questioning the basic structure that has been established for assisting the elderly. The only questions that need be raised concern the appropriate distribution of responsibility within the existing structure.

In contrast, when an analysis of policy begins by questioning the family's obligation to care for an elder, the patterns of caregiving can be interpreted differently. The predominant role of the family might be better viewed as the consequence of policy that imposes family responsibility rather than as an indicator of chosen values. Indeed, findings from numerous studies that have looked at caregiving patterns would suggest that the greater the choice a family member has, the less likely that family member will be to provide personal care for an elderly dependent person. Several studies have noted that spouses perform more tasks and provide more intensive care than do adult children (Cantor, 1983; Soldo and Myllyluoma, 1983; Montgomery and Borgatta, 1985). Certainly, one interpretation of this difference is that the two types of relationships are qualitatively different and spouses *choose* to do more. A second interpretation, and one that deserves serious consideration, is that spouses have less choice. Since the primary criteria for conferring the status of public dependence upon the elderly is the older person's level of income, the elderly do not have a right to assistance unless they are in financial need. Physical limitations that prevent an older person from performing daily living tasks are not sufficient criteria for obtaining public assistance. Persons needing this assistance must either pay for it, obtain it from a family member, or reduce their income to meet the income eligibility criteria for public dependency. It is clear that there are different consequences of this policy for adult children than for spouses. Since the income and financial resources of a spouse are tied to those of the dependent individual, their choice is to pay for tasks, perform the caregiving tasks, or share the poverty that is required to obtain assistance. In some situations even sharing a low income is not sufficient, although it is necessary. It is not uncommon for programs to require the absence of a family member in the household before assistance is provided. The options for adult children are to pay for assistance, let the elder pay for assistance, perform the helping tasks, or allow the older person's income to diminish to the point of meeting income eligibility criteria. Children not only have more choices, but they are not required to share in the poverty that is necessary to obtain services. The tendency of children to perform fewer and less intensive tasks and to utilize more formal services might well reflect this greater range of choices.

A number of other research findings support the argument that family members do not care for physically dependent elders because they value this role, but do so because other options are unavailable. Children who are primary caregivers tend to seek and use more formal services than do spouses. This pattern likely reflects the greater resources of children and the ability to use the elder's resources to pay for services without costs to the caregiver. Social class differences have also been found in caregiving patterns. Middle-class children provide more financial assistance and working-class children provide more direct services. This, too, suggests that when options are available, direct caregiving is not the option that is most often chosen.

Additional evidence that would suggest that caregiving is not a choice based on personal values but a consequence of values imposed by policy rests in the large literature concerned with caregiver burden. The most widely reported care-related costs are the loss of personal time and restriction of personal activities (Archbold, 1983; Frankfather et al., 1981; Horowitz, 1985). This burden or strain has consistently been shown to be greater for spouses than for children who can choose not to incur the costs (Horowitz, 1985). Spouses assume more tasks and greater costs because they are more obligated. This fact is supported by findings from our recent study that indicated that spouses reported a greater sense of *obligation* to care for the dependent person than did children. Interestingly, spouses did not report greater affection for the elder (Montgomery and Borgatta, 1985).

When considered together, the findings concerned with caregiving patterns and burden that have been described in the literature suggest that the role of caregiver is not assumed because of personal values but, instead, is assumed as a consequence of values imposed by public policy. If this is true, social scientists who purport an interest in the welfare of the family cannot defend their failure to question the assumption that families should be responsible by asserting that the value reflects individual choice.

The unwillingness to question the basic value that the family is responsible for the care of the elderly might better be attributed to an idealistic and sometimes romantic view of the family. Despite media hype about the disintegration of the American family, increased divorce rates, and family violence, most people associate the term family with images of love, warmth, sharing, and happiness. Social scientists are equally, if not more, prone to this perspective than is the general public. As a result, caregiving is often portrayed as an altruistic activity that a family member engages in because of love and affection. Although social scientists readily discuss the sacrifices and burdens of caregivers, the possibility that family members despise the role or would prefer not to provide care at all is really never entertained. Certainly there is considerable focus on services and programs that help ease the burden and strain, but there appears to be no recognition of the fact that many people, if given a true choice, would prefer to abstain from the caregiving role altogether. The more common picture that is painted is one of a loving spouse who tends to the needs of the disabled person and only gives up this role when personal resources are exhausted. The facts that the disabled person no longer functions as a companion, is demanding, and may even be abusive, are rarely acknowledged. While caregiving may be a choice when the disabled person responds with love and actively participates in a mutually rewarding relationship, there is considerable reason to believe that for many people caregiving is a relationship of bondage from which a spouse is unable to escape. Perhaps the most compelling support of this scenario are the findings from a recent study by the authors that show that the group of caregivers who had the least burden and the highest scores on a morale scale after 12 months of participation were those caregivers whose elderly relative died during that period (Montgomery and Borgatta, 1985). Caregivers whose relative had moved to the nursing home faired better than did those who continued to care for the older person. Regardless of the type of support service that was offered to a caregiver, the data suggest that the best way to relieve the caregiver of burden and to increase morale is to relieve the family of the responsibility for care.

If the obligation of the family for caring for dependent elders is questioned, it becomes clear that the basic dilemma is one of balancing the individual rights of family members with the public purse. Both policy and programs currently being advocated to "support" the family appear to protect the public purse as the cost of care for the elderly is delegated to a small segment of the population who are primarily older women. If this choice is questioned, then the types of policy options that can be entertained are expanded beyond those of sharing ratios between the family and the state. The question becomes, How does the state assume responsibility for the care of elderly persons who are unable to care for themselves? It is at this point that our discussion returns to the more basic value dilemma of entitlement versus charity. Are persons who are unable to care for themselves entitled to state resources? If so, how does the state assure this support?

It is not surprising that our discussion of policy related to the family of the elderly has come full circle to raise questions that parallel those raised by our discussion of economic supports, since both issues are tied to prevailing values. It is the failure of social scientists to recognize the fact that policy is grounded in values that has lead to narrow views of aging policy that tend to restrict our understanding of the issues. More important, failure to recognize values as the basis of policy decisions has impeded analysts' abilities to identify likely and/or viable options for policy change.

Changing Values and Policy

One of the facts of life that seems to be recognized most often only as a matter of convenience is that values change. There is often great emphasis on a given value until, for some reason, it is no longer considered to be all that important. So, policymakers should always be prepared to take a broad perspective. Things change, and thus a narrow perspective in approaches to policy is bound to lead to not anticipating changing needs and new demands. This is easily shown in major areas where there has been dramatic change. It is beyond the memory of most, but the institution of income taxes, something that had not existed at all, is a policy change in this century. Change in the tax structure, along with many other changes of what is to be controlled by government, have continued to occur with an acceleration during this century. The development of social security is now a half century old, and it has surely not reached its final form.

We point to this transitional nature of policy, of its propensity to change as the world and the nation change, to emphasize that at the "right" time things that would have been unthinkable at an earlier time suddenly can be defined as appropriate. So, for example, the Reagan Administration's emphasis on tax reform has involved many changes, some of them quite different from recent expectations. But some more common suggestions may be more radical in terms of their consequences. For example, in the debate of how new taxes should be developed, one suggestion that has been advanced is the use of a value-added tax, varieties of which have been used in Europe. This would be a change, but not a radical one for policy. However, the common criticism that such a tax would be regressive as it is basically a consumption (sales) tax requires that a method be advanced to protect the poor. In response, the Harvard economist Lester C. Thurow (*Seattle Times,* March 23, 1986) suggests a refund procedure. It is the implicit requirement of participation by all persons that is radical, because it effectively constitutes a continuous registration procedure for all persons or families in the United States. Although this development of continuous registration has been progressing through not only the tax system, social security, voter registration, and so forth, when fully applied such a system could eventually lead to enormous economies of record keeping. But, at this stage the notion that every person in the United States should be registered in some way is apparently alarming to many. Such a value may shift, quickly, as the complexity of government and its involvement in all aspects of life continues.

We make the above point because continuous registration is a fact in some other nations, and, for example, what are public records and private records may change in concept. In some nations it is possible to go check what income taxes one's neighbor has paid, as it is public record, while in the United States it is a closely guarded item of privacy. So, what of values in other domains? We have "peculiar" histories in this country such as the constitutional amendment remembered as "prohibition," which persons in other nations find difficult to understand. The United States orientation to some aspects of fertility control, such as contraceptives and abortion, was difficult for some to understand in earlier times. And, relevant here, some aspects of our attitudes and behavior with regard to death and dying may be viewed as "peculiar" by external observers. To put things crassly, a concept of triage is better understood in nations that have been poorer, in which the choice to do all has not always been available because limitations on resources have severely limited what was possible.

More to the point, there are other ways of doing things than those that are policy in the United States. Some are related to resources, but some are related simply to differences in values. It would take a massive ethnocentrism to suggest that only the values as they exist in the United States should be considered in examining the future of policy. We suggest, for example, that a notion of death and dying may eventually be revised quite substantially, and the meaning of life, considered in concepts of quality of life and contributions to sustenance of the society, could change quite radically in the future as the pressures of population on resources become more dramatic.

Conclusion

When analysis of aging policy is confined to options within existing frameworks and prevailing values, limits are placed upon the research questions and the research that is undertaken. As a consequence, the knowledge base that is critical to formulation of informed aging policy is often ignored and fails to be advanced. For example, as noted above, world demographic trends are overlooked as policymakers focus on the more immediate pressures of the aging baby boomers. Resources are directed toward designing and evaluating programs to assist family members in their caregiving efforts while accurate knowledge about the availability of such family members in the future is scarce and still unstudied. Resources are directed toward the creation of programs to ensure the well-being of the elderly and to study the impact of events and public policy on well-being, but minimal basic developmental work has been done in the conceptualization and measurement of well-being.

No book on policy can address all of the critical areas. In this book we have used a broad perspective of policy analysis to identify issues. In particular we view aging policy as an element of larger public policy that reflects cultural values that are subject to change. In addition to including chapters on such traditional issues as retirement and health policy, we have included issues that are sometimes not brought to the fore of policy considerations such as issues of conceptualization and measurement of key concepts. We have also opened up some new areas that have been totally ignored. For example, the chapter on crime addresses the influence of value systems on deviant behavior across the life cycle. With this context we can extrapolate about future trends in deviant behavior and begin to plan for them now. This perspective on the issue of aging and crime is quite different from the focus on elder abuse and other more narrowly defined areas.

It is our perspective that aging policy exists and is made within the larger context of cultural values and public policy. An adequate understanding of aging policy requires a broad perspective that acknowledges the role of values in the development of policy and enables the researcher to step back from prevailing values in the analysis of policy.

References

ACHENBAUM, W. A. (1983) Shades of Gray: Old Age, American Values, and Federal Policies Since 1920. Boston: Little, Brown.

ARCHBOLD, P. G. (1983) "The impact of parent-caring on women." Family Relations 32: 39-45.

BORGATTA, E. F. and M. B. LOEB (1981) "Toward a policy for retired persons: reflections on welfare and taxation," in N. G. McClusky and E. F. Borgatta (eds.) Aging and Retirement: Prospects, Planning and Policy. Newbury Park: Sage.

BURWELL, B. O. (1986) "Shared obligations: public policy influences on family care for the elderly." Medicaid Program Evaluation. New York: SysteMetrics/ McGraw-Hill.

CALLAHAN, J., L. DIAMOND, J. GIELE, and R. MORRIS (1980) "Responsibility of the family for their severely disabled elders." Health Care Financing Review 1: 24-48.

CANTOR, M. H. (1983) "Strain among caregivers: a study of experience in the United States." The Gerontologist 23: 597-604.

Department of Health and Human Services (1982) Annual Revision of Poverty Income Guidelines. Federal Register 47: 15418.

FRANKFATHER, D., M. J. SMITH, and F. G. CARO (1981) Family Care of the Elderly: Public Initiatives and Private Obligations. Lexington, MA: Lexington Books.

GARFINKEL, I. (1978) "Welfare reform." Social Welfare Forum 105: 80-95.

HOROWITZ, A. (1985) "Family caregiving to the frail elderly," pp. 194-246 in M. P. Lawton and G. L. Maddox (eds.) Annual Review of Gerontology and Geriatrics. New York: Springer.

LITWAK, E. and J. FIGUERIA (1968) "Technological innovation and theoretical functions of primary groups and bureaucratic structures." American Journal of Sociology 73: 468-481.

MARONEY, R. M. (1976) The Family and the State: Considerations for Social Policy. New York: Longmans.

MARONEY, R. M. (1980) Families, Social Services and Social Policy: The Issue of Shared Responsibility. Department of Health and Human Services. Washington, DC: Government Printing Office.

MONTGOMERY, R.J.V. and E. F. BORGATTA (1985) Family Support Project. Final Report to the Administration on Aging. Seattle, WA: Institute on Aging.

NELSON, G. M. (1982) "Support for the aged: public and private responsibility." Social Work 27: 137-143.

NOELKER, L. S. (1984) "Family care of elder relatives: the impact of policy and programs." Presented to the Conference on Families, Interstudy, Minneapolis, Minnesota.

Older American Reports (1982) April 23 issue, p. 8. Washington, DC: Capital Publishing.

President's Commission (1980) A National Agenda for the Eighties. Washington, DC: Government Printing Office.

President's Commission on Pension Policy (1981) Coming of Age: Toward a National Retirement Income Policy. Washington, DC: President's Commission on Pension Policy.

SHANAS, E. (1979) "The family as a social support system in old age." The Gerontologist 19: 169-174.

SOLDO, B. J. and J. MYLLYLUOMA (1983) "Caregivers who live with dependent elderly." The Gerontologist 23: 605-611.

SUSSMAN, M. B. (1979) Social and Economic Supports and Family Environments for the Elderly. Final Report to Administration on Aging.

THEOBALD, R. (1976) Beyond Despair: Directions for America's Third Century. Washington, DC: New Republic Book Company.

United Nations: Department of International Economic and Social Affairs (1985) The World Aging Situation. Strategies and Policies. New York: United Nations.

WHITFIELD, S. (1981) Report to the General Assembly on the Family Demonstration Program. State of Maryland: Office on Aging.

Introduction to Chapter 2

The formulation of rational public policy in any arena requires the capability of predicting future needs. While the definition of "need" is in part determined by values, all definitions of need require basic knowledge of the population characteristics. The ability to plan for the needs of the elderly rests upon knowledge of current and future distributions of the population by age, sex, marital and family status, and living arrangements. It is the work of demographers that has provided this critical information for gerontologists and policymakers.

DeVos's discussion of methods and contributions of demographers illustrates how demographic work has been able to inform gerontologists by analyzing the mortality, migration, marital, and household dynamics of this age group and by illuminating how different fertility, mortality, migration, and marital regimes affect the elderly's kin availability and living arrangements. In addition, demography's dynamic and long-range view sees today's youth as tomorrow's elderly, and has helped to clarify such concepts as age, period, and cohort.

Despite the extensive knowledge that demography has generated in the past and its potential for the future, its contribution to public policy is limited to the extent that appropriate research is supported and findings are employed. While policymakers have become painfully aware that the elderly portion of the nation's population has been growing and will continue to grow, they appear not to be equally informed about other important population characteristics and dynamics that will affect the needs of the elderly and the ability of the nation and the world to meet these needs. Whether the issue is health care, income, or general well-being, policymakers must know more than the absolute numbers of elderly. Critical information about the distribution of functional level, marital and family status, and income are also needed. Furthermore, policymakers must be able to take into account historical influences and social change. It is not sufficient for demographers to have dynamic and long-range views. This understanding must be extended to policymakers.

Equally important is DeVos's emphasis on the need to increase knowledge of the demographics on the elderly in less developed cultures. This gap in knowledge will prevent policymakers from adequately planning for the future. Just as policy for the elderly cannot be made in the absence of an understanding of the relationship between the elderly population and younger cohorts, future policy cannot ignore world trends.

2

Demography

A Source of Knowledge for Gerontology

SUSAN DE VOS

If asked what the demographic contribution to gerontology is, many gerontologists would list two factors. First, demographic work provides a basic description of society's elderly such as absolute number, proportion of the population, relative numbers of females to males, ethnic composition, health status, employment status, income, and living arrangement (Tibbitts, 1960: 15). Second, demography has provided an important insight unexpected in most circles: that the elderly proportion of the world's population has been growing and will continue to grow because of past and present trends in fertility and mortality. The implications of this for all aspects of social organization are immense, including the nature of such intergenerational transfers as social security (see, e.g., Decker, 1980; Schwartz and Peterson, 1979).

The demographic component of social gerontology goes well beyond describing population characteristics and analyzing age structure, however, to include the description and analysis of the elderly's vital

AUTHOR'S NOTE: I am grateful to David Featherman for his comments on an earlier draft of this chapter. Research for this chapter was supported in part by NIH postdoctoral training grant 5T32 HD07014 to the Center for Demography and Ecology of the University of Wisconsin—Madison. Core support to the Center from the National Institute of Child Health and Human Development Grant HD 05876 is also gratefully acknowledged.

functions, living arrangement, and kinship organization. The demographic perspective insists on viewing the elderly component of a population dynamically: The elderly constitute a cohort that has passed through other ages, and the individuals in changing cohorts of the elderly have had different life experiences. This in and of itself is an important factor in social change (Ryder, 1965). The nature of the future elderly population can be projected given information about the middle-aged population. Expectations about old age can affect young people's demographic behavior. The age denominator of many demographic rates represents a combination of biological age, historical age, and social age. Demographers decompose age variables into these different factors.

The purpose of this chapter is to survey the demographic component of gerontology, for less developed countries in particular. Relying primarily on recent research, it reports both on areas that have received attention and on areas that have not. The intent is to complement a 1980 review of the demography of aging by Jacob Siegel (Siegel, 1980) that focused on research and issues relevant to the United States. While it is the case that most demographic research in gerontology has been performed on the developed world,[1] the number of elderly in the developing world has been growing rapidly and will continue to grow. Countries that are successful in lowering fertility also face the challenge of an increasing elderly component of the population, or an aging population (see, e.g., Goldstein and Goldstein, 1984).

The chapter is limited to more or less formal as opposed to social demography because the latter topic is too extensive to be covered in one essay such as this. Formal demography is concerned with fertility, mortality, migration, population distribution, family status, and living arrangement. Social demography is concerned with the implications of a population's size or structure on economic, political, and social institutions and processes, and in how these institutions and processes affect the elderly population. On the micro level, social demography is concerned with how the characteristic of being aged affects an individual's attitudes, behavior, or well-being.[2]

My focus is on the aged population, as opposed to the aging process (see Featherman, forthcoming). While topics of gerontology and aging overlap, the first focuses on people over a specified chronological age (usually 55, 60, 65 or 70 years of age), whereas the study of aging is concerned with the process of human development at all ages. This includes the transition from childhood to adulthood as well as the transition into old age. The life-span approach to the aged is part of gerontology only insofar as it sees old age as a period following other life events (see Hogan, 1983). The influence of previous life events on demographic behavior in old age is an issue for both aging and gerontological research whereas the influences of the expected life situation in old age on demographic behavior at younger ages is an issue in aging research but not gerontological research.

Describing Population Characteristics

There has been a "growing consciousness among demographers and planners alike" that they need information on the elderly population to help plan for the needs of this group.

> The most common variables. . . are age, sex, race, marital and family status, income, labor force status and occupation, education, health status, and living arrangements. All of these are significant with reference to such matters as housing, pension programs, health facilities and services [Tibbitts, 1960: 15].

Data gathering by way of a census, survey, or population register requires a skilled and efficient bureaucratic infrastructure with resources. These capabilities are most developed in the Western world and Japan, and least developed in most of Africa, Latin America, and Asia (see, e.g., Palmore, 1975, 1980; Shanas, 1978; Siegel and Taeuber, 1982). The U.S. Census now publishes current population reports and special subject reports on the elderly population, and Japan's Ministry of Health and Welfare sponsors surveys on "old people."

However, gathering even such basic population information as age and sex taxes the census capabilities of many developing countries. Since it is often sufficient to know that one is younger, older, or of the same cohort as another individual, many people do not know their chronological age (see Howell, 1979; Seltzer, 1973). There is a tendency to exaggerate length of life at advanced ages. There is often differential completeness in reporting by sex, or sex bias in the reporting of age (see Shryock and Siegel, 1973).

Researchers sometimes resort to techniques of indirect estimation (Ewbank, 1981) so that the United Nations is now able to publish an annual *Demographic Yearbook* which contains population numbers by age and sex for most of the world. It is estimated for instance that in 1981 the population proportion 65 years and over ranged from about 3 percent in most parts of Africa to about 15 percent in Northern Europe (United Nations, 1982c: 164-165).

The sex ratio among the elderly has caught popular attention as there are increasingly more females than males in the elderly population. In the United States, for instance, the ratio of males to females over 65 years of age was greater than 1.0 in 1900, was only about .68 in 1979, and is projected to decline to about .66 by 2050 (Verbrugge, 1983: 140-142). A recent article on the aged in Latin America and the Caribbean reported that the actual and projected male proportion of the population above 60 years old was less than 1.0 in most countries since about 1950. Apparently, the differential has been greater in urban than in rural areas (Pelaez and Arguello, 1982). Siegel (1981) reports from United States Census Bureau Projections that the sex ratio for the entire "less developed regions" in 1975 was estimated to be .88, and was projected to drop to .85 by 2000 (1981: 101). Before presenting such figures however, Siegel duly cautioned the reader about "the limitations of the estimates" (1981: 94). Even in Latin America, the proportions fluctuate enough to make one wary of the data's accuracy, or the proportion of men to women is close enough to equality to make the ultimate conclusion sensitive to relatively small errors in data collection. Our knowledge of the sex ratio in less developed countries stays dubious.

Age Structure and the Elderly Population

The proportion of the population over such "old" ages as 55, 60, 65, or 70 years has been increasing in the developed world because of declines in fertility and mortality, and is projected to increase throughout the developing world as well. Fertility decline is the major cause (Coale, 1956; see also Keyfitz, 1977: chap. 4; Coale and Demmeney, 1966; United Nations, 1967, 1982a). The mechanism behind the structural change was demonstrated elegantly in a chapter by Philip Hauser (1976). He constructed five ideal typical demographic regimes corresponding to different stages in the demographic transition. The first stage had constantly high birth and death rates and a no-growth population. The second ideal regime had somewhat reduced mortality resulting in a net annual population growth rate of 1.0 percent. The third ideal type had the low mortality and high fertility typical of many less developed countries today. The annual growth rate was 3.0 percent per year. The fourth type had low birth and death rates, but still had a net growth rate of 1.0 percent similar to situations in many developed countries today. The final "modern-stationary" stage achieved equally low birth and death rates to experience no net population growth.

The beauty of this exercise is that it demonstrates the relative importance of fertility and mortality in affecting the elderly proportion of the population. Under the first demographic regime in which births and deaths were equally high, the proportion 65 years and older was 2.9 percent. When mortality dropped somewhat, the proportion only increased to 3.4 percent. Under the third regime in which mortality was much lower but fertility had increased slightly, the proportion of the elderly actually *dropped* to only 2.6 percent. On the other hand, the proportion increased radically in the fourth stage when the birth rate dropped from 45.7 to 20.4 per thousand. The elderly proportion increased to 10.3 percent of the population. In the final, stationary regime in which mortality was somewhat higher but fertility was still lower, the proportion increased to 18.5 percent of the population.

Initial declines in mortality tend to occur at the young (0-20 yrs.) ages and actually *increase* the proportion of the young population. The effect of mortality improvements has a significant effect on the elderly proportion of the population only *after* initial mortality reductions occur. It has been estimated that the increase in the proportion of the population 60-89 years old between 1900 and 1950 in the United States was due: 72 percent to fertility change,[3] 11 percent to mortality change, 5 percent to the interaction between fertility and mortality change, and 12 percent to immigration (Sheldon, 1960: 42-46).

After initial mortality declines improve the life chances at younger ages, continued mortality improvements among the elderly themselves—not yet experienced by much of the developing world—result in an important shift in the age composition of the "elderly population" from primarily under 75 years to a significant proportion 75 years and over. In the United States for instance, these "older old" comprised about 22 percent of the population 65 and over in 1900, but 38 percent by 1979. The proportion is projected to become 48 percent by 2050 (Verbrugge, 1983: 141). For most of the developing world, however, the major focus is still on the gross proportion of elderly in the population, not on the age distribution within the older population.

Projecting the size and proportion of a population that is elderly is related to describing current size and proportion. While this has included use of the exponential and logistic models, most commonly used at present is the "component method" because it is sensitive to the mortality, fertility, immigration, and emigration of different age and sex groups (Shryock and Siegel, 1973: 777). The basic idea is that numbers in each age-sex group are exposed to predetermined mortality, fertility, immigration, and emigration rates and then are moved forward into the next age category. The United Nations has periodically made projections of the population for regions and countries of the world using high, medium, and low assumptions of fertility and mortality. In a recent publication of the medium variant projections, the proportion 65 and over for the world is projected to increase from 5.7 percent in 1975 to 9.3 percent in 2025 (United Nations, 1982b: 58).

Mortality

Precise information about mortality among elderly people is difficult to obtain for a number of reasons. First, deaths have to be registered. Second, the demographic technique for calculating mortality rates presumes accurate age information for the population at large, and detailed age is often distorted or unknown among the old. It is still most common to talk about mortality in developing countries in terms of expectation of life at birth, which summarizes average mortality over the entire life span and is relatively insensitive to age misreporting at the older ages. Third, diagnoses as to cause of death can be difficult, especially if the body is afflicted by more than one disease. Many people are still considered to die from "old age."

One method for estimating age-specific mortality rates among populations with poor mortality data has been to match general population characteristics with a "model" life table population (e.g., from Coale and Demeney, 1966, 1983), and to use the corresponding mortality (Qx) values.[4] The idea is that there exists a general force of mortality, with some variation, among different societies. A recent evaluation of this method for estimating mortality in Asian countries however, found the west model life table to overestimate mortality rates at younger ages (under 35 or 40) and to underestimate mortality rates at the older ages. It was suggested that mortality decline has been more rapid at younger ages in Asia than had been observed in the countries upon which the model tables were based (Ueda, 1983: 63-66).

Data on mortality by age and cause for less developed countries is nigh impossible to obtain. The experience of developed countries seems to suggest that at high levels of mortality, death due to infectious disease is most important while at lower levels of mortality, cardiovascular diseases, cancer, and other degenerative diseases are the most significant causes of death (Preston, 1976: chap. 5). In general, the latter type of disease is thought to be the kind that afflicts the elderly. It was estimated recently that three-fourths of "older" people in the United States ultimately die from heart disease, cancer, or stroke (Verbrugge, 1983: 146). While there have been several attempts to correlate life expectancy with cause of death in Asian countries, the data do not appear accurate enough to evaluate the similarity of Asian and Western experience except in the case of Japan, which now has a relatively affluent population and high medical standards (Yamaguchi, 1983, as translated in Ueda, 1983: chap. 5).

The relationship between socioeconomic status, lifestyle, and mortality, especially at the older ages, remains a big question. To some, socioeconomic status means better access to medical care while to others its main impact on mortality is through nutrition, shelter, and other aspects of lifestyle. It is often argued that there is such poverty and poor understanding of hygiene in many parts of the world that simple improvements in nutrition and cleanliness would have an important impact on reducing mortality. Smoking and stress have also been found to significantly affect morality rates (see Kitagawa, 1977). I have been unable to find a study of this issue that focuses on the elderly in developing countries. The primary focus of mortality research there is still on infant and child mortality. For developed countries Siegel recently wrote,

> For purposes of planning the use of health resources and the financing of research on health matters, it is important to determine the extent to which the declines are due to new medical developments and the extent to which they are due to other factors, such as changes in the system of health practices. For example, the death rate from heart disease declined sharply in the 1968-77 period even though there were no new basic biomedical discoveries; this suggests the greater role of changes in life style or in health care delivery as illustrated by the mass screening for high blood pressure [1980: 348].

Differences in mortality by sex have been observed throughout the world, but the patterns have been different. Differences at the older ages in developing countries cannot be determined accurately because of poor data, but there seems to have often been an advantage for males (e.g., Stolnitz, 1956: 27-28). In developed countries, in contrast, among the elderly the mortality rates for males can be as much as twice the rates for females (Myers, 1978). For both sexes there, the mortality rates dropped until about 1950, stabilized between 1950 and 1970, and then began to drop markedly again during the 1970s. This last drop was important at the "younger" (old ages for persons in their 60s) and at the "older" (75 or over) ages. But the drop was bigger for females than for males, thus widening the gap between life expectancies. In fact, male rates actually increased in some countries, for instance Sweden and the Netherlands (Myers, 1978: 444). In the United States in 1978, expectancy of life at birth was 7.7 years less for males than for females (Verbrugge, 1983: 145). Reasons for these sex differentials in mortality are poorly understood. "They emerge from some combination of genetic risks for each sex, from risks acquired during life, and from attitudes that influence symptom perception and curative behavior" (Verbrugge, 1983: 139).

Migration and Spatial Distribution

Migration among the elderly has become of concern to most demographers only recently, and then primarily for developed countries (see Golant, 1980; Longino and Jackson, 1980; Harootyan, 1982; Parker and Serow, 1983). Most migration research has been concerned with the relationship between the labor market and the labor force between 15 and 64 years of age—factors that "push" young people out of rural areas—or the family-building and housing needs of younger individuals. A survey of recent articles in *International Migration Review* or of books on migration anywhere in the world would satisfy those skeptical of this assertion.

Some studies have noted that the proportion of the population 65 years and over varied considerably between localities, but they have emphasized the out-migration or in-migration of young people in causing concentrations at certain ages. For instance, a common observation in the post-World War II period in the United States was that younger people tended to move out into suburbs from central cities, leaving a concentration of older people in the city proper (see Heaton, 1983). In less developed countries too, the conventional wisdom is that it is predominantly the young who leave rural areas in search of employment while the old stay in the villages. However, in the United States at least, it has been observed that the concentration of elderly persons has changed from being predominantly nonmetropolitan to predominantly metropolitan. Also, this has increasingly been "driven by the elderly actively seeking a desired destination" rather than being merely "left behind" (McCarthy, 1983). The elderly seem to have greater choice of location than before due to higher incomes and earlier retirement. An increase in migration around retirement age compared to somewhat younger and older ages, has been observed in many developed countries (Rogers and Castro, 1981). Whether this may occur in less developed countries in the future is a natural question. There may be a number of differences in family and housing patterns between the developed and currently less developed countries that will result in different migration patterns among the elderly.

In the Western world at least, there appear to be push and pull factors motivating migration among the elderly that are distinct from those encountered by younger populations. Economic factors appear to have less importance while quality of life factors are more important. Among pull factors are warmer climates, social services, and cultural amenities (Rogers and Castro, 1981). Many older individuals are no longer tied to a locality for employment reasons, and have been found to be an important component of the recent metropolitan-nonmetropolitan turnaround (see also Lichter et al., 1981). For example, since 1950 in the United States, "the large metropolitan 'core' areas have consistently experienced a net outmigration of the elderly, and the trend has been most pronounced during the past decade" (Heaton, 1983: 96). Major push factors are poor health or marital disruption, usually the death of a spouse. Although often independent economically, many elderly persons move closer to kin when this occurs. It might be expected that the pattern is different in many developing countries if the elderly already live with children before poor health or a major disruption occurs, but this is an open question.

The reasons why older people are less likely to migrate than younger people "represents a serious gap in migration research" (Heaton, 1983: 102). On average older people probably have more invested in their current location materially, socially, and emotionally (Heaton, 1983: 101-102). In the developed countries, it is reasoned that if elderly individuals are on fixed incomes, they must move to a location with a lower cost of living if they are to improve their financial situation. That is, economic status, ethnicity, sex, and educational attainment help differentiate elderly migrants from nonmigrants. Migrants tend to be comparatively well-off, and this tends to increase with the distance of the move (Biggar, 1980; Parker and Serow, 1983: 197).

Parker and Serow (1983) note that much of the previous work on migration among the elderly in the United States has been dominated by life-satisfaction scales whereas an analysis of the economic effects of the migration for areas of origin and destination need much more analysis (1983: 195).

Marital Dynamics

Most people think of young adults when they think of marriage, middle-aged adults when they think of divorce, and the elderly when they think of widowhood. Yet the issue is obviously much more complicated than this, especially when one begins to consider marital patterns cross-culturally. There are young widows and widowers. Middle-aged divorcees eventually become elderly. There is substantial remarriage. Many of the elderly are still married. Yet demographic research on the marital dynamics or marital status of the elderly, especially for developing countries, appears thin.

For instance, four editions of the United Nations *Demographic Yearbook* have specifically included data on marriages and divorce, some of which were tabulated by age, sex, previous marital status, or duration of marriage (1958, 1968, 1976, 1982). While data from Latin America, Africa and Asia were notably slim in the first edition, information for significantly more countries was available by 1982 (see United Nations, 1983). However, I am unaware of a study that has systematically dealt with such data.

Many elderly persons are widowed, much more so for females than for males. In Egypt in 1976 for example, only 81 percent of the males and 23 percent of the females 65 years and older were married. The respective figures for the United States were 77 and 37 percent (United Nations, 1983: tab. 40).

Dynamics behind such a sex differential have only begun to be explored, and then only for industrialized countries. Noreen Goldman and Graham Lord (1983) recently used "simple formulas measuring life cycle characteristics of widowhood as a function of life table survivorship and age at marriage" to look at patterns of widowhood and widowerhood in the United States. They found that the "inequality in the risks of widowhood and widowerhood is mostly due to sex differences in mortality which currently imply an eight year difference in life expectancy at birth" (1983: 193). The common tendency for husbands to be older than their wives is also a contributing factor. The study assessed the probability of a wife outliving her husband according to a variety of characteristics. The study also reported implications of the findings for a stationary population that had no divorce or remarriage.

The elderly do marry, remarry, and divorce; and differential rates at all ages with respect to these contribute to the differential in the marital status of elderly men and women noted above. For instance, while remarriage among the elderly is lower than among other age groups, it is considerably higher among elderly men than women. Again, the United Nations data do not seem to have been explored in any detail, but a comparative analysis could prove illuminating if one could be confident in the comparability of the statistics. In the United States in 1971 the annual marriage rate (per 1,000 unmarried persons) for females 65 and over was 2.4 while the rate for males was 16.7 (Siegel, 1976: 47). It has been conjectured that this differential "is a result of social norms supporting marriage to younger women (and discouraging the opposite), a stronger motivation to remarry, and a male demographic advantage in the fact of a surplus of women in the marriage market" (Siegel, 1976: 47). But such conjecture has not been subjected to careful scrutiny.

Only the most rudimentary of statistics is known about the elderly with respect to divorce. For example, in Egypt in 1976, only .6 and .8 percent of men and women 65 years and older were reported as divorced compared to 2.7 and 2.8 percent of the 65 years and older population in the United States (United Nations, 1983: tab. 40). But what proportion of the elderly were ever divorced? In the United States in 1975, 10 to 13 percent of the elderly had "ever experienced divorce" (see Furstenberg, 1981; Cherlin, 1983). The figures for Egypt appear to be unknown. Yet for questions bearing on family or housing policy and law there would be considerable value in knowing this. There would be considerable value in knowing what the probability is that a married women of age X would be widowed or divorced within the next five years, or what the probability is that a widowed woman of age Y would be remarried within five years.

Kinship

In most societies, an individual's lot is determined largely by his or her kin group. Even in complex societies, the traditional norm has been for the elderly to be cared for by their families, whether or not this has been the *actual* situation. The norm presumes, of course, that elderly have family members on whom to depend but little is really known about the kinship arena of the elderly or how this might vary on the societal level with variations in fertility, mortality, or migration. Demography can inform social policies by providing information about the current kinship situation of the elderly, by projecting the kinship situation of future elderly, and by explicating the relationship between fertility, mortality, and migration on the one hand and kinship availability on the other, given certain rules of kinship formation. Such work is only beginning.

Censuses do not ask anyone of any age about kinship except, perhaps, to ask about children ever born and relationship to the household head. On rare occasions, surveys of the elderly that include questions on kinship have been conducted in developed countries (e.g., Shanas et al., 1968; Ministry of Health and Welfare, 1971; Rowland, 1984; Shanas, 1978). Shanas's national survey of the aged in the United States (1978) was exemplary on this score. The survey asked about such immediate kin as children, parents, siblings, grandchildren, great-grandchildren, and nieces and nephews. It asked about their residences relative to the elderly respondent, and about the social and economic relationship. The survey found that four of every five noninstitutional residents 65 years of age and over in the United States in 1975 had at least one surviving child; the proportion who had only one was 28 percent; more than one-third had great-grandchildren; and about one-tenth had children who were themselves 65 years of age or older.

Comparable information for other countries is rare. A recent study of household structure in Sri Lanka found 11 percent of the unmarried individuals 65 years or older to live alone, but whether this was due to the unavailability of kin or some other factor could not be determined (De Vos and Radhakrishnamurty, 1983). In her recent study of the elderly in China, Davis-Friedmann (1983) was required to call the number of childless elderly "a small minority" and then to refer to the number of residents in old-age homes (presumably because they were childless) in 1958 as 2,000,000!

What proportion of elderly are childless?[5] In want of direct data from censuses or surveys, several demographers have taken a more theoretical approach. Immerwahr (1967) used microsimulation to ask what the probabilities were that a father or mother would be outlived by a son "depending on (a) the number of sons, (b) the relative ages of father and sons, (c) the ages at which the probabilities are measured, and (d) the future mortality assumed." Independently, Heer and Smith (1968, 1969) asked what the probability was that at least one son would be alive when a father reached age 65 under different marriage, fertility, and mortality regimes. Bongaarts and Menken (1983) used macro-simulation to assess the number of children alive to a parent aged 65 given variations in fertility and child survival. Krishnamoorthy (1980) developed mathematical expressions for the probability that older individuals would have no surviving offspring, and the implications for this of different fertility and mortality regimes. It was determined that under conditions of high mortality and fertility (e.g., in Madagascar in 1966), 12 percent of the women surviving to age 50 would have no living daughter, compared to 6 percent in Venezuela (low mortality) and 30 percent in the United States (low mortality and fertility).

Goodman et al. (1974, 1975) have begun to develop a demographic theory of kinship that, although it does not focus exclusively on the elderly, uses age as a critical variable (see also Keyfitz, 1977). Focusing on the female population to avoid the "two-sex" problem common in demography,[6] the authors developed a model that predicted the number of daughters, granddaughters, sisters, nieces, and mothers still alive to women at different ages given different levels of mortality and fertility. Given the levels of fertility and mortality in the mid-1960s, for example, the expected number of daughters ever born and still alive to women 70 years old would be 1.25 and 1.15 in the United States, 3.13 and 2.66 in Venezuela, and 3.29 and 1.44 in Madagascar. The expected number of surviving granddaughters would be 1.42, 7.16, and 3.38, respectively. Unfortunately, the authors did not report distributions around these averages, which would be necessary to determine expected proportions of the elderly without any offspring. Herve La Bras independently derived a related model of kinship, deriving its implications for past and present France and for Venezuela (1973).

The only analytical study of the elderly's kinship universe, in specific, of which I am aware was performed by Hammel et al. on the United States (1981). Given the mortality, fertility, and nuptiality rates of the United States population since 1900 and projected up to 2000, the study estimated the expected number of living kin (children, grand-children, siblings, etc.) of an individual by his or her age. The study concluded among other things that persons "over 70 in 2000 can expect more children than could persons over 70 in 1950" and that "persons aged about 70 and over in 2000 can expect to have four or five grand-children, just about what persons of the same age had in 1950" (1981: 26, 28).

To date, none of the theoretical studies have tried to deal with issues of migration, preferring to concentrate on closed populations. They have avoided dealing with complications surrounding divorce and remarriage. Although all of these theoretical studies were constrained to make a number of simplifying assumptions, and although many only reported averages but not distributions, they demonstrate the kind of study that can be applied to populations of developing countries.

Living Arrangements

The living arrangements of the elderly is another demographic topic about which we know little, especially for developing countries. A major reason has to do with the way data for households are usually published. Censuses commonly obtain information on households as units, gathering such data as household material, number of rooms, and household size. These data, as well as any data on household com-position, are often reported in terms of the household head, perhaps his or her sociodemographic or economic characteristics. Information on individuals is absent.

Demographers are left to glean information about the household structure of the aged from age-specific headship rates (Myers and Nathanson, 1983). Age-specific headship rates are the proportion of individuals of a given age who are also recorded as household heads. The lower the rate for elderly, the more aged individuals live with another who is considered the head. Although the rates help indicate the extent to which older individuals live with others, this is confounded by the fact that older men are often considered to be household heads whether or not they live with children. Whether an older woman is considered household head depends on her marital status and, if she lives with others, the honorary position given an older woman. The symbolic meaning of "household head" is obviously ambiguous and may differ between social groups.

Still, comparison of headship rates can provide useful insights. For instance, female headship rates tend to be low at young ages and rise at the older ages, whereas male rates tend to drop. The rise in female rates probably reflects the increasing number of women who are widowed. The decline in the rate for men probably reflects declines in economic power and in health, and a greater likelihood of living in a household headed by another male (Myers and Nathanson, 1983).

Headship rates for older men and women tend to be higher in developed than in developing countries, indicating more independent living. This is thought to be due partly to economic factors, but factors such as custom, preference, emotions, and health care are probably also important (United Nations, 1981). Japan, the only industrialized non-Western country, has headship rates that are more similar to those in developing countries than to those in other developed countries. Low-income individuals and elderly persons in poor health have a greater tendency to live with relatives in the United States, but in other cultures living with children may be preferred (see Soldo, 1981; Palmore, 1975). Yet even in non-Western cultures such preferences may be changing as a consequence of modernization (see Kobayashi, 1977). Little is known about the actual living arrangements of the elderly in developing countries, either about those with children or about those with no surviving offspring.

Studies have found that age differences among the elderly themselves are an important determinant of living arrangements, at least in developed countries. They have also found that living arrangements are quite different on average for older males and older females; and that the living arrangement situation of older nonwhites differs considerably from that of whites. The number of children an older woman had correlates with her type of living arrangement in old age (Soldo, 1981). Whether there would be similar relationships in less developed countries is unknown.

Age as Biology, Society, and History

It is common to attribute different demographic rates between age groups at one point in time to biological "age." However, different age groups at one point in time were born at different times (different cohorts), experienced different environmental stimuli (different time periods), and experienced the same environmental stimuli differently because of past experiences and because of differences in their place in the life cycle (see Hobcraft et al., 1982). For example, older people now migrate less than younger people. Yet theoretically, people who are older now could have migrated less when they were young than younger people do now. And they could be migrating less than people who were in a previous cohort. That is, age differences could be due to cohort or period effects as well as to age effects.

The problem is that in any comparison, be it cross-sectional or longitudinal, there are two decomposable factors (age and either cohort or period), but three conceptual factors (age, cohort, and period). The decomposition of any observable "age" difference into two factors will be biased with respect to the third factor. There appear at present to be three ways to deal with this problem of "overidentification." One way is to eliminate one of the factors, for instance reducing a "three-factor developmental model to a two-factor model incorporating age and cohort" (Maddox and Wiley, 1976: 21). For instance, the analyst may be most interested in differentiating between the effect of biological age and social and historical factors. A second way is to construct a "three-factor model with special restrictions that circumvent the usual consequences of dependence among the three components" (Maddox and Wiley, 1976: 21; see also Mason et al., 1973). Maddox and Wiley cite a study of American political party affiliation by Knoke and Hout (1974) as an example of this. Of particular importance for demography, a third way disentangles the biological age component from the other two components by combining empirical and mathematical procedures. "Age patterns present in a particular population or cohort are viewed as a simple statistical transformation of a 'standard' age pattern that is empirically specified" (Hobcraft et al., 1982: 14; see also Coale, 1971). Presumably, this pattern can be specified and the deviations from it accorded to period and cohort effects. Each of these solutions appears applicable to certain research questions but is only a partial solution. None is satisfactory for all questions. Actually, since age, period, and cohort are often surrogates for factors that cannot be measured directly, the best approach is to measure the underlying variables, when possible.

Conclusion

Demography makes a significant contribution to the study of older people by describing and projecting their basic characteristics, by exploring the determinants and consequences of these characteristics (including their kinship universe and living arrangement), and by identifying and understanding such vital processes as mortality, migration, marriage, divorce, and widowhood. Demographers have helped clarify the concepts of age, period, and cohort.

Much more demographic information is known about the elderly in developed countries compared to developing countries. This is tied in large part to the relative proportion of the elderly in those societies: The population 65 years and older in 1980 varied from 3 percent in much of Africa to 15 percent in Northern Europe.

Demographers use census enumeration, population registration, and surveys to describe the elderly population in terms of its size, proportion of the total population, and such characteristics as age, sex, race, marital and family status, income, labor force status and occupation, education, health status, and living arrangements. Generally, high fertility populations have a small proportion in the elderly years whereas populations with low fertility and low mortality have a large proportion. One of the striking aspects of the elderly, in developed countries at least, is the greater number of females compared to males. This phenomenon appears to be increasing in less developed countries as well. The population can be projected from knowledge of younger populations via a component method, for the elderly proportion of the total population results from past trends in fertility, mortality, and migration.

Two factors that stand out in our current knowledge of mortality among the aged in developed countries may or may not be true in less developed countries: (1) the considerably higher mortality of males compared to females, and (2) the causes of death being due primarily to degenerative disease—cancer and cardiovascular problems. While most migration studies focus on the population 15 to 64 years of age, migration patterns of the elderly seem to be distinct from this group. Migration among the elderly appears to be less tied to employment or financial considerations and more strongly associated with retirement or family considerations. The marital dynamics of elderly appear little explored, either in developed or developing countries. The most evident "fact" is that a much larger percentage of older men are married compared to women; and their remarriage rate is higher.

We know little about the kin of the aged in either developed or developing countries. Recently, the noted demographer Jacob Siegel wrote that "a national survey on kinship networks is needed" (1980: 356). Demographers have also gone about studying kinship by developing a theory of kinship—mathematical expressions for the number of kin of various sorts depending on different fertility and mortality regimes. Other studies have used simulation or dynamic programming techniques. Such studies have estimated the proportion of the elderly population that will be childless according to different fertility and mortality rates. One study in particular used microsimulation to estimate the kinship arena of elderly in the United States in 1950 and 2000.

Since most household data for less developed countries are at best reported in terms of the household head, demographers have tried to glean information about the household characteristics of the elderly by using age-specific household headship rates. Such measures give indirect information at best. Work in the United States by Beth Soldo and others has done much to further our understanding both of the living arrangements, and the determinants thereof, of the elderly population; but the situation in less developed countries could well be quite different. For instance, it has been well established that most elderly prefer to live separately from other kin in the United States, but this preference may not exist in other cultures. It is often presumed that elderly live with kin, but other studies suggest that a substantial number of elderly may be left childless.

Demography has much to offer an international gerontology in terms of describing and understanding the elderly population and its dynamics. However, the elderly proportion of the population in these countries is still quite low compared to more developed countries (3 percent compared to 10 percent), and demographic research is still focusing on infant and child mortality, high fertility, rural to urban migration, and international migration with respect to these countries. Research on the elderly population remains slim. This chapter has tried to outline the demographic topics and review recent research in this area. A main conclusion is that we do not yet know very much, and that much more research is needed. The number of elderly in developing countries has been increasing at a rapid rate, and will increase even more rapidly in the future. Those countries that are successful in reducing their fertility face the additional challenge of an aging population. This affects the entire world. We need to know more about this process, and about the aged in these countries, if we are to meet this challenge successfully.

NOTES

1. That is, Western countries and Japan. In other countries, investigations into the elderly population that have been made tend to be performed by governmental agencies that report findings in difficult-to-obtain bureaucratic documents, and in languages ranging from Korean to Spanish, making it difficult for any one researcher to integrate the diverse findings (see International Center of Social Gerontology, 1982; Palmore, 1980, 1982).

2. For instance, economic demographers are concerned with the effect of population aging on the dependency ratio, labor force dynamics, patterns of consumer spending, and patterns of savings and investments. They are concerned with the material well-being of older persons. Political scientists are concerned with the implications of population aging for the general political climate, for age patterns of elective office, and for the political mobilization of the elderly as a distinguishable and powerful constituency. They are also concerned with the relationship between age and political attitude. Sociologists are concerned with the relationships between population aging and the elderly's prestige or social status within the larger society and the family. They are concerned with "social disengagement" and life satisfaction (see, e.g., Binstock and Shanas, 1976; Kiesler et al., 1981; and Riley et al., 1983).

3. Sheldon refers to an increase in births between 1860 and 1890 compared to 1810 to 1840 rather than to change in the fertility rate before and after 1900 to take into account fertility change. But he would have come to similar conclusions if he had looked at the fertility rate at different time periods. His method of decomposition relied on the use of actual figures rather than on a theoretically derived formula, but more theory-based decompositions are also possible.

4. The model populations have been revised as new information about mortality, especially mortality at the older ages, has become available (Coale and Demeney, 1983).

5. In fact, a desire for many children has sometimes been linked to the perceived necessity of having children to provide for one's support in old age (e.g., Cain, 1977; Willis, 1981; De Vos, 1984).

6. As Hogan explained recently,

On average, men marry later than females, and their mean age at parenthood is later. In formal models of population growth, the mean age at fertility is interpreted as the mean length of a generation. The sex ratio at birth typically is in the range of 102-106 males per 100 females. Thus, for any given rate of fertility fathers have more sons than mothers do daughters. In combination, the mean age at fertility and the reproduction rate determine the growth rate of the population. Therefore, formal models of population translation project different (and inconsistent) results for population change depending on whether female or male experiences are modelled. This is referred to as the "two sex" problem in demography. Although a number of solutions for the two sex problem have been proposed, formal demographers typically have dealt with it by restricting attention to the experience of females. [1983: 4-5].

References

BIGGAR J. C. (1980) "Who moved among the elderly, 1965 to 1970: a comparison of types of older movers." Research on Aging 2: 73-91.

BINSTOCK, R. H. and E. SHANAS [eds.] (1976) Handbook of Aging and the Social Sciences. New York: Van Nostrand.

BONGAARTS, J. and J. MENKEN (1983) "The supply of children: a critical essay," pp. 27-60 in R. A. Bulatao et al. (eds.) Determinants of Fertility in Developing Countries. New York: Academic Press.

CAIN, M. (1977) "The economic activities of children in a village in Bangladesh." Population and Development Review 3, 3: 201-228.

CHERLIN, A. (1983) "A sense of history: recent research on aging and the family," pp. 5-24 in M. W. Riley et al. (eds.) Aging in Society: Selected Reviews of Recent Research. Hillsdale, NJ: Lawrence Erlbaum.

COALE, A. J. (1956) "The effects of changes in mortality and fertility on age composition." Milbank Memorial Fund Quarterly 34: 79-114.

COALE, A. J. (1971) "Age patterns of marriage." Population Studies 25, 2: 193-214.

COALE, A. J. and P. DEMENEY (1966) Regional Model Life Tables and Stable Populations. Princeton, NJ: Princeton University Press.

COALE, A. J., and P. DEMENEY, with B. VAUGHAN (1983) Regional Model Life Tables and Stable Populations. New York: Academic Press.

DAVIS-FRIEDMANN, D. (1983) Long Lives: Chinese Elderly and the Communist Revolution. Cambridge, MA: Harvard University Press.

DECKER, D. L. (1980) Social Gerontology. Boston: Little, Brown.

DE VOS, S. (1984) "The old age economic security value of children in the Philippines and Taiwan." Paper 60-G of the East-West Population Institute. Honolulu: East-West Center.

DE VOS, S. and K. RADHAKRISHNAMURTY (1983) "Life course characteristics and household structure in Sri Lanka, 1975." CDE Working Paper 83-17. Madison: Center for Demography and Ecology, University of Wisconsin—Madison.

EWBANK, D. C. (1981) Age Misreporting and Age-Selective Underenumeration: Sources, Patterns, and Consequences for Demographic Analysis. Report No. 4 of the National Academy of Science Committee on Population and Demography. Washington, DC: National Academy Press.

FEATHERMAN, D. L. (forthcoming) "Individual development and aging as a population process," in J. Nesselroade and A. v. Eye (eds.) Individual Development and Social Change: Explanatory Analysis New York: Academic Press.

FURSTENBERG, F. F., Jr. (1981) "Remarriage and intergenerational relations," pp. 115-142 in R. W. Fogel et al. (eds.) Aging: Stability and Change in the Family. New York: Academic Press.

GOLANT, S. M. (1980) "Future directions for elderly migration research." Research on Aging 2: 271-280.

GOLDMAN, N. and G. LORD (1983) "Sex differences in life cycle measures of widowhood." Demography 20, 2: 177-196.

GOLDSTEIN, A. and S. GOLDSTEIN (1984) "The challenge of an aging population in the People's Republic of China." Presented at the Population Association Meetings, May.

GOODMAN, L., N. KEYFITZ, and T. PULLUM (1974) "Family formation and the frequency of various kinship relationships." Theoretical Population Biology 5: 1-27.

GOODMAN, L., N. KEYFITZ, and T. PULLUM (1975) "Addendum to 'family formation and the frequency of various kinship relationships.' " Theoretical Population Biology 8: 376-381.

HAMMEL, E. A., K. W. WACHTER, and C. K. McDANIEL (1981) "The kin of the aged in A.D. 2000: the chickens come home to roost," pp. 11-39 in S. B. Kiesler et al. (eds.) Aging: Social Change. New York: Academic Press.

HAROOTYAN, R. A. (1982) "Aging population research: suggestions for a model data system for service planning." The Gerontologist 22, 2: 164-169.

HAUSER, P. M. (1976) "Aging and world-wide population change," pp. 58-86 in R. H. Binstock and E. Shanas (eds.) Handbook of Aging and the Social Sciences. New York: Van Nostrand.

HEATON, T. B. (1983) "Recent trends in the geographical distribution of the elderly population," pp. 95-114 in M. W. Riley et al. (eds.) Aging in Society: Selected Reviews of Recent Research. Hillsdale, NJ: Lawrence Erlbaum.

HEER, D. M. and D. D. SMITH (1968) "Mortality level, desired family size, and population increase." Demography 5, 1: 104-121.

HEER, D. M. and D. D. SMITH (1969) "Mortality level, desired family size and population increase: further variations on a basic model." Demography 6, 2: 141-149.

HOBCRAFT, J., J. MENKEN, and S. PRESTON (1982) "Age, period and cohort effects in demography: a review." Population Index 48, 1: 4-43.

HOGAN, D. P. (1983) "The demography of life span transitions: temporal and gender comparisons." Presented at the American Sociological Association Meetings, Detroit.

HOWELL, N. (1979) Demography of the Dobe !Kung. New York: Academic Press.

IMMERWAHR, G. E. (1967) "Survivorship of sons under conditions of improving mortality." Demography 4: 710-720.

International Center of Social Gerontology (1982) International Bibliography of Social Gerontology: An Annotated Core List By Country. Paris: International Center of Social Gerontology.

KEYFITZ, N. (1977) "The demographic theory of kinship," pp. 273-302 in Applied Mathematical Demography. New York: John Wiley.

KIESLER, S. B., J. N. Morgan, and V. K. OPPENHEIMER (1981) Aging: Social Change. New York: Academic Press.

KITAGAWA, E. M. (1977) "On mortality." Demography 14, 4: 381-389.

KNOKE, D., and M. HOUT (1974) "Social and demographic factors in American political party affiliation: 1952-1972." American Sociological Review 39: 700-713.

KOBAYASHI, K. (1977) "Attitudes towards children and parents," chap. 6 in Japanese Organization for International Cooperation in Family Planning (ed.) Fertility and Family Planning in Japan. Tokyo: Mainichi Newspapers Press.

KRISHNAMOORTHY, S. (1980) "Effects of fertility and mortality on estimation of family and number of living children." Social Biology 27, 1: 62-69.

LE BRAS, H. (1973) "Parents, grandparents, bisaieux." Population 28-9-37. Trans and revd. pp. 163-188. in K. W. Wachter et al. [eds.] (1978) Statistical Studies of Historical Social Structure. New York: Academic Press.

LICHTER, D. T. et al. (1981) "Components of change in the residential concentration of the elderly population: 1950-1975." Journal of Gerontology 36, 4: 480-489.

LONGINO, C. F., Jr., and D. J. JACKSON [eds.] (1980) Migration and the Aged: special issue of Research on Aging 2, 2.

MADDOX, G. L. and J. WILEY (1976) "Scope, concepts and methods in the study of aging," pp. 3-34 in R. H. Binstock and E. Shanas (eds.) Handbook of Aging and the Social Sciences. New York: Van Nostrand.

MASON, K. O., H. H. WINSBOROUGH, W. M. MASON, and W. K. POOLE (1973) "Some methodological issues in cohort analysis of archival data." American Sociological Review 38: 242-258.

McCARTHY, K. F. (1983) The Elderly Population's Changing Spatial Distribution Patterns of Change Since 1960. Santa Monica, CA: Rand.

Ministry of Health and Welfare (1971) Survey of Old Persons. Tokyo: Ministry of Health and Welfare.

MYERS, G. C. (1978) "Cross-national trends in mortality rates among the elderly." The Gerontologist 18, 5: 441-447.

MYERS, G. C. and C. A. NATHANSON (1983) "Aging and the family," in World Health Statistics Quarterly. Geneva, Switzerland: World Health Organization.

PALMORE, E. (1975) The Honorable Elders: A Cross-Cultural Analysis of Aging in Japan. Durham, NC: Duke University Press.

PALMORE, E. [ed.] (1980) International Handbook on Aging. Contemporary Developments and Research Westport, CT: Greenwood Press.

PALMORE, E. (1982) "Cross-cultural research: state of the art." Presented at the American Sociological Association Meetings, San Francisco.

PARKER, J. R. and W. J. SEROW (1983) "Migration of the elderly: a needed new dimension in research." International Topics in Gerontology 17: 194-202.

PELAEZ, C. A. and O. ARGUELLO (1982) "El envejecimento de la poblacion en America Latina: tendencias demograficas y situacion socioeconomica." Notas de Poblacion 30: 9-96.

PRESTON, S. H. (1976) Mortality Patterns in National Populations. New York: Academic Press.

RILEY, M. W., B. B. HESS and K. BOND [eds.] (1983) Aging in Society: Selected Reviews of Recent Research. Hillsdale, NJ: Lawrence Erlbaum.

ROGERS, A. and L. J. CASTRO (1981) Model Migration Schedules. International Institute for Applied Systems Analysis RR-81-30, Laxenburg, Austria.

ROWLAND, D. T. (1984) "Old age and the demographic transition." Population Studies 38: 73-87.

RYDER, N. B. (1965) "The cohort as a concept in the study of social change." American Sociological Review 30: 843-861.

SCHWARTZ, A. N. and J. A. PETERSON (1979) Introduction to Gerontology. New York: Holt, Rinehart & Winston.

SELTZER, W. (1973) "Demographic data collection: a summary of experience." New York: The Population Council.

SHANAS, E. (1978) A National Survey of the Aged. Final Report to the Administration on Aging. Washington, DC: Department of Health, Education and Welfare.

SHANAS, E., P. TOWNSEND, D. WEDDERBURN, H. FRIIS, P. MILHOJ, and J. STEHOUWER (1968) Old People in Three Industrial Societies. New York: Atherton.

SHELDON, H. D. (1960) "The changing demographic profile," pp. 27-61 in Clark Tibbitts (ed.) Handbook of Social Gerontology: Societal Aspects of Aging. Chicago: University of Chicago Press.

SHRYOCK, H. S., J. S. SIEGEL et al. (1973) The Methods and Materials of Demography. Washington, DC: Government Printing Office.

SIEGEL, J. S. (1976) "Demographic aspects of aging and the older population in the United States." Current Population Reports, Special Studies Series P-23, No. 59. Washington, DC: Bureau of the Census.

SIEGEL, J. S. (1980) "On the demography of aging." Demography 17, 4: 345-364.

SIEGEL, J. S. (1981) "Demographic background for international gerontological studies." Journal of Gerontology 36, 1: 93-102.

SIEGEL, J. S. and C. M. TAEUBER (1982) "The 1980 census and the elderly: new data available to planners and practitioners." The Gerontologist 22, 2: 144-150.

SOLDO, B. (1981) "The living arrangements of the elderly in the near future," pp. 491-512 in S. B. Kiesler et al. (eds.) Aging: Social Change. New York: Academic Press.

STOLNITZ, G. (1956) "A century of international mortality trends: II," pp. 17-42 in Population Studies Vol. 10, Pt. 1.

TIBBITTS, C. (1960) "Origin, scope and fields of social gerontology," in C. Tibbitts (ed.) Handbook of Social Gerontology: Societal Aspects of Aging. Chicago: University of Chicago Press.

UEDA, K. (1983) Recent Trends of Mortality in Asian Countries. Tokyo: Southeast Asian Medical Information Center.

United Nations, Department of Economic and Social Affairs (1967) Manual IV: Methods of Estimating Basic Demographic Measures from Incomplete Data. New York: United Nations.

United Nations, Department of International Economic and Social Affairs (1981) "Estimates and projections of the number of households by country, 1975-2000," ESA/P/WF. 73. New York: United Nations.

United Nations, Department of Economic and Social Affairs (1982a) Model Life Tables for Developing Countries. New York: United Nations.

United Nations, Department of Economic and Social Affairs (1982b) Demographic Indicators of Countries: Estimates and Projections as Assessed in 1980. New York: United Nations.

United Nations (1982c) 1981 Demographic Yearbook. New York: United Nations.

United Nations (1983) 1982 Demographic Yearbook. New York: United Nations.

U.S. Bureau of the Census (1976) Demographic Aspects of Aging and the Older Population in the United States. Current Population Reports, Series P-23, No. 59. Washington, DC: Department of Commerce.

U.S. Bureau of the Census (1978) Social and Economic Characteristics of the Older Population: 1978. Current Population Reports Series P-23 No. 85. Washington, DC: Department of Commerce.

VERBRUGGE, L. M. (1983) "Women and men: mortality and health of older people," pp. 139-174 in M. W. Riley et al. (eds.) Aging in Society: Selected Reviews of Recent Research. Hillsdale, NJ: Lawrence Erlbaum.

WILLIS, R. J. (1981) "The old age security hypothesis and population growth," in T. K. Burch (ed.) Demographic Behavior: Interdisciplinary Perspectives. Boulder, CO: Westview.

Introduction to Chapter 3

The social well-being or morale of the elderly has been and continues to be extensively studied by social scientists. In particular, attention has been given to the correlates and causes of well-being. Although it is rarely made explicit, this focus on well-being apparently reflects an underlying assumption that a positive well-being is valued for the elderly and that knowledge of predictors will enable the development of policy to promote the well-being of older persons. In terms of broad social policy, findings may translate into policies concerning retirement, health care, and income maintenance. At the programmatic level, information about the predictors of well-being may be used to design social programs such as senior centers and activities, living environments, and pre-retirement programs. Whether or not the design of such programs has been guided by research on well-being, the promotion of well-being has been the expressed purpose of many programs, as witnessed by the language in the Older American's Act. Furthermore, it is common practice to use measures of well-being as outcome measures in the evaluation of programs.

This central role of well-being as both the goal of social policy and a measure of success suggests a common understanding of the concept and the ability to measure it reliably. Yet Stull's chapter clearly illustrates that the definition, conceptualization, and measurement of well-being and related concepts are problematic. It appears that much of public policy, both as it is defined and at the programmatic level, is guided by findings that are questionable and difficult to interpret. This chapter raises numerous questions about the meaning and measurement of well-being and provides a much-needed synthesis of the theoretical and methodological issues in the literature. One of the most important issues addressed by the chapter concerns the extent to which well-being is amenable to change. If well-being is a stable attribute of an individual, the use of well-being both as a goal for policy and a measure of success is questionable and deserves serious attention.

In contrast, if it is determined that well-being is subject to change, a number of questions about values arise that deserve serious attention. For example, should the goal of a policy be to promote a minimum standard of well-being for the largest number of persons or should the goal be to maximize the well-being for selected populations? The answer to that question leads to others such as what should a minimum standard be and which segments of the population should be given priority? While important, questions about values cannot be addressed in an informed manner in the absence of conceptual clarity and adequate measurement of the concept of well-being.

3

Conceptualization and Measurement
of Well-Being

Implications for Policy Evaluation

DONALD E. STULL

Well-being, and related measures of happiness, life satisfaction, and morale, are a group of concepts that have received much attention in gerontology. There is seldom an issue in a major journal of the field that does not include an article that looks at correlates or predictors of well-being. A parallel line of inquiry has developed more recently that is concerned with issues of conceptualizing and measuring well-being, happiness, life satisfaction, and morale. It is time to bring together research from several disciplines that has focused on the concept of well-being, take stock of where researchers are in this endeavor, and see where future research must be directed.

In the past two decades, a great deal of research has been conducted in the United States and around the world on assessing well-being in different populations (e.g., Andrews and Withey, 1976; Campbell et al., 1976; Hall, 1976). A fair question that might be posed to researchers in this area is, Why try to predict such things as well-being, happiness, or life satisfaction? One reasonable response comes from the social indicators research. Just as the gross national product is inter-

AUTHOR'S NOTE: I would like to thank Karl D. Kosloski, Laurie Russell Hatch, and Kyle Kercher for comments on an earlier draft.

preted as a measure of the functioning and health of the economy, measures of happiness and satisfaction are an indication of the mental health or well-being of particular groups of people (see, for example, Campbell, 1976; Campbell et al., 1976).

While the measure of the GNP provides us with useful, objective, summary information about the economy, the question must be asked, How well do these economic data represent the quality of life? It is doubtful that these objective measures capture the true experience or impact of life circumstances. As Campbell (1976: 118) has stated,

> If we are primarily concerned with describing the quality of the life experience of the population, we will need measures different from those that are used to describe the objective circumstances in which people live. We will have to develop measures that go directly to the experience itself.

In terms of applied concerns, measures of well-being can be used to assess the impact of programs or changes in service delivery for client populations. This means, of course, that measures of well-being are important to those carrying out evaluation research and to policymakers. Thus, conceptualization and measurement of well-being are important to the development and evaluation of social and health policy.

One of the biggest problems in this area is the lack of consistency in the usage of the terms "well-being," "happiness," "life satisfaction," and "morale" (see George, 1979; Horley, 1984; Larson, 1978; Wilcox, 1978). A substantial amount of research has shown that while these measures are related, they are not identical (e.g., Andrews and McKennell, 1980; Campbell et al., 1976; Horley, 1984; Lohmann, 1977; McKennell, 1978; McKennell and Andrews, 1980; Michalos, 1980). For example, a number of authors (e.g., Andrews and McKennell, 1980; Campbelll et al., 1976; McKennell, 1978; McKennell and Andrews, 1980) have argued that life satisfaction has a more cognitive component to it, while happiness has a more affective or emotional component to it. If this is true, then one would not expect variables of interest to be related in the same way to both of these measures. Any assumptions or expectations of identical correlates or predictors would most likely not be met. Yet many researchers continue to treat the concepts and measures as interchangeable and fail to note that differences in findings among studies may be due to the choice of dependent measure. The failure to treat these measures as distinct but related has led to problems of comparability between studies and may contribute to confusion.

A second and related problem concerns the way in which these various measures fit into a larger scheme. It has been suggested (Horley, 1984; George, 1978; Stones and Kozma, 1980) that happiness, life satisfaction, and morale are measures of well-being. While this seems a reasonable place to start, it is necessary to specify how such things as domain satisfactions, overall life satisfaction, happiness, morale, and well-being all fit together.

This chapter discusses a number of central issues and problems regarding conceptualization and measurement of well-being and related measures. First, definitions of happiness, life satisfaction, and morale are presented along with issues of what is actually being measured (e.g., attitudes, personality traits, moods). Second, research that has looked at the underlying components of the various concepts will be discussed. Third, measures that have commonly been used will be discussed and briefly compared. Finally, a number of models of the structure of well-being will be presented. The purpose here is to provide a sense of the work that has been done to date and to clarify issues.

How Should We View Measures of Well-Being?

Definitions

For centuries philosophers have discussed the distinctions between and the desirability of various states of human condition (for example, happiness and virtue; see Stones and Kozma, 1980). For over 20 years researchers in gerontology have acknowledged the multidimensional nature of well-being. Nevertheless, these concepts are often used interchangeably—an unfortunate and confusing practice. A critical look at the definitions of these concepts suggests that they are not identical.

Happiness has been defined as transitory moods of "gaiety and elation" that reflect the affect that people feel toward their current state of affairs (Campbell et al., 1976). It has also been defined as the extent to which positive feelings outweigh negative feelings (Bradburn, 1969). This latter definition often includes the time dimension of "the past few weeks." (The issue of time will be discussed below.)

Life satisfaction generally refers to some overall assessment of one's life or a comparison reflecting some perceived discrepancy between one's aspirations and achievement (Campbell et al., 1976). In this regard, satisfaction suggests a cognitive process, while happiness implies an affective or mood state. Life satisfaction questions usually include some explicit or implicit comparison group ("compared to others") or some time referent ("life as a whole" or "compared to two years ago"). In addition to overall life satisfaction, questions regarding satisfaction with certain domains of life are often asked.

The concept of morale is perhaps the most poorly defined and measured concept of the three. Kutner et al. (1956) equate adjustment and morale and define morale as "a continuum of responses to life and living problems that reflect the presence or absence of satisfaction, optimism, and expanding life perspectives." Lawton (1972, 1975) has defined morale as a basic sense of satisfaction with oneself, a feeling that there is a place in the environment for oneself, and an acceptance of what cannot be changed. As can be seen, these definitions include the concept of satisfaction. A final definition of morale, a dictionary definition, has been presented by George (1979) and by Stones and Kozma (1980): a mental or moral condition "with respect to courage, discipline, confidence, enthusiasm."

One rationale for using the concept of happiness rather than morale is given by Stones and Kozma (1980). They state that based upon dictionary definitions, happiness and morale are quite different, and life satisfaction is closer in meaning to happiness than to morale. They argue that the construct of happiness is preferable to that of morale due to the long history of its usage. Happiness has roots in antiquity, while the notion of morale is as recent as the nineteenth century; and the term life satisfaction is even more recent in origin than morale. A more convincing argument is presented by Bradburn (1969). He states that happiness corresponds most closely to subjective well-being, which is at the root of mental health. Additionally, happiness appears to be more narrowly conceptualized than either life satisfaction or morale scales. These are, however, weak reasons for choosing one measure over the other. The choice must be based upon what the researcher wants to measure and what each of these constructs is measuring.

Attitudes, Affect, and Cognition

Some researchers have suggested that measures of well-being are measures of attitudes. According to Andrews and McKennell (1980), previous research on attitudes has suggested at least two underlying components: cognition and affect (see, for example, Campbell et al., 1976; McKennell, 1978). They then state that measures of well-being "are fundamentally measures of attitudes, and hence can be expected to reflect cognitive and affective elements" (1980: 127). What is at issue here is not whether these measures differentially tap cognitive and affective dimensions, for this has been addressed by several authors (Andrews and McKennell, 1980; Campbell et al., 1976; McKennell, 1978; McKennell and Andrews, 1980; Michalos, 1980; Stones and Kozma, 1980). Rather, the issue is whether or not some or all of these measures are measures of attitudes and whether they should be conceptualized as such.

Attitudes have been viewed as multidimensional, including cognitive, affective, and conative (behavioral) components (see, for example, Rosenberg and Hovland, 1960). They have been variously defined as "a mental and neural state of readiness, organized through experience, exerting a directive or dynamic influence upon the individual's response to all objects and situations with which it is related" (Allport, 1935) and as "a learned predisposition to respond in a consistently favorable or unfavorable manner with respect to a given object" (Fishbein and Ajzen, 1975). However, other constructs such as personality traits also account for consistencies in behavior (Brannon, 1976). Personality traits have been defined as differing from attitudes in that they have no particular object of reference (e.g., assertiveness; see Brannon, 1976). The question is, then, whether such things as optimism or happiness represent moods or personality traits, or whether they represent attitudes toward life (George, 1979).

The reason for this concern centers on how much variability within individuals is to be expected over time. Happiness, life satisfaction, and morale may not exhibit changes over time in the same way if some of these are attitudes and others are personality traits. That is, people who have a generally happy disposition may show slight changes in happiness with the occurrence of certain life events (e.g., retirement or widowhood) but little variation in the long run. On the other hand, life satisfaction, which some consider to be the result of a comparison between aspirations and achievements (e.g., Campbell et al., 1976), may only show changes over an extended period of time, when differences between aspirations and achievements become salient. An additional point is that different factors may account for any change that might be exhibited in a particular measure depending upon whether the underlying dimension is an attitude or a personality trait. That is, attitudes are presumed to be susceptible to processes of cognitive dissonance, while it is questionable that personality traits are affected by this process.

Other discussions seem to indicate that some of these measures should be considered indicators of moods, emotions, or dispositions (e.g., Wessman and Ricks, 1966). Wessman and Ricks argue that happiness/unhappiness is a reflection of one's changing subjective feelings of elation or depression. Consequently, while there may be day-to-day changes in happiness, over an extended period of time one's responses would reflect a general mood or disposition.

High stability measures have been reported by a number of authors (r = .38 to .60) for both single-item measures of happiness and life satisfaction (see Campbell et al., 1976; Smith, 1979).[1] Using a reinterview subsample of 285 and a test-retest period of eight months, Campbell et al. (1976) report a higher stability measure for overall life satisfaction than for happiness. This finding supports the contention that life satisfaction is affected only after a long period of time, when comparisons can be made.

These stability measures can be interpreted in at least two ways: (1) The measure is reliable (this is the usual interpretation); and (2) people are fairly stable in regard to these dimensions of their lives. A third possible interpretation is that people develop a pattern of consistency in answering such questions independently of the actual level of the measure. It is possible that all of these interpretations are true.

This leads to the additional concern of time. What period of time must transpire before changes in these various measures become observable or meaningful? The inclusion of time referrents such as "compared to two years ago" or "taking all things together...life as a whole" or "taking all things together, how would you say things are these days" may result in different kinds of assessments. Comparing one's life after retirement with life before retirement (e.g., "two years ago") requires a different assessment than does one referring to "life as a whole these days." This is a particularly important issue in longitudinal designs with repeated measures. Different amounts of intervening time may lead to different results and interpretations. Many life events may be upsetting in the short run, but new patterns become established and levels of happiness or satisfaction may return to their previous level or close to that level. Hence, measurement points that are temporally close to the event of interest would yield different results than would measurement points that are farther apart.

Additional Issues

Two other issues should be mentioned regarding global measures of happiness. Smith (1979) has stated that there appears to be seasonal variation in the global measure of happiness, with happiness highest in the spring, declining in the summer and fall, and dropping to its lowest point in the winter. The other issue concerns the positivity bias of global measures of happiness due to social desirability. This is a problem particularly when the number of response categories is small, and the responses cluster at one end, reducing variance. Unfortunately, Smith did not look at global measures of life satisfaction, so comparisons cannot be made with overall happiness.

Underlying Dimensions of Measures of Well-Being: Cognition, Affect, Disposition

Early work regarding the distinction between underlying dimensions of cognition and affect is commonly traced back to two researchers: Cantril (1965) and Bradburn (Bradburn and Caplovitz, 1965; Bradburn, 1969). Cantril conceptualized well-being as a cognitive experience in which individuals compared achievements with aspirations. The discrepancy between these two, then, is a measure of satisfaction/dissatisfaction—a measure of well-being.

The other approach has been to conceptualize well-being as largely affective. Bradburn was primarily concerned with the "subjective feeling states that individuals experience in their daily lives." He identified two orthogonal dimensions, which he called positive and negative affect. These scales varied independently and were correlated to different sets of variables. The degree to which positive feelings outweigh negative feelings (the affect balance) determined the degree of happiness one felt. The choice of the name "positive affect" or "negative affect" was, however, an unfortunate one, since the two factors contain items that have little or nothing to do with affect. This will be evident later in this section and in the discussion of the various measures of well-being in the next section.

It should be pointed out that neither of these conceptualizations is either purely cognitive or purely affective. Rather, they appear to share a certain degree of both elements, but include more of one than of the other. A substantial amount of research has centered around this distinction (e.g., Andrews and McKennell, 1980; Campbell et al.,

1976; McKennell, 1978; McKennell and Andrews, 1980; Michalos, 1980). In this regard, McKennell (1978: 395) has noted that

> it is not simply the semantic distinction between satisfaction and happiness that is at issue, nor even between the rating-scale indicators that bear these labels. What is important is the distinction between the underlying dimensions of cognition and affect which...are only imperfectly tapped by these indicators.

Related to this issue of conceptualization is the issue of correlates of the various measures of well-being. Reviews of the literature (e.g., Larson, 1978) show that the different measures have different correlates, though these measures are often treated an synonymous and the terms happiness and satisfaction are used interchangeably. Indeed, McKennell (1978) found that when looking at the area of non-overlap between happiness and life satisfaction ratings, a number of variables were found to be differentially related. These differences were not apparent using simple correlations. Additionally, Lohmann (1977) has shown that many of the major scales used in studies of well-being are highly intercorrelated. It appears, as McKennell (1978) notes, that these measures tap both cognitive and affective components, though to different degrees. The correlations between these measures can be accounted for by the factor loadings they have in common on the underlying factors. Similarly, Wilson (1967) has stated that one of the problems of measures of mental health is not that they fail to measure happiness, but rather that they also measure other things. This is a note of caution suggesting that these different concepts may be associated with different sets of correlates or predictors.

Some writers have identified three-factor models. For example, Beiser (1974) obtained two components that corresponded very closely to Bradburn's positive and negative affect, and a third factor that appears to be a dispositional factor. Stones and Kozma (1980) argue that Neugarten et al. (1961) and Lawton (1972) "intended a dispositional component as part of their respective formulations" (1980: 275). However, neither was able to sufficiently separate the affective and dispositional factors.

It has been pointed out by a number of authors (e.g., Knapp, 1976; Stones and Kozma, 1980) that most researchers in this area acknowledge the multidimensional nature of these measures. Indeed, many factor analytic studies have been conducted that show that many of the popular scales are not unidimensional (e.g., Adams, 1969; Bigot,

1974; Lawton, 1975; Morris and Sherwood, 1975). However, subsequent researchers have not always remained faithful to the structure reported and have occasionally treated the scales as unidimensional, thus confounding the underlying dimensions (e.g., Collette, 1984; Liang, 1982; Liang et al., 1980). In contrast to these measures, the Kutner Morale Scale (Kutner et al., 1956) and global measures of happiness and satisfaction imply a unidimensional construct.

Other interpretations of underlying dimensions of some of these measures have been discussed. For example, Cherlin and Reeder (1975) argue that the simple two-component model of Bradburn's Affect Balance Scale (positive and negative affect) is incorrect insofar as it includes items that are not affective items but rather refer to levels of activation (for example, "excited or interested in something"). Bradburn (1969) and Cherlin and Reeder (1975) have stated that the notions of positive and negative affect may not be adequate to cover the full range of emotions involved in well-being.

Burt and his colleagues (1978) explore what they call the third aspect of well-being, the first two being absolute levels of well-being in society and feelings of power over individual well-being (i.e., alienation). They refer to this third aspect as the "structure of well-being" (1978: 365) and conclude that it has four dimensions: positive affect, negative affect, satisfaction with domains, and general satisfaction. In addition to the items from Bradburn's Affect Balance Scale, they include domain satisfaction items, making their analyses clearly different from those of Cherlin and Reeder (which included only the Affect Balance Scale).

Finally, Lawton (1983) has hypothesized that subjective well-being is composed of four first-order dimensions: congruence between expectation and attainment (basically, life satisfaction), happiness, positive affect, and negative affect. Lawton and his colleagues (Lawton et al., 1984) and Liang (1985) have put this conceptualization to fairly rigorous empirical tests, confirming that this is one possible underlying structure.

Common Measures of Well-Being

Descriptions and Shortcomings

A review of the literature indicates that well-being has been measured by four major scales or global items: Life Satisfaction Index A

(Neugarten et al. 1961),[2] Philadelphia Geriatric Center Morale Scale (Lawton, 1975), Bradburn Affect Balance Scale (Bradburn and Caplovitz, 1965; Bradburn, 1969),[3] and global items of happiness and life satisfaction (see, for example, Campbell et al., 1976; Smith, 1979). Each of these scales or items are discussed below and are presented in the Appendix.

The Life Satisfaction Index A and the related scale known as the Life Satisfaction Index B were developed in order to have a relatively short, self-report measure of life satisfaction. The two scales differ only slightly in content but differ greatly in form (see Table 1 in the Appendix). The Life Satisfaction Index A has a checklist of 20 items, statements with which the respondent either agrees or disagrees. The Life Satisfaction Index B, on the other hand, has 17 open-ended questions that are given a score based upon the content of the answers. Neugarten et al. (1961) state that these two instruments can be used together or separately. The Life Satisfaction Index A appears to have been used more than its counterpart, the Life Satisfaction Index B, probably due to ease of administration.

One can see from the items that a great variety of content areas are tapped by each of these scales. For example, questions regarding happiness, life satisfaction, and what could be considered "activation level" (Cherlin and Reeder, 1975)—question 10 in the Life Satisfaction Index A—are all included. Since scores are summed over all items in each of the indices, ratings of happiness, satisfaction, and activation level are combined, thus confounding the separate dimensions. This aspect of the scales has crucial implications for correlates and predictors of well-being. Since these scales (and variations of them) are the most common indices used in research of well-being in the field of gerontology (Larson, 1978; Stull, 1985), this leaves at issue what is being predicted: happiness, life satisfaction, activation level, or some combination of these. Similar measurement issues can be raised concerning the other two scales discussed in this chapter.

The Affect Balance Scale has been subjected to a great deal of analysis (see note 3; also see Knapp, 1976). The Affect Balance Scale is composed of 10 items, 5 referring to "positive affect," and 5 referring to "negative affect" (see Table 2 in the Appendix). According to Bradburn, these two subscales were found to be independent, though both correlated with happiness. In addition, these subscales had different correlates.

According to Bradburn, "balance" refers to the balance between positive and negative affect that an individual's score on the scale should reflect. This balance, however, is the result of an additive process—Bradburn and others since him have stated it as a difference between the negative and positive scales. Hence, the score on the scale is a combination of the positive and negative affect scales. When correlated with other items, it is unclear whether the correlation is due to the relationship between positive affect and the other item, negative affect and the other item, or some combination of positive and negative affect.

An additional concern is the underlying structure of the Affect Balance Scale. Cherlin and Reeder (1975) argue that this two-dimensional structure is not correct. They contend that there is an additional component—activation level—included in the items. The item, "particularly excited or interested in something," could be considered an indicator of some level of activation. Cherlin and Reeder state that

> the Positive Affect Scale is as much a measure of levels of activation or engagement as of pleasantness or happiness. The Negative Affect Scale, on the other hand, seems to be more closely associated with the pleasantness-unpleasantness aspect of emotions [1975: 202].

Additionally, some of the items in the positive affect scale appear to be measuring instrumental aspects (e.g., accomplishments). Thus it may not be the case that the two-dimensional structure is incorrect but rather that the label "positive affect" is inappropriate for this factor.[4]

These two issues raise an important question: To what extent does the Affect Balance Scale help us to understand the way in which well-being (or more specifically, affect or happiness) is constructed? Since these components are orthogonal, combining them will result in different correlates than when the subscales are treated independently. Additionally, "positive affect" and "negative affect" imply a bipolar construct, yet these scales have been shown to the orthogonal. This latter issue would seem to indicate that more appropriate labels for the factors are needed.

The Philadelphia Geriatric Center Morale Scale (Lawton 1972) and the Revised Philadelphia Geriatric Center Morale Scale (Lawton, 1975) were developed on the assumption that well-being (Lawton uses the term "morale") is multidimensional. In addition, two other properties were considered important: applicability to older, institutionalized populations, and optimal scale length allowing reliability without respondent fatigue (Knapp, 1976; Lawton, 1975).

The scale originally contained 22 items, but with subsequent analyses was reduced to 15 (Morris and Sherwood, 1975) and 17 (Lawton, 1975), the latter being the Revised Philadelphia Geriatric Center Morale Scale. Earlier analyses produced a six-factor solution, but with the reduced number of items, three major factors were obtained: Agitation (6 items), Attitude Toward Own Aging (5 items), and Lonely Dissatisfaction (6 items). These items and factors are shown in Table 3 in the Appendix.

This scale is subject to the same limitations as those of the Affect Balance Scale. For example, the inclusion of items measuring both happiness and life satisfaction is questionable given the definition of morale presented earlier. This is made even more problematic by the difference in time referent for each of these items ("I am as happy now as when I was younger" and "How satisfied are you with your life today?"). In addition, the practice of combining these factors into a single scale, rather than treating them as separate variables, is problematic. The very fact that Lawton has explicitly treated morale as a multi-dimensional construct should suggest to other researchers that the Philadelphia Geriatric Center Morale Scale represents at least three underlying components of morale.

The final set of measures to be discussed are global measures of happiness and life satisfaction. Table 4 in the Appendix presents most of the variations of these questions that have been used. Overall measures of happiness and life satisfaction have been used in major studies since the 1950s (e.g., Andrews and Withey, 1976; Gurin et al., 1960; Bradburn and Caplovitz, 1965; Cantril, 1965; Campbell et al., 1976). Smith (1979) points out that between 1946 and 1977 nearly 50 surveys have asked respondents in national samples about their happiness.

The choice to use either measures of happiness or life satisfaction, or both, depends upon the interests of the researcher. As discussed above, these two measures appear to tap differentially the underlying dimensions of affect and cognition. In addition, a researcher may have a particular interest in measuring one or the other of these concepts. For example, Campbell et al. (1976) state that their overriding concern was with measuring the quality of American life. Consequently, measures of satisfaction (in terms of need satisfaction) would be of particular interest to legislators and policymakers. It should be noted, however, that Campbell et al. included global measures of both happiness and satisfaction, as well as measures of domain satisfaction.

Obviously, one of the advantages of these overall questions is their brevity. One can get a global assessment of a respondent's well-being (either happiness or life satisfaction) with one or two questions rather than a whole battery of questions. There are, however, problems with these global measures. For example, there appears to be a positivity bias resulting from a number of sources, including social desirability, comparisons with others, and associations of the terms "happiness" and "satisfaction" with positive rather than negative feelings. Additionally, the small number of response categories fails to yield sensitive findings since variance is usually limited to three categories (see Smith, 1979). Further, since two of the three answer categories are stated positively (e.g., "very happy" and "pretty happy" versus "not at all happy"), the questions encourage primarily positive responses.

One additional problem concerns contextual effects. Smith (1979) reports that the National Opinion Research Center (NORC) General Social Surveys from 1973 through 1977 placed a question asking about marital happiness immediately prior to the global question of happiness. This appears to have resulted in a slightly more positive response on the global happiness question than would otherwise be obtained. The effect of question order in measuring overall life satisfaction has not been explored.

Comparisons

Lohmann (1977) has shown that many of the major scales used in research on well-being are correlated quite substantially. Additionally, a global measure of satisfaction ("How satisfied are you with your life?") was found to be moderately correlated with all of the measures tested. Lohmann concludes that these correlations suggest that the measures "are directed toward a common underlying construct" (1977: 74). As stated earlier, McKennell (1978) has argued that happiness and life satisfaction measures differentially tap cognitive and affective components, and that correlations between these measures result from loadings on underlying factors that the measures have in common.

Related to this is the fact that many of the questions in the various scales are similar or identical. Thus, there is a certain degree of overlap between the scales, accounting for their intercorrelations. For example, of the four measures presented in the present paper, the correlation between the Philadelphia Geriatric Center Morale Scale and Life Satisfaction Index A is one of the largest reported by Lohmann (r =

.76). Closer examination of the scales reveals that the two scales either share identical items ("As I get older things seem better than I thought they would," "I am as happy now as when I was younger") or the content area is the same (e.g., each contains a question about current satisfaction, each has a question about sadness or unhappiness).

One final note of caution should be reiterated regarding the construction of the various scales. There is some question as to whether or not it is wise to combine the subscales (e.g., positive and negative affect) into a larger scale when they represent distinct constructs. Factor analysis is only a data reduction tool; ultimately, the researcher has to rely on theory and common sense in determining the final contents of the scale and defining it in terms of what it is measuring.

Models of Relationships of Measures of Well-Being

This section presents a number of models of the structure of well-being. Some of the earlier work in this area (Bradburn, 1969; Campbell et al., 1976; McKennell, 1978) was concerned with the distinction between the underlying dimensions of happiness and satisfaction— that is, affect and cognition. Subsequent researchers recognized that these two dimensions and their indicators were not sufficient to account fully for the underlying structure of well-being. Domain satisfactions, positive and negative affect, life satisfaction, and happiness had to be included. These were found to have differential impact on one another as well as on evaluations of life as a whole. A number of complex models have been developed and tested with sophisticated procedures (e.g., LISREL). These models, some of them simple and others more complex, will be presented below.

Burt and his colleagues (1978) have stated that the most commonly assumed structure of well-being consists of general satisfaction with one's situation. A slightly more complex construct consists of positive and negative affect (e.g., Bradburn and Caplovitz, 1965; Bradburn 1969; Cherlin and Reeder, 1975). A still more complex model treats affect as one of possibly two dimensions, the other being cognition (e.g., McKennell, 1978). In this case, affect and cognition represent two dimensions that are orthogonal to one another. Work by researchers from the Survey Research Center at the University of Michigan (e.g., Andrews and Withey, 1976; Campbell et al., 1976) suggests that the structure of well-being consists of a number of different domain satisfactions that affect evaluations of overall life situation. However, these models generally do not include global measures of happiness, leaving unanswered the question of how happiness fits into a model of the structure of well-being. This issue has been dealt with in several of the models presented below.

Campbell and his colleagues (1976) present two basic models that guided their research. The first model, presented in Figure 3.1, postulates that various comparison situations ("most liked experience," "relatives," "typical American," "other comparisons") affect one's aspiration level, which is compared with the assessment of one's current situation. This comparison, in turn, affects satisfaction with a particular domain. The second model, presented in Figure 3.2, postulates direct relationships between various attributes of a domain, evaluations of those attributes, satisfaction with those domains, and finally how those related to life satisfaction.

One drawback to each of these models is that only the cognitive or comparison aspect is included and the influence of affect is not considered. Subsequent researchers recognized the joint influence of both affective and cognitive components. Thus more recent models have incorporated both of these aspects.

The investigation by Burt et al. (1978) was prompted by the lack of accurate knowledge concerning the structure of well-being. These researchers test four models representing the four postulated structures of well-being discussed above. In the first model (Figure 3.3), a single dimension of general satisfaction is assumed to be the underlying structure. In the second model (Figure 3.4), the underlying dimensions of positive and negative affect represent the structure of well-being. The third model (Figure 3.5) is a combination of the first two in which general satisfaction, positive affect, and negative affect are the three underlying dimensions of well-being. Using data from the NORC Continuous National Survey, chi-square approximations testing for the goodness of fit showed that these three models significantly depart from the observed structures. A fourth structure was found to have a better fit. This model has four main components: general satisfaction, satisfaction with domains (for example, housing, neighborhood, finances, work, leisure), positive affect, and negative affect. However, while this model showed a better fit than the other three, it still showed a significant lack of fit. Thus while this model appears to be an improvement over the earlier two-factor models (e.g., Bradburn, 1969;

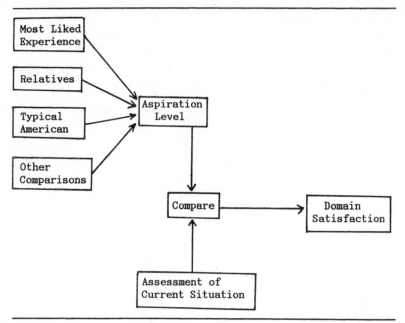

Figure 3.1

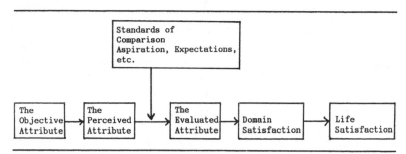

Figure 3.2

Cherlin and Reeder, 1975), it still fails to present an adequate picture of the structure of well-being.

More complex models have been tested by McKennell and Andrews (1980; Andrews and McKennell, 1980). For example, they tested a number of alternative models that included various combinations of affect, domain satisfactions, and "cognition," and their effect on evaluations of life as a whole. Using LISREL (Jöreskog, 1969, 1973;

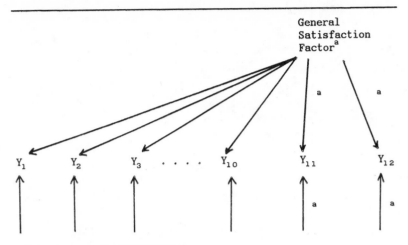

a. Refers to parameters held constant.
Y_1 = Bradburn Positive Affect Scale.
Y_2 = Bradburn Negative Affect Scale.
Y_3 to Y_{10} = evaluations of various domains.
Y_{11} = overall satisfaction with life.
Y_{12} = overall happiness.

Figure 3.3

Jöreskog and Sörbom, 1978) a maximum-likelihood procedure, they tested the fit of a number of models. Two basic models were considered (Figures 3.6 and 3.7). In these models Affect includes both positive and negative affect; D_i and D_j represent domain evaluations; Cognitive is a factor of global cognition (discussed in more detail below). LAW represents a single-item evaluation of life as a whole.

In Figure 3.6 Affect does not directly affect LAW but, rather, operates through domain evaluations. This implies that the evaluations of life as a whole do not include direct influences of emotional aspects of one's life. McKennell and Andrews point out that the absence of a direct influence seems unlikely. In addition, there is no cognitive factor involved in this process, another omission that seems incorrect. A more appealing model is presented in Figure 3.7. In this model both Affect and Cognition have direct and indirect effects on evaluations of life as a whole. Domain satisfactions affect evaluations of life as a whole through association with Affect and Cognition. Results of analyses gave stronger support to this model than to the first.

One drawback to the analyses that still leaves in question the

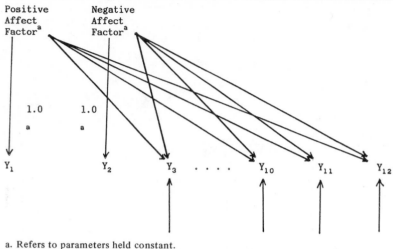

a. Refers to parameters held constant.
Y_1 = Bradburn Positive Affect Scale.
Y_2 = Bradburn Negative Affect Scale.
Y_3 to Y_{10} = evaluations of various domains.
Y_{11} = overall satisfaction with life.
Y_{12} = overall happiness.

Figure 3.4

specification of the model is the fact that the Cognition factor was derived through a process of residualizing. Since no observed measures of global cognition were available, McKennell and Andrews removed the variance explained by Affect and the methods effect (correlated error) and treated the residual variance as Cognition. This lack of observed measures means, of course, that any number of other dimensions could also be implied by the residual variance. Consequently, a number of other models could be equally correct.

In contrast to other researchers who have treated psychological well-being and subjective well-being as synonymous, Lawton et al. (1984) consider psychological well-being to be one of four dimensions of subjective well-being. The other three dimensions are behavioral competence, perceived quality of life, and objective environment. In their analyses they sought to determine the underlying dimensions of psychological well-being. The dimensions that emerged were negative affect, congruence between expectation and attainment, and positive affect. Happiness was also a possible factor. These findings are consistent with past research.

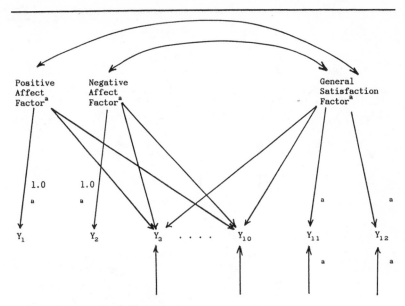

a. Refers to parameters held constant.
Y_1 = Bradburn Positive Affect Scale.
Y_2 = Bradburn Negative Affect Scale.
Y_3 to Y_{10} = evaluations of various domains.
Y_{11} = overall satisfaction with life.
Y_{12} = overall happiness.

Figure 3.5

In subsequent analyses Lawton et al. found that two factors emerged that seemed to represent "basic" aspects of subjective well-being. The first factor includes items that the researchers view as representing "inner modes" of subjective well-being. Such items as negative affect, self-esteem, and self-rated health are included in this factor. In addition, satisfaction with family loads on this factor, while happiness and satisfaction with friends (which is a quality of life domain) loads on both factors one and two. Lawton et al. interpret this pattern as suggesting that satisfaction with family has an impact on inner states of well-being, while happiness and satisfaction with friends has an impact on inner states as well as outer states. Factor two appears to represent an "outer mode" of subjective well-being. Included in this factor are such items as residential satisfaction, positive affect, and a wish to move. In addition, happiness and satisfaction with friends load highly

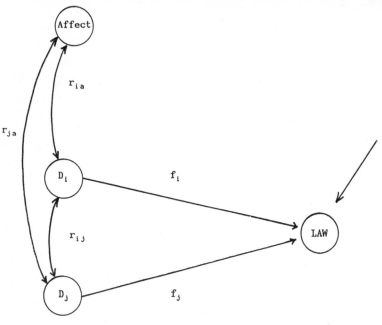

D_i and D_j = domain factors.

Figure 3.6

on this factor as well as factor one. Lawton et al. infer from these analyses that happiness appears to be contingent on both inner psychological well-being and satisfying external stimulation. They conclude that "while the good life model exactly asserts that there is much more to life than happiness, the present research does not let us forget how central happiness is" (1984: 94).

Liang (1985) attempts to integrate two of the scales discussed earlier, the Life Satisfaction Index A and the Affect Balance Scale. He selected 7 items from the Life Satisfaction Index and 8 items from the Affect Balance Scale as measures of the four dimensions discussed by Lawton (1983). The model he proposes to test is presented in Figure 3.8. He reports that, for the most part, the model remains a plausible one—the correlations among the four first-order factors (congruence, happiness, positive affect, and negative affect) could be accounted for by the second-order factor labeled subjective well-being.

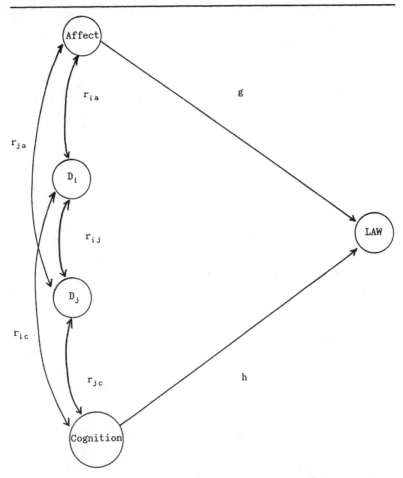

D_i and D_j = domain factors.

Figure 3.7

While Liang's analysis is representative of the sophistication that researchers are applying to this area, one serious drawback remains. An attempt to integrate existing measures without adequate conceptualization of subjective-psychological well-being and underlying dimensions, and without adequate operationalization, will only compound the problems already facing the area. Indeed, Liang acknowledges this issue when he states that

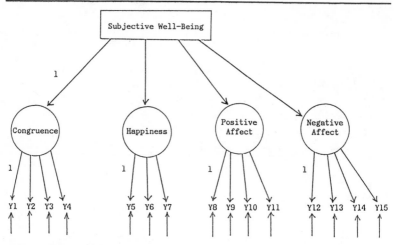

1. Factor loadings set = 1.
Y1 = As I look on my life, I am fairly well satisfied.
Y2 = I would not change my past life even if I could.
Y3 = I have gotten what I expected out of life.
Y4 = I have gotten more of the breaks in life.
Y5 = I am just as happy as when I was younger.
Y6 = My life could be happier.
Y7 = These are the best years of my life.
Y8 = Feel excited.
Y9 = Feel pleased.
Y10 = Feel on top of the world.
Y11 = Feel things are going your way.
Y12 = Feel restless.
Y13 = Feel very lonely.
Y14 = Feel bored.
Y15 = Feel depressed.

Figure 3.8

what seems to be lacking is a continuity between the theoretical conceptualization of subjective well-being and its operationalization. As
observed by Sauer and Warland (1982), most instruments were developed
with only a general conceptual definition, and the sampling of the item
domain is usually based on intuition, experience, and empirical experi-
mentation [1985: 553].

To what extent Liang's model would have remained unchanged had
a larger universe of items originally been sampled for inclusion is a
potentially important empirical question. This is a criticism that must
be leveled at researchers in this area in general and not at any one study

in particular. It is a reflection of the current state of conceptualization and measurement of well-being.

Conclusions

It is obvious from this review that the concern with measures and underlying dimensions of well-being is not limited to the field of gerontology. Indeed, many of these scales or items have been used originally with nonelderly populations. Thus the concerns discussed here have a more general application, and gerontologists should look outside of their field for developments in this area.

Four major points have been made in this review. First, conceptual and definitional distinctions between dimensions of well-being need to be made carefully and explicitly. One problem with past research has been the lack of consistency in the usage of the terms "happiness," "life satisfaction," "morale," and "well-being." These concepts are not identical in meaning, yet the terms have been used interchangeably for distinct concepts and measures.

A second problem concerns the measures of the relevant concepts. If a larger universe of items had been used, to what extent would there be changes in the measures currently being used? It is unclear whether this would result in additional factors, items being rearranged among new factors, or whether existing factors would remain but would be more amenable to appropriate labels.

Third, labels for factors should take into account the content of the items. The desire of the researcher to have a measure that includes the term "life satisfaction" or "morale" may fail to capture the essence of each of the factors. Similarly, the use of labels such as "positive" and "negative" affect for measures that are not, in fact, symmetrical may obscure the true composition of the factors. In addition, combining orthogonal factors may not add to predicitive ability and may obscure the relative contributions of each factor.

Fourth, alternative models to those presented here are still viable. This is particularly important given the construction of the measures and the factors used in the models. The inclusion of additional items in measures or additional measures in models can change the model and thus change the nature of the relationships between the measures under consideration. Additionally, the use of goodness-of-fit tests can yield identical results for any number of different models, and if underlying dimensions are not measured but are merely assumed or implied, then results become particularly tenuous. Since goodness-of-fit tests are sensitive to sample size, different sample sizes can lead to different and perhaps incorrect conclusions about the model under consideration. That is, large samples can be expected to produce significant differences (i.e., lack of fit) while small samples may not produce such results. While LISREL and confirmatory factor analytic techniques are in vogue, they will not compensate for poor conceptualization or poor measurement.

The central issue that researchers in this area must now address is one of conceptualization—that is, whether or not the underlying dimensions of well-being are attitudes, personality traits, or mood states, and whether or not well-being is best represented by some combination of these. Andrews and McKennell seem convinced that these underlying dimensions are attitudes when they state that

> the fact that different measures show somewhat different patterns of relationships raises the fundamental question, Why? It would seem reasonable to suppose that the measures are tapping different components of people's attitudes about their own well-being [1980: 130].

However, it can also be argued that the different patterns of relationships are due to these measures tapping something other than, or in addition to, attitudes (for example, personality traits or mood states). If one or more of these underlying dimensions is an attitude, we could question whether or not attitudinal change has some relevant referent in behavior. Stated differently, does attitudinal change manifest itself in some change in behavior or well-being? If one or more of these underlying dimensions is a personality trait, it is probably unrealistic to expect much change over time. However, whether or not change takes place and the conditions under which change could occur remain empirical questions. If some of these dimensions are mood states, changes could reflect either true variance or unreliability of measurement. The events that bring about changes in mood states are likely to differ substantially from those that affect the more enduring personality or dispositional traits.

It is clear that what constitutes an appropriate measure depends upon how the investigator conceptualizes well-being and its underlying dimensions. Additionally, the investigator's choice of phenomena to study will determine the appropriateness of a particular measure. For example, the choice of positive affect as a dependent variable is probably not meaningful in situations of catastrophic events, such as a stroke. Consequently, it is unlikely that a standard measure of well-being applicable to all gerontological studies can be constructed.

These issues should be of concern to policymakers. As discussed above, the choice of dependent measure may affect interpretations of the data, which will affect policy. For example, if a measure that taps into a personality trait or mood state is used and shows little or no change, researchers and policymakers may interpret this as a failure of the program to have any impact on the clients. Similarly, if a measure of satisfaction is used and the time period between measurement points is short, little or no change may be apparent. Since satisfaction is hypothesized to represent a comparison between aspirations and achievements, a short time period may not allow for sufficient change in life circumstances for an adequate comparison. Clearly, then, issues of conceptualizing and measuring well-being are of importance to both researchers and policymakers.

NOTES

1. Campbell et al. (1976) report a stability measure for their overall measure of happiness of .38. However, they also report that 10 percent of their test-retest subsample had moved in the interim. They state that this appears to have dampened the stability measures of a number of domain satisfaction measures. It is possible that selecting out this group of people would increase the stability measure of happiness, thus placing it more in line with the values reported by Bradburn and Caplovitz (1965) and Bradburn (1969): $r = .48$.

2. Related to the Life Satisfaction Indices is the Life Satisfaction Rating developed by Neugarten et al. (1961). This scale includes five components: zest versus apathy, resolution and fortitude, congruence between desired and achieved goals, positive self-concept, and mood tone. The Life Satisfaction Rating is used much less than either the Life Satisfaction Index A or the Life Satisfaction Index B due to the requirement of long, detailed interviews (the Life Satisfaction Index A and Life Satisfaction Index B) are relatively short, self-report instruments). Thus the Life Satisfaction Rating will not be discussed here.

3. The Bradburn Affect Balance Scale has been subjected more to scrutiny than to actual usage, particularly in the field of gerontology (this scale was developed for use on the general population rather than an elderly population). Larson (1978) and Stull (1985) indicate that the Affect Balance Scale has been used primarily as a dependent measure for only a few studies in gerontology (e.g., George, 1978; Moriwaki, 1974), while it has been subject to considerable discussion regarding its structure (e.g., Bradburn, 1969; Bradburn and Caplovitz, 1965; Burt et al., 1978; Campbell et al., 1976;

Cherlin and Reeder, 1975). Because of this latter interest in the Affect Balance Scale and the influence it has had on conceptualizing well-being, it will be discussed in this chapter.

4. It should be noted that the factor loadings for these variables placed them solidly in their respective factors. That is, the loadings for the variables that appeared to measure activation level or instrumental aspects were not loading marginally on either of the factors in the findings presented by Cherlin and Reeder (1975). Consequently, it is not unreasonable to assume that these variables are part of these factors. However, the labels "positive affect" and "negative affect" are misleading, given the particular items in each factor.

APPENDIX

Table 1

Life Satisfaction Index A:

Here are some statements about life in general that people feel differently about. Would you read each statement on the list, and if you agree with it, put a check mark in the space under "AGREE." If you do not agree with a statement, put a check mark in the space under "DISAGREE." If you are not sure one way or the other, put a check mark in the space under "?." PLEASE BE SURE TO ANSWER EVERY QUESTION ON THE LIST.

(Key: score one point for each response marked X.)

	AGREE	DISAGREE	?
1. As I grow older, things seem better than I thought they would be.			
2. I have gotten more of the breaks in life than most of the people I know.			
3. This the dreariest time of my life.			
4. I am just as happy as when I was younger.			
5. My life could be happier than it is now.			
6. These are the best years of my life.			
7. Most of the things I do are boring or monotonous.			
8. I expect some interesting and pleasant things to happen to me in the future.			
9. The things I do are as interesting to me as they ever were.			
10. I feel old and somewhat tired.			
11. I feel my age, but it does not bother me.			
12. As I look back on my life, I am fairly well satisfied.			
13. I would not change my past life even if I could.			

(continued)

14. Compared to other people my
    age, I've made a lot of foolish
    decisions in my life.

15. Compared to other people my
    age, I make a good appearance.

16. I have made plans for things
    I'll be doing a month or a
    year from now.

17. When I think back over my
    life, I didn't get most of the
    important things I wanted.

18. Compared to other people, I
    get down in the dumps too
    often.

19. I've gotten pretty much what
    I expected out of life.

20. In spite of what people say,
    the lot of the average man is
    getting worse, not better.

Life Satisfaction Index B:
        (with scoring key)

   Would you please comment freely in answer to the
following questions?

   1. What are the best things about being the age you
      are now?
         1.....a positive answer
         0.....nothing good about it

   2. What do you think you will be doing five years
      from now? How do you expect things will be dif-
      ferent from the way they are now, in your life?
         2.....better, or no change
         1.....contingent--"It depends"
         0.....worse

   3. What is the most important thing in your life right
      now?
         2.....anything outside of self, or pleasant inter-
               pretation of future
         1....."Hanging on"; keeping health, or job
         0.....getting out of present difficulty, or "nothing
               now," or reference to the past

   4. How happy would you say you are right now, com-
      pared with earlier periods in your life?
         2.....this is the happiest time; all have been
               happy; or, hard to make a choice
         1.....some decrease in recent years
         0.....earlier periods were better, this is a bad time

5. Do you ever worry about your ability to do what people expect of you--to meet demands that people make on you?
   2.....no
   1.....qualified yes or no
   0.....yes

6. If you could do anything you pleased, in what part of_____would you most like to live?
   2.....present location
   0.....any other location

7. How often do you find yourself feeling lonely?
   2.....never; hardly ever
   1.....sometimes
   0.....fairly often; very often

8. How often do you feel there is no point in living?
   2.....never; hardly ever
   1.....sometimes
   0.....fairly often; very often

9. Do you wish you could see more of your close friends than you do, or would you like more time to yourself?
   2.....O.K. as is
   0.....wish could see more of friends
   0.....wish more time to self

10. How much unhappiness would you say you find in your life today?
    2.....almost none
    1.....some
    0.....a great deal

11. As you get older, would you say things seem to be better or worse than you thought they would be?
    2.....better
    1.....about as expected
    0.....worse

12. How satisfied would you say you are with your way of life?
    2.....very satisfied
    1.....fairly satisfied
    0.....not very satisfied

Source: Neugarten et al (1961)

(continued)

APPENDIX Continued

Table 2

Bradburn Affect Balance Scale:

Question: We are interested in the way people are feeling these days. During the past few weeks did you ever feel:

Positive Affect

1. pleased about having accomplished something?

2. that things were going your way?

3. on top of the world?

4. proud because someone complimented you on something you had done?

5. particularly excited or interested in something?

Negative Affect

6. very lonely or remote from other people?

7. upset because someone criticized you?

8. so restless that you couldn't sit long in a chair?

9. bored?

10. depressed or very unhappy?

Source: Bradburn (1969)

Table 3

Philadelphia Geriatric Center Morale Scale:

Factor 1 – Agitation:

[b]Little things bother me more this year (No)
[b]I sometimes worry so much that I can't sleep (No)
I have a lot to be sad about (No)
[b]I am afraid of a lot of things (No)
[b]I get mad more than I used to (No)
Life is hard for me most of the time (No)
[b]I take things hard (No)
[b]I get upset easily (No)

Factor 2 – Attitude Toward Own Aging:

[b]Things keep getting worse as I get older (No)
[b]I have as much pep as I had last year (Yes)
Little things bother me more this year (No)
[b]As you get older you are less useful (No)
[b]As I get older, things are better/worse than I thought they
would be (Better)
I sometimes feel that life isn't worth living (No)
[b]I am as happy now as when I was younger (Yes)

Factor 3 – Lonely Dissatisfaction:

[b]How much do you feel lonely? (Not much)
[b]I see enough of my friends and relatives (Yes)
[b]I sometimes feel that life isn't worth living (No)
[b]Life is hard for me much of the time (No)
[b]How satisfied are you with your life today? (Satisfied)
[b]I have a lot to be sad about (No)
People had it better in the old days (No)
A person has to live for today and not worry about tomorrow
(Yes)

----

[b] = Items which consistently loaded highly on its respective factor
     for several studies. Source: Lawton (1975)

(continued)

APPENDIX Continued

<u>Table 4</u>

<u>Happiness and Life Satisfaction Question Wordings</u>:

A. Happiness: AIPO Standard
   In general, how happy would you say you
   are--very happy, fairly happy, or not very
   happy? ("Not at all" additional precoded
   response)................................

   In general, how happy would you say that
   you are--very happy, fairly happy, or not
   very happy? ("Not at all" additional precoded response)..........................

   In general, how happy would you say you
   are--very happy, fairly happy, or not at all
   happy?...................................

   In general, how happy would you say you
   are--fairly happy, very happy, or not very
   happy?...................................

   In general, how happy would you say you
   are--very happy, fairly happy, not very
   happy, or not at all happy?..............

   In general, how happy would you say you
   are--very happy, fairly happy, or not
   happy? ("Not at all" additional precoded
   response)................................

   In general, how happy would you say you
   are--very happy, fairly happy, or not
   happy?...................................

B. Happiness: SRC/NORC Standard

   Taking things all together, how would you
   say things are these days--would you say
   you're very happy, pretty happy, or not too
   happy these days?........................

   Taken all together (altogether), how would
   you say things are these days--would you
   say that you are very happy, pretty happy,
   or not too happy?........................

   Taking all things together, how would you
   say things are these days--would you say
   that you're very happy, pretty happy, or
   not too happy these days?................

C. Happiness: NORC Variant

   Taken all together, how would you say things
   are these days--would you say that you are

. . .completely happy, very happy, moderately happy, slightly happy, or not at all
happy. (CARD used)

D. Happiness: AIPO Variant

Please tell me how far up the scale or how far
down the scale you would rate how happy
you are in general. (5+, 4+, 3+, 2+, 1+,
-1, -2, -3, -4, -5)

E. Andrews' and Withey's 7-Point Happiness
   Item (G32)

How do you feel about how happy you are?

Card lists following responses:

1. Delighted, 2. Pleased, 3. Mostly Satisfied, 4. Mixed (about equally satisfied
   and dissatisfied), 5. Mostly dissatisfied,
   6. Unhappy, 7. Terrible,
   A. Neutral (Neither Satisfied nor dis-
       satisfied)
   B. I never thought about it.
   C. Does not apply to me.

Source: Smith (1979)

AIPO = American Institute of Public Opinion (Gallup)
SRC = Survey Research Center, University of Michigan
NORC = National Opinion Research Center, University of Chicago
Andrews and Withey (1976)

References

ADAMS, D. L. (1969) "Analysis of a life satisfaction index." Journal of Gerontology 24: 470-474.

ALLPORT, G. W. (1935) "Attitudes," in C. Murchison (ed.) A Handbook of Social Psychology. Worcester, MA: Clark University Press.

ANDREWS, F. M. and A. C. McKENNELL (1980) "Measures of self-reported well-being: their affective, cognitive, and other components." Social Indicators Research 8: 127-155.

ANDREWS, F. M. and S. B. WITHEY (1976) Social Indicators of Well-Being: Americans' Perceptions of Life Quality. New York: Plenum Press.

BEISER, M. (1974) "Components and correlates of mental well-being." Journal of Health and Social Behavior 15: 320-327.

BIGOT, A. (1974) "The relevance of American life satisfaction indices for research on British subjects before and after retirement." Age and Ageing 3: 113-121.

BRADBURN, N. M. (1969) The Structure of Psychological Well-Being. Chicago: Aldine.

BRADBURN, N. M. and D. CAPLOVITZ (1965) Reports on Happiness. Chicago: Aldine.

BRANNON, R. (1976) "Attitudes and the prediction of behavior," pp. 145-158 in B. Seidenberg and A. Snadowsky (eds.) Social Psychology: An Introduction. New York: Free Press.

BURT, R. S., J. A. WILEY, M. J. MINOR, and J. R. MURRAY (1978) "Structure of well-being: form, content, and stability over time." Sociological Methods and Research 6: 365-407.

CAMPBELL, A. (1976) "Subjective measures of well-being." American Psychologist (February): 117-124.

CAMPBELL, A., P. E. CONVERSE, and W. L. RODGERS (1976) The Quality of American Life: Perceptions, Evaluations, and Satisfaction. New York: Russell Sage Foundation.

CANTRIL, H. (1965) The Pattern of Human Concerns. New Brunswick, NJ: Rutgers University Press.

CARP, F. M. and A. CARP (1983) "Structural stability of well-being factors across age and gender, and development of scales of well-being unbiased for age and gender." Journal of Gerontology 38: 572-581.

CHERLIN, A. and L. G. REEDER (1975) "The dimensions of psychological well-being: a critical review." Sociological Methods and Research 4: 189-214.

COLLETTE, J. (1984) "Sex differences in life satisfaction: Australian data." Journal of Gerontology 39: 243-245.

FISHBEIN, M. and I. AJZEN (1975) Belief, Attitude, Intention, and Behavior: An Introduction to Theory and Research. Reading, MA: Addison-Wesley.

GEORGE, L. K. (1978) "The impact of personality and social status factors upon levels of activity and psychological well-being." Journal of Gerontology 33: 840-847.

GEORGE, L. K. (1979) "The happiness syndrome: methodological and substantive issues in the study of social-psychological well-being in adulthood." The Gerontologist 19: 210-216.

GURIN, G., J. VEROFF, and S. FELD (1960) Americans View Their Mental Health. New York: Basic Books.

HALL, J. (1976) "Subjective measures of quality of life in Britain: 1971-1975. Some developments and trends." Social Trends 7. HMSO.

HORLEY, J. (1984) "Life satisfaction, happiness, and morale: two problems with the use of subjective well-being indicators." The Gerontologist 24: 124-127.

JÖRESKOG, K. G. (1969) "A general approach to confirmatory maximum likelihood factor analysis." Psychometrika 34: 183-202.

JÖRESKOG, K. G. (1973) "A general method for estimating a linear structural equation system," pp 85-112 in A. Goldberger and O. D. Duncan (eds.) Structural Equation Models in the Social Sciences. New York: Seminar Press.

JÖRESKOG, K. G. and D. SÖRBOM (1978) LISREL IV: Analysis of Linear Structural Relationships by the Method of Maximum Likelihood. Chicago: National Educational Resources.

KNAPP, M.R.J. (1976) "Predicting the dimensions of life satisfaction." Journal of Gerontology 31: 595-604.

KUTNER, B., D. FANSHEL, A. M. TOGO, and T. S. LANGER (1956) Five Hundred Over Sixty. New York: Russell Sage Foundation.

LARSON, R. (1978) "Thirty years of research on the subjective well-being of older Americans." Journal of Gerontology 33: 109-125.

LAWTON, M. P. (1972) "The dimensions of morale," in D. Kent et al. (eds.) Research Planning and Action for the Elderly. New York: Behavioral Publications.

LAWTON, M. P. (1975) "The Philadelphia Geriatric Center Morale Scale: a revision." Journal of Gerontology 30: 85-89.

LAWTON, M. P. (1983) "The varieties of well-being." Experimental Aging Research 9: 65-72.

LAWTON, M. P., M. H. KLEBAN, and E. diCARLO (1984) "Psychological well-being in the aged: factorial and conceptual dimensions." Research on Aging 6: 67-97.

LIANG, J. (1982) "Sex differences in life satisfaction among the elderly." Journal of Gerontology 37: 100-108.

LIANG, J. (1985) "A structural integration of the Affect Balance Scale and the Life Satisfaction Index A." Journal of Gerontology 40: 552-561.

LIANG, J., L. DVORKIN, E. KAHANA, and F. MAZIAN (1980) "Social integration and morale: a re-examination." Journal of Gerontology 35: 746-757.

LOHMANN, N. (1977) "Correlations of life satisfaction, morale and adjustment measures." Journal of Gerontology 32: 73-75.

McKENNELL, A. C. (1978) "Cognition and affect in perceptions of well-being." Social Indicators Research 5: 389-426.

McKENNELL, A. C. and F. M. ANDREWS (1980) "Models of cognition and affect in perceptions of well-being." Social Indicators Research 8: 257-298.

MICHALOS, A. C. (1980) "Satisfaction and happiness." Social Indicators Research 8: 385-422.

MORIWAKI, S. (1974) "The affect balance scale: a validity study with aged samples." Journal of Gerontology 29: 73-78.

MORRIS, J. N. and S. SHERWOOD (1975) "A retesting and modification of the Philadelphia Geriatric Center Morale Scale." Journal of Gerontology 30: 77-84.

NEUGARTEN, B. L., R. J. HAVIGHURST, and S. S. TOBIN (1961) "The measurement of life satisfaction." Journal of Gerontology 16: 134-143.

ROSENBERG, M. J. and C. I. HOVLAND (1960) "Cognitive, affective, and behavioral components of attitudes," in M. J. Rosenberg et al. (eds.) Attitude Organization and Change. New Haven, CT: Yale University Press.

SMITH, T. W. (1979) "Happiness: time trends, seasonal variations, intersurvey differences, and other mysteries." Social Psychology Quarterly 42: 18-30.

STONES, M. J. and A. KOZMA (1980) "Issues relating to the usage and conceptualizations of mental health constructs employed by gerontologists." International Journal of Aging and Human Development 11: 269-281.

STULL, D. E. (1985) "Correlates, predictors, and causal models in research on well-being of the elderly." (unpublished)

WESSMAN, A. E. and D. F. RICKS (1966) Mood and Personality. New York: Holt, Rinehart & Winston.

WILCOX, A. R. (1978) "Dissatisfaction with satisfaction: subjective social indicators and the quality of life." Presented at the seventy-fourth Annual Meeting of the American Sociological Association, Boston.

WILSON, W. R. (1967) "Correlates of avowed happiness." Psychological Bulletin 67: 294-306.

Introduction to Chapter 4

Within the gerontological literature there is a considerable concentration on the correlates, causes, and consequences of social support or the informal support system. The benefits of social support for both physical and psychological well-being have been widely purported and frequently studied. The role of the informal support system in caring for the elderly has been debated, and programs have been advocated and implemented to facilitate, augment, or substitute for social support. Yet, as with social well-being, there is little agreement about the definition and measurement of social support or informal support.

In this chapter, Lawton and Moss provide an extensive review of the literature and clarify the concept of social support. The authors not only explore differences between the quantity and quality of social supports, but provide a compendium of functions of relationships. Using data collected from 236 older persons, the authors report differential relationships between dimensions of well-being and dimensions of social support. The analysis is particularly important because it illustrates the clarity in understanding that can be gained when complex concepts are separated into component variables. It also calls into question the utility of current debates about the merits of social support for well-being and of programs aimed at enhancing the informal support system. Given the present lack of conceptual clarity, it is nearly impossible to draw conclusions about which elements or aspects of a social relationship are important and should be promoted through public policy and programs.

4

The Social Relationships of Older People

M. POWELL LAWTON and MIRIAM MOSS

It is very possible that the most ubiquitous theme of gerontology today is social support or the informal support system. Indeed, the theme is in great danger of wearing out its welcome if corrective measures are not applied both to curb the excess enthusiasm over the presumed merits of social support and to sharpen the amorphous constructs that are sometimes used in research on social support. This chapter will be devoted, first, to a critical analysis of some aspects of social relationships that are in need of better understanding. Second, some new data that add further to this understanding will be presented and interpreted in light of the theoretical introduction.

In fact, in the last year or so the state of the art in comprehending older people's social relationships has shown signs of substantial improvement as critical scientists have begun to identify the conceptual problems in this area. This chapter will attempt particularly to identify such published critiques that pursue individual theoretical and methodological issues in greater depth than can the present discussion.

The Key Concepts in Social Relationships

A number of recent articles have attempted to clarify the relationships among the many concepts that have been used in studying social

AUTHORS' NOTE: This research was supported by grant MN-35312 from the National Institute of Mental Health.

relationships (Heller and Swindle, 1983; Quinn, 1983; Thoits, 1982; Ward, 1985). The present discussion will distinguish among the interpersonal environment, social interaction, the perceived quality of the interpersonal environment, and the functions of the interpersonal environment. Each of these constructs has its own internal structure and subclasses. Furthermore, the subclasses are sometimes by no means as distinct as the names given them. These constructs may in turn be anchored within the larger framework of "the good life" (Lawton, 1983). Three of the suggested sectors that constitute the good life are the objective environment, behavioral competence, and perceived quality of life. The present discussion will consider how the social domains within each of these three sectors are in turn related to the fourth sector, psychological well-being. We shall suggest that objective structural factors in the social environment lead to social competence and to high perceived quality of social relationships.

Interpersonal Environment (Social Network)

For heuristic purposes, the objective environment consists of all that lies outside the skin of the person (Lawton, 1982). One domain of the objective environment sector is the interpersonal environment, defined here as the aggregate of significant others who have some individual relationship (face-to-face, symbolic, or other two-way relationship) with the target person. This definition is identical to the term "social network," which will be used hereafter because of its common currency. According to Adams, a social network is the set of people with whom one "maintains contact and has some form of social bonds" (1967: 64). Wellman (1981) uses the term "social connection" while Berkman and Syme (1979) speak of a "social tie" to refer to this aggregate of people with whom the individual interacts. These terms already connote a chink in the armor of any tight insistence that the interpersonal environment may be defined in purely objective terms. There are almost 5 billion people in the world, but this aggregate clearly is no person's social network. "Contact" is necessary to define a network. Further, a network consists of persons nonrandomly selected by some means that includes the target person's perceptual, cognitive, affective, and behavioral systems, as connoted by the term "bonds." Thus the ideal of the "out-there" aspect of the interpersonal environment is compromised by the intrapersonal factors involved in the selection of such a network.

The out-there quality is perhaps more evident if we think of a family relationship as defining one subclass of social network. As everyone who has ever tried to construct a quantitative index of kin knows, however, even here ambiguities arise. Are second cousins, great-nieces, in-laws, great-great-grandchildren, or relatives not contacted for 30 years to be considered part of the network? Even more ambiguous are nonkin. The usual questions that result in a social network list are "Who are the people that you are close to?"; "Who are the people you are most in contact with?"; or "Who are the people who matter the most to you?" "Close," "in contact with," and "matter the most" connote intrapersonal processes that are not objective.

A subjective element thus intrudes strongly no matter which term we use to delimit network members from nonmembers. The result is that what stands for the network in most research is strongly biased toward closeness and toward the positively valued relationship because of the phrasing of the questions used to generate the network. There is as yet no truly neutral question that can successfully elicit not only friends and family but coworkers, unchosen associates, neighbors, enemies, casual contacts, or other types of individuals with whom we interact and who influence the totality of our experience, but whom we simply do not think of when asked to name our network in any of the usual ways. It is thus obvious that the inherent distortion in constructing a network for research use must be kept in mind as one interprets the results. Less obvious is another type of distortion that confounds the independent and dependent variables in social-relationship research. The respondent has already ascribed some value or affective quality to the people in the network simply by naming them. Thus it might be no surprise that a positive correlation exists, for example, between whether a person was named as a confidant (i.e., a member of the interpersonal environment) and the rating of that person's warmth expressed to the subject (a member of another sector of the good life—perceived quality of life).

Social network theorists have been very explicit in defining formal, or structural, qualities of networks (Hammer, 1981; Homans, 1974; Mitchell, 1969). These constructs have been very useful in operationalizing and understanding social relationships. However, it is suggested here that further conceptual distinctions need to be made among some of these formal characteristics. Interaction, or amount and type of contact between network members, is a structural component of the social network included in most writers' definitions. It is suggested here that interaction is a behavioral attribute that is different from and requires separate consideration from the other structural characteristics. Social interaction is best considered a domain of the behavioral competence sector of the good life. Further, as suggested by Heller and Swindle (1983), some structural network characteristics are "morphological" while others are interactional.

The morphology of a network includes the number of people in the network, their spatial dispersion, and the dominant characteristics of the aggregate of people in the network, if any, such as age, gender, race, or health. (This type of attribute, when applied to all people in spatial proximity to a target individual, was termed "the suprapersonal environment" by Lawton, 1970.) Morphological characteristics exist independently of transactions among members of the network.

Some structural interactional characteristics of a network include, first, reciprocity: Is an interaction one-way or do actors engage in a given behavior or affect as both initiator and receiver? Second is the attribute of symmetry: How many pairs (or larger multiples) of network members interact with one another out of all possible, given the total network size?

The distinction between morphology and interaction again draws attention to the blurring of the lines between the person and the network outside the person. One could make a case for the morphological characteristics existing independently of the person, but the interactional characteristics, while nominally attributes of the network, clearly include both person and other.

Another dimension of the social network, termed the "components" by Ward (1985), has been implied by the foregoing discussion. Family, friends, neighbors, and sometimes professionals or casual contacts, are the usual components into which the network is divided. The spouse is a special instance of the family component. Household members might constitute another way of designating a component. Although the literature provides ample demonstration that the components are well worth distinguishing for both conceptual and analytic purposes, one still occasionally comes across analyses where simple numbers of people in the network, irrespective of class of network member, constitutes the analytic variable. More, rather than less, differentiation among components is desirable for future research. For example, the differential functions of and outcomes associated with whether one has a spouse, children, siblings, or other relatives are clearly worth determining separately. As mentioned earlier, explorations that attempt to incorporate neutral, negative, or casual associates into the research definition of network are desirable.

Social Interaction

Social interaction is suggested as belonging in a conceptually different class from other social network characteristics because the term is reserved for the externally observable behavior of the target person. In our view of the good life, social interaction is an instance of "behavioral competence," which is distinguished from the other sectors comprising the good life—objective environment quality, perceived quality of life, and psychological well-being. An interaction may be defined as a communication between one person and another, whether the medium for communication is behavioral, verbal, affective, or symbolic. An interaction may be either unilateral or reciprocal. While not all interactions occur with members of one's network, one could argue that if a significant interaction occurs with a non-network member, that fact should logically define the stranger as now a member of the network.

Interaction count. The most usual indicator of interaction has been and will continue to be some combination of number of people in one's network with whom one interacts and the frequency of interaction with them. Some examples are the number of people seen three or more times per week; the summed weekly frequencies of interaction across all network members; or the number of instances named in response to the open-ended question, "In an average day, how many people do you see, talk to on the phone, or correspond with?" Such interaction counts may be stratified by network component, separated by specific network member, or aggregated to represent the entire network.

The type of interaction may also be a basis for stratifying interaction counts. To the extent that the type of interaction is exhibited in observable behavior that may be reliably coded, this interactional dimension is unproblematic. For example, observable behaviors such as conversation, letters, touching, personal distance, and caregiving acts are common objects of naturalistic research. Interactions may be reported either by the observer or the person. While there is probably greater error in self-report, these behaviors would still represent instances of interactions that can be counted.

Attempts to characterize types of interaction may sometimes move from the objectively observational to include types that impute motivations, needs, or outcomes in the actor in their definitions (for example, "a comforting interaction"). Such qualitative categories belong in the next major class to be discussed below, perceived quality of life.

The concept of social competence belongs in the social interaction category. Competence in social behavior is defined by values and normative judgments (and thus is qualitative), but the criteria for such normative judgments may be specified clearly enough to allow reliable ratings of observable behavior. Heller and Swindle (1983) cite some examples of social competence, all of which seem to be capable of observational study: conversational skill, role-taking skill, reading cues in Other, adjusting own behavior to these cues, allocating listening and talking behaviors, initiation and response, and so on. Social competence, for the present purpose, may be defined as the quality of behavior exhibited by the target person toward other people, where quality is judged by normative criteria that define desirable interpersonal goals. It should thus be noted that it is contemporary behavioral acts, not their outcomes, that are being judged. For example, the response of the Other is not a factor in the criterion for evaluation of the social competence of a behavior. Some indicators of social competence when viewed as interactions (i.e., initiation and response) are structural network properties.

Perceived Quality of the Interpersonal Environments

One of the canards of the social-support literature is that "it isn't how much interaction that counts, it's the quality of the interaction." Although the evidence for the tenability of this conclusion is incomplete, it is sufficient to note that the importance of distinguishing between quantity (i.e., number of people or frequency of interaction) and subjectively perceived quality of social relationships is firmly established.

Ward (1985), however, has called our attention to the meager fashion by which account has so often been taken of the qualitative aspects of social relationships. The most frequently used index of quality has been the response to a question that elicits an undifferentiated rating of overall satisfaction with the relationship or aggregate of relationships (for example, "How satisfied are you with your friends?"). Sometimes the indicator is a similar rating of satisfaction with the quantity of social interaction ("Do you see enough of your family?").

Ward is certainly correct in finding such evaluations as inadequate representations of all that might be called "perceived quality of relationships." It is nonetheless very important that such overall judgments be obtained. One's evaluation of social relationships (or more specific roles such as those of marital partner, child, friend, or neighbor) constitute a major domain of perceived quality of life (Campbell et al., 1976), one of the four sectors defining the good life (Lawton, 1983). The Campbell study, another by Andrews and Withey (1976), and many others, have shown that such domain-specific evaluations of limited aspects of one's total life have validity in their own right as indicators of satisfaction with life as well as being related to a variety of antecedent and consequent conditions. The tasks for researchers are, first, to improve the psychometric quality of such domain indicators (for example, strive for multiple-item indices with norms rather than the ubiquitous single items quoted above) and, second, to deal more adequately with quality in a broader sense than mere perceived satisfaction.

The salience or importance of a social relationship, a network, or an interaction is a facet of quality that is independent of satisfaction but is a troublesome construct. The importance of importance is not at issue. A person can rank others in terms of how important that person finds them. Further, people may indicate the degree to which they value social relationships among all other domains of their daily lives. What is problematic is the adequacy of the usual methods used to factor in salience along with evaluated quality as predictors of other outcomes. This is a familiar problem in both quality of life and environmental research. It is easy for subjects to indicate their preference for, or evaluation of, a series of attributes—for example, the list of individuals comprising their social networks. However, it would be possible for a subject to rate all network members highly on a scale for "liking" but have only one who is truly salient to the subject's well-being. Thus it would be reasonable to suggest that every object be rated both in terms of quality and importance. Unfortunately, in quality of life research attempts to improve the prediction of life satisfaction through weighting domain ratings (such as measures of perceived quality of life) in terms of perceived salience sometimes do not succeed (Campbell et al., 1976). When tried with older people, we found that it was hard for older subjects to maintain the distinction between quality and salience as they attempted to rate a series of objects in terms of both satisfaction and importance.

It may be desirable in future research to use more sophisticated preferential methods such as paired comparisons or trade-off games (Robinson et al., 1975) to try to approximate better the subjective weighting processes used as people judge the overall quality and significance of other people to them.

The Functions of the Interpersonal Environment

The most difficult construct category has been saved for last. As will be discussed in detail, even naming the category is difficult. Because functions typically are defined by subjective assessments of characteristics of relationships or interactions, this category may be thought of as an aspect of perceived quality of life. The functions category is in one sense the residual of the larger category, quality of social relationships, after the gross, purely evaluational perceived quality features discussed above have been eliminated. Part of the confusion is due to the separate meanings of the term "quality." The first meaning is synonymous with "evaluative," as in perceived quality of social relationships as discussed above. "Quality," however, also has the dictionary definition "character, as belonging to or distinguishing a thing." The residual use here defines quality of social relationships as the characteristics of a relationship or set of relationships described in terms referring to nonevaluative features along which relationships with others may differ. Although this definition succeeds in distinguishing the two types of quality, the semantic confusion caused by the two different meanings of "quality" is intolerable. Thus in deference to its use by a number of investigators, the term "functions of interpersonal relationships" will be defined as above, despite the new set of conceptual problems that the term "function" introduces.

This section will begin by reviewing what many investigators have posited as the major functions of social relationships. Because thinking in this area has been so diffuse, it is essential to see exactly how a variety of scientists have attempted to deal with this concept. Following the review, we will suggest a new set of functions, with definitions, that integrates some of the efforts of others. Finally, we will reintroduce the question of exactly what category it is whose members we are trying to classify when we speak of social relationships.

Functions as Suggested in the Literature

Classical sociology, followed by a latter-day assist from a psychologist (Brown, 1965), posited status and solidarity as the basic dimensions of social relationships. Status represents the social comparison process whereby Self and Other are ranked with respect to any socially desirable dimension. Recognition by the Other that one is of equal or superior status is affirming to that person. Thus the aspects of social relationships that enhance the person's feelings of adequacy in ways that are personally or socially valued constitute a major dimension by which people view themselves and others.

Solidarity, on the other hand, represents a dimension whereby security, commitment, communality, affection, and attachment are evidenced. The competitiveness, aggression, and vulnerability to loss of esteem that characterize relationships among unequals is minimized in situations of solidarity; solidarity is fostered by status equality. It is possible to subsume many other functions of social relationships, such as power or support, under these two rubrics.

More recently, as the tradition of social-support research has become established, there has been a tendency toward elaboration and differentiation among a larger number of different though related characteristics. For example, Weiss (1974) posited six "provisions" of social relationships. First, *attachment* is a link to others that affords the person a feeling of security. Schachter (1959), for example, suggested that emotional arousal or fear led to gregarious behavior, the presumption being that the perceived safety of affiliation would allay anxiety. Second, *social integration* represents the gratification gained from being a part of the larger society, from doing what others are doing or complementing what others are doing. Shared interests and similarity are characteristic of people and the social networks into which they are integrated. *Opportunity for nurturance* describes relationships where the person assumes the role of helper for the Other. Conversely, *guidance* represents relationships in which the Other provides information, counsel, understanding, and other forms of assistance. A related provision is *reliable alliance,* which is the knowledge that a person will be ready to extend assistance if needed—dependability, whether called upon or not. Finally, *reassurance of worth* characterizes relationships in which the Other recognizes and provides affirmation of the person's desirable qualities. Russell and Cutrona (1984) developed measures of these provisions whose factorial independence was confirmed.

Cobb (1976) defined social support as information leading the person to believe that he is *cared for, esteemed* or *valued,* and *belongs to a network* of communication and mutual obligation.

House (1981) posited four major components of social support. First is *emotional concern,* which includes love, empathy, caring, and trust. *Instrumental support* includes concrete assistance such as help in performing tasks and financial help. *Provision of information about the environment* includes teaching, role modeling, and accessing resources through knowledge. Finally, *appraisal* is the actions and judgments made by Other designed to furnish self-regulating information to the person about his or her acts, attitudes, and feelings.

Five "social needs" met by personal relationships were described by Thoits (1982): affection, approval (or esteem), belonging, identity, and security. The gratification of these needs constitutes social support. The needs have not, however, been operationalized separately.

Brim (1974) was one of the first to attempt to define empirically the dimensions of social relationships. He factored responses to 23 items describing "likely behavior" of the subject in relation to a good friend, a casual acquaintance, and a close relative. Factors emerged that were named assistance, value similarity, concern, trust, and desired interaction. Most of the same factors were replicated in another sample.

An empirical approach was also used by Gottlieb (1978) to identify the terms in common parlance that people used to define social support. These dimensions included *emotionally sustaining behavior* (sharing confidences, closeness, admiration); *problem solving behavior* (either direct material aid or advice); *indirect personal influence* (the belief that a person would be ready to offer support if required); and *environmental action* (behavior of Other designed to diminish stress in the person).

Kahn and Antonucci (1980) used aid, affect, and affirmation to represent the major forms of support in their study of older people. As operationalized in interview items, *aid* was reflected in giving care in sickness, discussing health, and talking with the person about things that made him or her upset. *Affect* included self-disclosure and reassurance of the person's value to Other. Affirmation was measured by an item denoting respect for the person's qualities.

Another study of family relationships in later life (Quinn, 1983) utilized measures of *affection, consensus,* and *communication.*

Many of the above functions were defined in a priori fashion, and some have never been operationalized. Candy (1977) began with a conception of functions of social relationships and proceeded to test the conception with exploratory factor analyses of items designed as indicators of the functions. She hypothesized the following functions:

gregariousness, status, compatibility, power, communality, assistance, and intimacy. Subjects ranging from age 14 through 80 rated the importance of the functions for each of their five best friends. Factors derived for males and females separately (across all ages) did not differ. The factors were named *intimacy/assistance, power,* and *status.*

The above review suggests that while there are dimensions that appear repeatedly in the work of different investigators, the last word clearly has not been said. It is notable that while some have investigated the functions of friends and some the functions of family, efforts to compare the functions served by these two groups have not come to light. Some of these writers have specified social support as their focus (for example, Thoits, 1982), while others have specified social relationships generally (Weiss, 1974). The question of whether the functions of supportive relationships versus other classes of relationship differ has apparently not been asked. Some have stated or implied "closeness" as an assumed delimiter of those who perform these functions, while others have been silent on this issue.

A Consolidated Set of Functions of Social Relationship

In light of the foregoing review it may be useful to compose yet another list that integrates the many functions discussed by others. The aim is to be complete rather than parsimonious and to provide definitions and synonyms to describe the functions. The purpose of such a list is to guide future researchers who try to go more deeply into this descriptive task of determining the dimensions of social relationships. The majority of these functions may be viewed as bipolar— that is, an opposing function or withholding of the positive function may occur.

Affection: The extent to which the Other gives or evokes in the person positive affects such as love or warmth. This dimension refers to affect, to the extent that feelings can be distinguished from the more cognitively toned evaluations implied by some of the other dimensions.

Affirmation: The Other's overt or implied evaluation of the person in terms that describe highly valued social characteristics (for example, looks, character, personality, social standing). Affirmation is the cognitive companion of affection.

Assistance: Behavioral acts of material assistance performed by the Other in behalf of the person, whether the assistance is in the form of money or task performance. Assistance is to be distinguished from counsel, which does not involve material assistance, and nurturance, which is assistance given *to* Other.

Commitment represents an attitude toward the relationship as enduring over time and requiring less reciprocity than an intrinsic willingness to help or interact under many conditions.

Compatibility represents the perception of a smooth, relatively conflict-free relationship. Although we find "compatibility" an evaluative statement about a relationship, it is listed tentatively as a function because people seem often to view the sheer absence of conflict as a characteristic that supports the attainment of other life goals.

Counsel is assistance delivered by the Other to the person in a psychological, often verbal, manner, including advice, listening, or empathy. Weiss's (1974) "guidance" or Murray's (1938) "succorance" thus is assistance if material, counsel if nonmaterial.

Dependability is the belief, presumably based upon experience, that the Other will be ready and willing to assist if needed. Thus where assistance and counsel refer to acts that have been performed, dependability represents an expectation that future assistance will be forthcoming if needed.

Entertainment represents the capacity of the Other to help pass time pleasantly, divert, or stimulate the person mildly. Despite early attention to the "play" aspects of social relationships (Simmel, 1949), social-relationship researchers appear to have ignored this function.

Homophily is the cognition of similarity between the Other and the person, whether the common attribute is background, personality, interests, goals, status, or other differentiating characteristics.

Integration is either acts or information provided by the Other that encourage the person to be aware of and use the resources of the social world and to adapt to its norms and expectations. While assistance and counsel imply support given to compensate for the person's material need or lack of personal competence, integration relates either to knowledge, role modeling, or mutual obligations that may be exchanged reciprocally with no implication of unequal status between the Other and the person.

Intimacy is the person's sharing or readiness to share knowledge about oneself, one's feelings, or one's thoughts with the Other, usually accompanied by the perception that the Other shares the feeling of intimacy.

Nurturance is the function of offering assistance, counsel, or security to the Other. As in Murray's (1938) and Weiss's (1974) systems, nurturance is help flowing in the direction opposite to that of assistance and counsel.

Security is the person's belief that one is safe in the Other's presence whether in the form of protection from a hostile world or from criticism, competition, or intrusiveness by others.

Social monitoring is behavior of the Other that provides feedbac reflecting a social evaluation of the person's behavior. While such feec back may be used as assistance, it is not necessarily designed to ! helpful; rather, the monitoring represents normal positive and negati social reinforcement. This is different from affirmation, which unconditional approval and has no such normative connotatio.

Status represents the function that distinguishes the person f the Other on the basis of any criteria for personal or social valuat: The status comparison may evaluate the person either favorabl; unfavorably with respect to the Other. Homophily reflects the pres of a perceived characteristic that is similar in the person and the O without the implied comparison and social evaluation that characteri status. Affirmation represents the Other's positive evaluation of ι. person but does not imply inequality between person and Other, whi status does.

Missing from most writers' conceptions of the functions of social relationships are explicitly negative features, although, of course, the opposites of many of the above functions implies a negative judgment about the Other. Since support, rather than the more broadly conceived quality of social relationships, is the basis for many of the conceptions reviewed here, the absence from the list of attributes not relevant to support such as conflict, incompatibility, and boredom, is not surprising. It is also difficult to elicit research subjects' negative feelings about the other people, particularly family members, in interview-based research. However, it is clear that neither social support nor social relationships are uniformly positive and that negatively toned aspects of relationships nonetheless serve various functions for the person. Thus another direction for future research is the exploration of such negative functions (Rook, 1984).

What Is a "Function of a Social Relationship"?

The foregoing discussion as well as the new set of definitions of functions of social relationships suggest a number of problematic issues concerned with the meaning of "functions." First is the perennial question regarding interactional processes: Is the function a property of the person, Other, or of the supraordinate dyad? Some of the functions can be, and are defined as, unidirectional—that is, characteristics of the Other acting on the person: affection, affirmation, assistance, counsel, dependability, entertainment, integration, and social monitoring. Nurturance is one-way behavior, thought, or affect flowing from the person to the Other. However, homophily and status imply a comparison between person and Other. Intimacy and security cannot exist without dyadic participation. Since viewing the entire set of functions as lodged in either party is unsatisfactory, an alternative is to see if all can fit into the dyadic level.

A second issue is the objective versus subjective dichotomy. The functions as defined above (perceived quality) imply that they are the result of subjective judgments by person and Other. Yet with sufficient attention to definition and operationalization, observable behaviors should be usable as indicators of each of the functions. This task is difficult, of course; whether subjective and objective assessments of the functions of social relationships can be made with acceptable levels of mutual agreement remains to be established.

A third issue is the time frame of the functions of social relationships. The temporal quality of the function may vary grossly from a single seconds- long interactional sequence to an episode or relationship of hours, days, months, or years. Viewed as a dyadic property, a function may characterize the entire lifetime of the relationship; as a property of a person the function may be seen in the short term as a behavior or in longer term as a personality trait or personal goal.

A fourth issue is the question of whether a function represents an antecedent condition, a contemporary condition, or a consequence. Thoits (1982) and Ward (1985) in referring to "social need" seem to identify a sequence that begins with an internal motivation of the person (antecedent) that leads to action of the person in relation to the Other (contemporary event) and is followed by a consequence. If we examine some functions—for example, affection—we would infer that some internal motivational state of the person was the source of a search for an interaction or relationship where affection was expressed or exchanged. The proximal consequence is the reduction of the motivational state. More distal consequences may be the establishment of a friendship, an affair, or a lifelong commitment that is perceived as a continuing source of satisfaction of affectional needs. The function that has been labeled "affection" could apply equally well to the antecedent, the contemporary event, or the short- and long-term consequences. This use of the term "need" ascribes the origin of a function to the person exclusively, which does not do justice to the transactional nature of social relationships.

It would thus seem that the overall term "function" could include any of the following constructs:

- a need or a plan (Miller et al., 1960) of the person, reported by the person;
- an action of the person in relation to the Other;
- a need or plan of the Other, reported by the Other;
- an action of the Other in relation to the person;
- an interactional sequence between person and Other;
- the person's perception and evaluation of the person's need, plan, behavior, or the interactional sequence;
- the Other's perception and evaluation of the person's need, plan, behavior, or the interactional sequence;
- any of the above observed or rated and summated over any of a variety of temporal periods, including consequent conditions over the same varieties of time periods.

It is the latter meaning that characterizes the usual approach to measurement, for example, "Would you say that your family pays enough attention to you?" Such a question does not specify the time frame; it implies an action of the Other; "enough" clearly involves the person's needs as well as the person's evaluation of the behavior. Furthermore, it requires the respondent to summate across all people considered family and weight those perceived as most important.

It is easy to conclude that there is a need to disentangle these different elements now subsumed under the term "function" and to cease using the term "need" unless the inquiry is framed in that way. Kelley et al. (1983) make a strong case for limiting the study of relationships to observable interactions before attempting the more error-prone causal analyses of higher-order abstractions such as needs, plans, global perceptions of relationship quality, and consequences. This short-term interaction analysis approach has been almost totally missing from gerontological research.

In the meantime, however, since there is such a dearth of even gross-level data on how relationships are perceived, exploratory work that deals even with overgeneralized constructs such as "functions of relationships" must be pursued. The next section of this chapter describes an attempt to extend previous efforts to determine those dimensions or functions as perceived by the older person.

The Perceived Qualitative Dimensions
of Personal Relationships

The overall purpose of the research reported here was to study the effects of sex, marital status, and living arrangements of older people on the quantity and quality of personal relationships and their joint effects on psychological well-being. The qualities of social relationships and their dimensions will be discussed in relation to the conceptual and methodological problems considered above.

Method

Subjects

Older people were recruited from a variety of sources to participate in this research. An attempt was made to draw roughly equal numbers of married men and women and never-married and widowed men and women living alone from an eight-year-old local area probability sample (Gottesman et al., 1975). Attrition was so great in this residual sample, however, that referrals from many other sources were necessary, especially to complete the never-married and widowed male subgroups. These referrals came by word of mouth, from an in-home service agency run by the Philadelphia Geriatric Center, and from some announcements placed in the media. The sample of 236 older persons thus is representative of no known universe. While parametric estimates would be inappropriate, the focus of the research on covariation patterns is appropriate for such a convenience sample. Table 4.1 shows some of the basic characteristics of the sample.

Procedure

Subjects were requested to participate in a study of the lifestyles of older persons. Interviewers were recruited from university social science and gerontology programs and were trained for one week in interviewing techniques and the use of this interview schedule. Interviews were done by appointment in the homes of the subjects, who were paid $15 for their help.

The interviews lasted from 60 to 100 minutes. The major components to be analyzed here included the following:

Functional health—five questions on instrumental activities of daily living that constitute the short functional health index of the Philadelphia

TABLE 4.1
CHARACTERISTICS OF SUBJECTS

	All subjects	Never Married		Married		Widowed		F
		M	F	M	F	M	F	
Age (mean)	74.5	73.5	73.2	75.4	71.9	77.9	74.8	5.71*
Race (1 = white; 2 = nonwhite)	1.06	1.09	1.03	1.03	1.03	1.05	1.11	0.97
Education (number of years)	11.6	11.3	13.5	10.9	11.2	11.3	11.1	2.68*
Income (categories 2 - 11, high = high income)	7.1	6.9	7.8	7.3	7.1	7.1	6.7	0.63
Nativity (1 = foreign; 2 = born U.S.)	1.86	1.91	1.92	1.83	1.91	1.78	1.83	1.18
WAIS Comprehension (mean raw score)	19.4	19.9	20.5	20.4	18.3	20.0	17.8	3.00*
Closest relative								
Frequency see	4.55	4.00	3.75	4.57	4.97	4.88	4.95	2.85
Frequency phone	5.80	4.87	5.36	5.37	6.03	6.20	6.59	3.61*
Solidarity	0.00	-2.79	-1.46	-1.01	1.59	0.77	1.91	4.44*
Status	0.00	-1.71	-1.51	0.68	0.79	1.04	0.28	1.66
Closest friend								
Frequency see	5.42	5.68	5.03	5.69	4.59	6.26	5.35	2.99
Frequency phone	5.34	4.55	6.05	4.31	5.21	5.37	6.12	3.75*
Solidarity	0.00	-1.85	2.24	-2.50	0.28	-1.64	1.92	3.16*
Status	0.00	-1.67	-0.41	0.62	0.79	-0.59	0.96	0.82
All relatives								
Number named (mean)	7.47	5.00	4.95	8.56	10.14	7.44	8.63	5.04*
Frequency see	17.73	12.12	11.73	20.81	22.97	19.05	19.54	8.94*
Frequency phone	22.07	14.50	17.10	23.78	26.63	23.07	26.30	7.42*
Solidarity	0.00	-5.11	0.79	-0.65	2.03	-0.66	2.52	5.83*
Status	0.00	1.60	0.31	-0.46	0.94	0.04	0.46	2.10
All friends								
Number named	7.47	7.06	9.60	5.47	7.46	6.66	8.20	1.14
Frequency see	15.91	15.76	17.05	15.14	15.63	16.39	15.41	0.29
Frequency phone	15.06	11.65	19.60	11.58	15.66	12.49	18.22	6.97*
Solidarity	0.00	-0.68	0.81	-1.13	1.02	-0.95	0.68	3.82*
Status	0.00	-1.29	1.59	-1.69	1.59	-0.91	0.48	4.06*
Health	47.2	47.3	47.0	47.0	47.8	47.8	46.6	3.47*
Mastery	25.7	25.0	25.6	26.3	24.6	27.0	25.6	0.87
Positive affect	0.00	-5.86	0.73	0.28	2.66	-0.50	1.89	5.99*
Negative affect	0.00	-0.92	0.78	0.72	0.69	0.07	-1.15	2.29

*$p < .05$.

Geriatric Center Multilevel Assessment Instrument (MAI; Lawton et al., 1982).

Number of relatives named and *number of friends* named in response to the Kahn-Antonucci (1980) network naming procedure. People were asked to name "the people who are important in your life right now." People could name as many individuals as they wished and received one prompt if fewer than four friends were named.

Frequencies of interaction with closest friend and closest relative, and the summed frequencies of interactions with all relatives and all friends named in the network.

Qualitative aspects of social relationships were measured by a series of (a) 27 rating items dealing with the closest relative named in the network, (b) 29 closest-friend items, (c) 22 items dealing with "your family...the relatives you listed on your network as well as other relatives who come to mind," and (d) 27 items dealing with "your friends that you listed on your network as well as other people with whom you are friendly." (The content of these items is displayed below in Tables 4.2 and 4.3.)

Mastery, seven five-point ratings of the degree to which the person feels in control of his or her own life versus feeling like a pawn (Pearlin and Schooler, 1978).

The Affect Balance Scale (ABS; Bradburn, 1969) and the short-form MAI psychological symptoms subscale provided items for measuring psychological well-being. Two analytic indices were used: the five-item Positive Affect Scale; and a composite of four items from the five-item Negative Affect Scale (the "feeling lonely and remote from others" item was removed to avoid confounding with the social quality predictors) plus the three MAI items from the psychiatric symptom subindex (depression, anxiety, suicidal thoughts). The seven-item cluster will be termed "negative affect."

In addition, the interview included the remainder of the short MAI (time use, social behavior, and environmental satisfaction), the comprehension subtest of the Wechsler Adult Intelligence Scale (Wechsler, 1958), items dealing with loneliness, uplifts (Kanner et al., 1981), feelings about one's home, help given and received, and special sections for subgroups dealing with feelings about living alone, widowhood, relationships with children, the fact of having never married, and one's current marriage.

Data Analysis

The composition of the item pools representing the qualitative social relationship items will be described first. The results of a principal-components analysis of these four item sets will then be presented and discussed. Finally, the results of a causal analysis relating these qualitative relationship components to the other constructs described above (Lawton et al., 1985) will be summarized and used in a further discussion of the meaning of the dimensions.

Measuring the Functions of Social Relationships

No existing item pool was satisfactory to represent the breadth of the functions of social relationships. Therefore some individual items from other investigators' research were combined with a much larger number written for the present purpose. Piloting reduced the number somewhat by eliminating items that were ambiguous (others were rephrased to remove the ambiguity) and that elicited low variability.

The pool was composed so as to represent some of the functions that had been posited by others as being central to social relationships. Thus affection, status, commitment, compatibility, intimacy, and affirmation were represented liberally. Assistance was covered in a behavioral sense in another section of the interview, but not in an item structure that would allow people to characterize their important relationships in this way. We found nurturance and security hard to phrase as items that people could accept as characterizing their relationships and ended with no items in these categories. Underrepresented (one item each) were dependability, counsel, social monitoring and integration (all friends only), while entertainment and homophily were each represented by two items. We had originally viewed reciprocity in exchange between dyads as another function and thus included some items expressing this feature of relationships. Later it seemed more appropriate to think of reciprocity as a structural feature rather than a function, but these items were included in the component analysis. Given the relatively small number of subjects and the exploratory nature of the present study, breadth rather than depth in item coverage seemed appropriate. The function designated for each item is shown beside the item in Tables 4.2 and 4.3

Results

Tables 4.2 and 4.3 show in their far left columns the percentages of people endorsing each item in the direction indicated by the phrasing of the item in the table. All items were three-, four-, or five-point rating

TABLE 4.2
Response Frequencies and Factor Loadings of Items Describing the Closest Relative (R) and Closest Friend (F)

Percentage		Item	Function	R					F			
R	F			I	II	III	IV	h^2	I	II	III	h^2
70	67	Are times when you and R/F have trouble getting along?.... (never).	Compatibility	70				53	71			51
56	40	Do you find it hard to understand the way R/F feels?.... (never).	Affirmation	47				27	48			35
55	60	Even though you're close, would you say you argue with R/F?.... (never).	Compatibility	52				39	68			54
33	33	Does R/F pay attention to what you have to say?.... (all the time).	Affirmation	46				34	34	41		35
66	71	Does R/F accept you just the way you are?.... (all the time).	Status	56				42	52			40
69	76	If R/F says will do something, how often can depend?.... (all the time).	Dependability	31				32	40			37
74	74	R/F is comfortable to be with.... (all the time).	Compatibility	62				58	55			41
33	33	Does R/F find it hard to understand the way you feel?.... (never).	Affirmation	47				29	55			35

(Continued)

111

TABLE 4.2 (Continued)

Percentage R	Percentage F		Function	R I	R II	R III	R IV	R h^2	F I	F II	F III	F h^2
72	80	Would you say R/F puts you down? . . . (never).	Status	51				40	60			43
84	82	R/F tries to tell you what to do. . . . (not at all).	Social monitoring			72		43	45			33
75	80	Does R/F try to change you? . . . (not at all).	Status	35		54		45	57			39
92	89	R/F sometimes too nosy about my business. . . . (disagree a lot or little)	Status			48		35	49			38
55	50	Does R/F make you feel good about yourself? . . . (all the time).	Affirmation	49	47			52	36	54		43
33	46	Does R/F think the same way you do about. . . (most everything)?	Homophily		33			28	30	48		39
52	50	Would you say you and R/F . . . (a lot) in common?	Homophily		60			45		54		34
55	38	Does R/F do small favors for you . . . (very often)?	Assistance		62			41		40		30
42	31	S confides in R/F.	Intimacy		43			28		45	-36	43
27	31	R/F confides in S.	Intimacy		42			33		41		45

Item	Dimension							
R/F worries about me too much (agree a lot or a little).	Affection	41	33	45	-33	38	38	35
R/F feels you're . . . (one of the most important people in the world).	Affection	32	18	66		47	60	47
S is familiar with R/F's real worries and concerns . . . (all the time).	Intimacy	37	30	52		44	52	38
How often does R/F show affection to you? (all the time).	Affection	56	41	60		47	57	44
Is R/F familiar with your real worries and concerns . . . (all the time)?	Intimacy	35	32	63		45	61	45
The thing I like best about F is that I learn a lot from F (agree a lot or a little).	Integration	NA	68	NA			40	31
I am too proud to ask R/F for help even when need (disagree a lot or a little).	Status	64	68	39	24		37	25
I see R/F mostly as someone to pass time with (disagree a lot or a little).	Entertainment	73	58	44	31		49	27
The thing I like best is that R/F is an entertaining companion (agree a lot or a little).	Entertainment	67	76	43	32			24
I like R/F mainly because we've known each other so long (agree a lot or a little).	Commitment	NA	57	NA			50	24

TABLE 4.3
Response Frequencies and Factor Loadings of Items Describing All Family (RR) and All Friends (FF)

Percentage RR	Percentage FF	Item	Function	Factor RR I	Factor RR II	Factor RR III	h²	Loadings FF I	Loadings FF II	Loadings FF III	Loadings FF IV	h²
19	9	Are you familiar with your RR/FF's real worries and concerns?... (all the time).	Intimacy		43		41		52			33
41	22	How often do your RR/FF show affection to you? ... (all the time).	Affection		65		53	31	45			35
88	70	I make excuses to avoid RR/FF taking too much of my time (disagree).	Compatibility		35		25			34		26
55	35	It's better not to discuss personal things with RR/FF (disagree).	Intimacy	36	41		33			32		28
21	6	Everything in my life revolves around my RR/FF. ... (agree).	Affection		54		44		59			42
89	80	My RR/FF are sometimes too nosy about my business (disagree).	Status		44		35			44		37
42	38	You and your RR/FF have (a lot) in common.	Homophily	45	56		53	38	40			45
28	31	RR/FF think the same way you do about.... (most everything).	Homophily	35	39	34	40		30			33
44	42	Mostly I see RR/FF only when I want to (agree).	Status	30			23	32				18
69	69	My RR/FF often forget to include me in their plans (disagree a lot or a little).	Affirmation	51	37		43	55				46
49	54	My RR/FF visit me only when it's convenient	Status	50	31		34	61				42

		Category	Item						
63	62	Status	I'm usually the one to get in touch with RR/FF (disagree).	71		42	43	31	34
65	57	Affirmation	RR/FF lose contact with you when you get older (disagree).	60		39	42		40
44	34	Dependability	If RR/FF say will do something, can depend on them to do it ... (all the time).	44	44	34	50	58	42
71	67	Entertainment	When you get together with RR/FF, how often do you laugh and have fun? (often).	32	50	42	42	30	36
36	22	Assistance	How often do RR/FF do small favors for you? (very often).	39	50	44	52	32	43
44	42	Compatibility	Argues with RR/FF ... (never).		58	27		63	35
69	76	Compatibility	How many RR/FF do you have trouble getting along with? (no one).		55	32		59	32
49	45	Compatibility	RR/FF comfortable to be with ... (all the time).	51	45	46	39		32
NA	38	Reciprocity	If FF does favor I'm uneasy until I repay the favor (disagree).	NA			44	37	23
79	60	Entertainment	RR/FF are mostly people to pass time with (disagree).			17	36	45	40
NA	45	Reciprocity	I like to do favors for FF because I might need a favor some day (disagree).	NA				56	32
NA	86	Commitment	FF help me without expecting anything in return (agree).	NA			35	36	44
NA	88	Commitment	FF are still FF even if don't see for long time (agree a lot).	NA				36	31
33	22	Affection	RR/FF worry about me too much (agree).					-34	18
NA	55	Commitment	My FF were more important to me when I was younger (disagree a lot or a little).	NA				30	28

scales except the two "confidant" items for closest relative and closest friend, which were dichotomies. Detailed analyses of the similarities and differences between friends and relatives and between closest versus all relatives or friends will not be presented here. However, it is of interest to note that similarities are more evident than differences when one compares the closest relative with closest friend (Table 4.2) or all relatives with all friends (Table 4.3). Not unexpectedly, the prevalence of positive perceived qualities was usually greater for relatives than for friends and always greater for the closest compared to the aggregate.

Separate principal components analyses were performed on each of the four item pools. Varimax rotations were performed using factors with eigenvalues above 1.00. Table 4.2 and 4.3 show only loadings of .30 and above (those .40 and above are underlined) for those factors that contained at least three items with loadings of .30 or higher.

Closest relative. The 27 closest-relative items yielded four components, which accounted for 43.7 percent of the total variance. However, only the first two factors contained enough high-loaded items to use in forming composite item clusters for later analyses. The largest factor includes items denoting affirmation, status, and compatibility. A relative perceived as high in these items shows high acceptance of the person, respect, and a generally conflict-free relationship. One item, "makes me feel good about myself," loaded highly on both of the first two factors; one of its meanings is clearly a feeling of respect and equal status.

The second factor's items were characterized primarily as affection and intimacy, with one each from the functions of assistance and homophily. Warmth, sharing, and self-disclosure are evidenced by relatives high in this cluster. The "makes me feel good about myself" item is very consistent with the affective warmth connoted by the other items.

The third factor's three items could fit completely into the status function because they indicate respect for the person's individuality and the assumption of equality between the person and the Other. However, as a trio their meaning is even more specific in denoting a perceived lack of need on the part of the Other to control the person and they are statistically different from the status cluster.

The fourth very weak factor's items suggest a perceived distance or superficiality in the relationship.

Closest friend. The three significant factors emerging from the 29 items describing the functions of the closest friend accounted for 36.7

percent of the total variance. The content of the first factor was very similar to that for the closest relative, emphasizing affirmation, compatibility, and status. The absence of a need to control was a strong facet of status in the best friend, as compared to its emergence as a separate factor in the closest relative. Perceived dependability is also an aspect of acceptance by the closest friend.

The second factor was almost identical to that for closest relative, composed of affection, homophily, and intimacy. The third factor seems to be similar to the superficiality factor found in the closest-relative rating.

All relatives. As indicated in Table 4.3, three usable factors emerged from the 22 items for relatives in general, including 34.6 percent of the total variance. By far the largest first factor includes a cluster of four items denoting attention (versus neglect), which falls into the more general affirmation category. A number of items falling into the second factor also have non-trivial loadings on factor one. Other items in the first factor belonged to the intimacy, dependability, homophily, entertainment, and assistance domains.

Factor two has a cluster of high-loaded items that makes it very similar to the second factors observed for closest relative and closest friend: affection, assistance, intimacy, entertainment, and homophily. Unlike the closest-associate factor however, compatibility was represented in the all-relatives' cluster that generally connoted warm sharing, affection, and intimacy.

The third factor was a very specific compatibility factor (three items) with marginal loadings on items that loaded more highly on the first two factors.

All friends. Four factors emerged for all friends, accounting for 47.3 percent of the total variance. The first was identical to the attention and neglect factor for relatives, including the pattern of non-trivial loadings that also were relatively high on the second factor. Thus this factor was strongest in status but also included single high-loaded items in the dependability, entertainment, and assistance domains and secondary loadings on an item in the homophily domain. Despite this diversity, the strength of the attention-neglect items mark the factor clearly as related to status.

The second factor shows the same four-item cluster in the domains of affection, intimacy, and homophily that characterized the warm sharing factor of each of the other relationship item pools. Secondary loadings occurred on items denoting the entertainment function, assistance, and commitment.

A third factor evidenced only two loadings above .40, representing entertainment ("pass time") and reciprocity ("I do favors for friends because I might need a favor done some day"), but a third loading of .37 on another reciprocity item ("I'm uneasy until I've repaid a favor") implies a casual and utilitarian basis for friendships in general.

The Meaning of the Factors

Because this research was an exploratory effort to determine whether there was statistical order across a wide range of content representing the functions of social relationships, a confirmatory, hypothesis-testing factor analysis was not appropriate. There was obviously no expectation that the long list of functions would be reproduced in the empirical factor structure. Because items were written to be specifically applicable to the four reference relationship categories, the four item pools differed among themselves and thus identical factor structures for every social object could not have been produced. The appropriate questions are whether there is any apparent communality among factors from the four groups and, if so, what the character of the major factor is.

The item pools for closest relative and closest friend were very similar, as were those for all relatives and all friends. It is thus not surprising that similarities within each of these pairs of groups were relatively obvious. The similarity was not artifactual. All questions about relatives were asked serially before the questions about friends; common method variance was thus less than it would have been had people rated relative and friend sequentially on each of the same items.

Despite differences in item composition, acceptance and respect appear to be the common thread for the first factors describing both closest relative and closest friends. In fact, the only real difference between relative and friend lies in the merging of the three control items ("tell me what to do," "try to change me," and "nosy") into the acceptance factor where closest friend is concerned, while these items form a separate factor for closest relative. A possible interpretation of this difference might be that perceived respect for the person's individuality precludes behavior by a close friend that might try to control the person. In the case of a close relative, however, control and intrusiveness may be able to coexist with any degree of acceptance and respect in other ways. In fact, it has often been suggested that interaction with friends (but not relatives) is associated with psychological wellbeing because people are more free to pick and choose friends that suit their personal preferences, while there is no such choice where familial ties are concerned (Hess, 1979; Wood and Robertson, 1978). Speculating from the present results, it might seem that choice of a friend would have more constraints on it because if one wished general acceptance one would have to seek friends who also exhibited no controlling tendencies. More concretely, the parent-child relationship continues on the basis of the lifelong bonding and commitment. Age, biological decline of the older person, and the forces of ageistic attitudes combine to cast the child in the role as controller of the parent.

Turning now to the factor underlying functions of relatives and friends in the aggregate, the differences in item pools preclude close matches between the factors representing the closest as compared to the aggregates. These item differences were necessary because one simply could not characterize all of one's relatives (or friends) in identical terms, for example, "confidant" or "never puts me down," terms that easily describe an individual. Thus the content of the largest aggregate factors for relatives and friends refers to behavioral attention or neglect, for the most part. We shall argue that this dimension is another facet of acceptance and respect.

The second factors for relatives and friends share four items. Three of these items also appear in the closest-relative and closest-friend factor and the fourth, with a change in phrasing appropriate to the closest versus aggregate referent, expresses the same judgment of centrality in the person's life. Thus it would seem that the warm sharing factor appeared in all four contexts.

The fact that "compatibility" items were included in the acceptance factors for closest relative and friend but tended to cluster somewhat independently of other factors for all relatives and all friends adds to our feeling that compatibility, satisfaction, and dissatisfaction with one's associates should be considered outcomes of functions rather than functions themselves. Not surprisingly, for one to feel accepted by one's closest relative or friend, one must also be compatible with the Other; the two dimensions could cluster statistically into a single factor even if one were cause and another effect. In the case of the aggregates, one may well judge that the weighted sum of either attention or warm sharing is composed of many complex influences across so many people that it would be difficult to demonstrate that compatibility is a simple function of either. Thus we suggest that the domain of compatibility should be the focus of more research designed to test its dimensionality and its relationships to other social dimensions in causal analyses.

The Dimensions of Social Relationships:
An Empirical After-View

The results of the component analyses offer an extraordinarily good validation of Brown's (1965) assertion that status and solidarity are the basic material from which social relationships are constructed. The largest factors of all four social objects may be viewed as representing some implied judgment or comparison in relation to others. Sometimes the implied comparison is in relation to the Other, as in the behavioral neglect items of the aggregate relative and friend factor: forgetting the person diminishes his or her status. In other instances, the Other confers status through respect, listening, and general compatibility.

The second factor provides an excellent match for the solidarity concept. In contrast to competition and status, this factor reflects the irrelevance of defensiveness, the assumption that openness will allow the flow of affect and the mutual recognition of communality in the relationship. Thus these two relatively independent factors seem to characterize the way both relatives and friends are perceived. Neither function is sufficient alone to explain the functions of social relationships. We suggest that a satisfying social life requires both status and solidarity, in varying mixes at different times (and very probably in different relationships).

It should be noted that the independence of the two factors is far from complete. Tables 4.2 and 4.3 demonstrate ample cross-loadings. As scored in composites the correlations between status and solidarity were .24 for closest relative, .23 for closest friend, .65 for all relatives, and .56 for all friends.

It seems almost self-evident that status and solidarity are desirable functions of relationships and must therefore be related to favorable outcomes. However, because the two functions were partially independent of one another, it seemed likely that they would also be associated with different aspects of psychological well-being.

Beginning with Bradburn's (1969) two-factor theory of affect, we hypothesized that mechanisms that enhance the perceived status of the person would be associated with the mental health aspect of psychological well-being, or, in Bradburn's terms, "negative affect." That is, if we think of mental health as the absence of anxiety, depression, worry, and other dysphoric subjective symptoms, then relationships that bolster the person's stature in relation to others should be "hygienic" (Herzberg et al., 1959).

On the other hand, a large body of research in psychological well-being, including a recent study of older people (Lawton et al., 1984), has suggested that the factors that lead to positive affect are quite different from those that counteract negative affect. Among the factors associated with positive affect are stimuli from the environment, such as social participation and friendships. Lawton(1983) speculated that the origin of negative affect, by contrast, was more likely to be in factors that diminshed the Self. In short, feelings falling above the affectively neutral adaptation-level (Helson, 1964) point are more apt to originate from diversion, novelty, and other stimuli that draw people out of themselves. An affectively neutral point may be the desirable equilibrium state for evaluations of the Self. A favorable evaluation of the Self leaves one's affective state at rest by protecting the person from anxiety and depression. The person is thus free to engage in effective cognitive activity and the adaptive behaviors that are necessary to everyday life.

It thus seemed reasonable to hypothesize that solidarity, being composed of factors that lead the person out of the Self—shared confidences with the Other, warmth, and perceived similarity—should show a unique relationship with positive affect.

Path-analytic results from this study, described in greater detail elsewhere (Lawton et al., 1985), showed the following:

(1) For closest relative and all relatives and all friends, low status in social relationships was significantly associated with negative affect. Status had a direct effect on positive affect only for all friends.

(2) For all four social relationship categories, solidarity was significantly associated with positive affect but not with negative affect.

An adequate measure of self-esteem with demonstrable discriminant validity does not exist. A closely related construct, mastery, was used as an indicator of self-esteem. Mastery (Pearlin and Schooler, 1978) is an attribute that includes a sense of personal control, the ability to handle most situations, and the capacity to shape one's environment in a proactive way. We hypothesized that status in social relationships would lead to greater mastery and that both would contribute independently (and inversely) to negative affect. This prediction was borne out for closest relative, closest friend, and all friends. For relatives collectively, greater mastery was strongly associated with lower levels of negative affect; but status did not enhance mastery. Solidarity, on the other hand, was hypothesized to be unrelated to mastery. This prediction was borne out for all four classes of social objects. Mastery was related significantly to both negative affect and positive affect, although the path coefficients were considerably higher in the case of negative affect. Thus status did have a significant indirect effect on positive affect through mastery.

This set of findings enables the two-factor conception of psychological well-being and its determinants to be extended to the qualitative aspects of social relationships and to the place of conceptions of the Self in the total scheme. If we see overall psychological well-being as consisting of a mix of both pleasant feelings and the absence of negative feelings—the latter leaving the person free to behave "competently"—there are undoubtedly many endogenous and exogenous factors leading to such well-being. It is very likely that future research will continue to identify such factors and their differential effects on positive and negative affect. Among the possible factors are biological health, cognitive functions, instrumental activities, elective uses of time or "effectance" (White, 1959), social behaviors, and the whole array of environmental influences (see Lawton, 1983, for a more general discussion of "the good life"). The present research has demonstrated the gain in predictability of psychological well-being that results from differentiating also within domains of the independent-variable realm. The domains of social relationship quality defined through exploratory factor analysis are consistent with theoretical conceptions of the functions of social relationships as well as being differentially associated with two outcomes.

Moving on to a far more speculative mode, we suggest that social relationships based on warmth, intimacy, and shared attributes give positive enjoyment to people's lives partly because these functions are free of concerns over status and social comparison. The feelings thus evoked bypass the Self and are enjoyed for their own sake. The bad news is that they are apparently less easily stored for future compensation against loss. Solidarity is contemporaneous and hedonistic in the sense that self-esteem does not seem to be fortified by the existence of solidary relationships.

We may do well to examine the course of solidarity as a temporally appraised state. Solomon (1980) has suggested that the positive effects of some kinds of highly enjoyable stimulation are not only short-lived but are diminished quickly over time by the operation of an "opponent process" that produces a negatively toned state, which in turn requires more positive stimulation to counteract. Habituation to the positive stimulus thus brings about a diminishing pleasureable effect of normal levels of positive stimulation. Relatively mild positive affect is maintained by continued stimulation; the cessation of such stimulation leads to a much more intense negative affect. Does solidarity as an element of social relationships fit into this framework?

Berscheid (1983) has hypothesized that the opponent process may explain how the disturbance of a longstanding relationship, even though few emotional peaks occur in it, can produce devastating effects on mental health; she cites the example of an affectively neutral or even negative long-term marital relationship broken by bereavement or divorce. The interdependence of the husband and wife represents the trace of a habituated affective relationship. Interdependence involves reciprocal role-playing and fulfilled behavioral expectations. When the positive stimuli of the interdependent behavior sequences cease, the opponent process cannot be reversed and intense negative affect ensues.

Our data do not speak directly to this issue, of course. One may offer the tentative hypothesis, however, that *loss* of a solidary relationship may provide a link to negative affect that is not evidenced in the steady, adapted state that was captured by our cross-sectional data.

There is, however, a link between status and positive affect that must be viewed as potentially significant. The indirect path from status to positive affect through mastery confirms what seems intuitively obvious: Social relationships that affirm our social standing make us feel good, but they do so not directly but because they fortify our sense of mastery. There is such a phenomenon as exhilaration stemming from a sense of power, effectance, or autonomy; this affect may begin with behaviors in others that attest to such competence. To contrast this casual sequence once more with that seen for solidarity, solidarity evokes a positive feeling without the mediation of the social comparison and the "matching to sample" of our expectations of our Selves. Nonetheless, one must wonder, does feeling loved not make our social comparison more likely to come out in our favor? The answer, intuitively speaking, has to be yes, though the data do not support this conclusion. It may well be that later research will show that solidarity needs to be partitioned into a purely affective component and another more cognitive, socially comparative component that does augment status.

References

ADAMS, B. N. (1967) "Interaction theory and the social network." Sociometry 30: 64-78.

ANDREWS, F. M. and S. B. WITHEY (1976) Social Indicators of Well-Being. New York: Plenum Press.

BERKMAN, L. F. and S. L. SYME (1979) "Social networks, host resistance, and mortality." American Journal of Epidemiology 109: 186-204.

BERSCHEID, E. (1983) "Emotion," pp.110-168 in H. H. Kelley et al. (eds.) Close Relationships. New York: W.H. Freeman.

BRADBURN, N. M. (1969) The Structure of Psychological Wellbeing. Chicago: Aldine.

BRIM, J. A. (1974) "Social network correlates of avowed happiness." Journal of Nervous and Mental Disease 158: 432-439.

BROWN, R. (1965) Social Psychology. New York: Free Press.

CAMPBELL, A., P. G. CONVERSE, and W. RODGERS (1976) The Quality of American Life. New York: Russell Sage Foundation.

CANDY, S. (1977) "A comparative analysis of friendship functions in six age groups of men and women." Ph.D. dissertation, Wayne State University, Department of Psychology.

COBB, S. (1976) "Social supports as a moderator of life stress." Psychosomatic Medicine 38: 300-314.

GOTTESMAN, L. E., M. MOSS, and F. WORTS (1975) "Resources, needs, and wishes for services in urban middle class older people." Presented at the tenth International Congress of Gerontology, Jerusalem, Israel.

GOTTLIEB, B. H. (1978) "The development and application of a classification scheme of informal helping behaviors." Canadian Journal of Behavioral Science 10: 105-115.

HAMMER, M. (1981) "Social supports, social networks, and schizophrenia." Schizophrenia Bulletin 7: 45-57.

HELLER, K. and R. W. SWINDLE (1983) "Social networks, perceived social support, and coping with stress," pp. 87-103 in R. D. Felner et al. (eds.) Preventive Psychology: Theory, Research, and Practice in Community Interventions. New York: Pergamon Press.

HELSON, H. (1964) Adaptation Level Theory. New York: Harper & Row.

HERZBERG, F., B. MAUSNER, and B. B. SNYDERMAN (1959) The Motivation to Work. New York: Wiley.

HESS, B. B. (1979) "Sex roles, friendship, and the life course." Research on Aging 1: 494-515.

HOMANS, G. C. (1974) Social Behavior: Its Elementary Forms. New York: Harcourt Brace Jovanovich.

HOUSE, J. S. (1981) Work, Stress and Social Support. Reading, MA: Addison-Wesley.

KAHN, R. L. and R. C. ANTONUCCI (1980) "Convoys over the life course," pp.254-286 in P. B. Baltes and O. Brim (eds.) Life Span Development and Behavior. New York: Academic Press.

KANNER, A. D., J. C. COYNE, C. SCHAEFER, and R. LAZARUS (1981) "Comparison of two modes of stress measurement." Journal of Behavioral Medicine 4: 1-39.

KELLEY, H. H., E. BERSCHEID, A. CHRISTENSEN, J. H. HARVEY, T. L. HUSTON, G. LEVINGER, E. McCLINTOCK, L. A. PEPLAU, and D. R. PETERSON (1983) Close Relationships. New York: W.H. Freeman.

LAWTON, M. P. (1970) "Ecology and aging," pp.490-567 in L. A. Pastalan and D. H. Carson (eds.) Spatial Behavior of Older People. Ann Arbor: Institute of Gerontology, University of Michigan.

LAWTON, M. P. (1982) "Competence, environmental press, and the adaptation of older people," pp.33-59 in M. P. Lawton et al. (eds.) Aging and the Environment: Theoretical Approaches. New York: Springer.

LAWTON, M. P. (1983) "Environment and other determinants of well-being in older people." The Gerontologist 23: 349-357.

LAWTON, M. P., M. H. KLEBAN, and E. diCARLO (1984) "Psychological well-being in the aged: factorial and conceptual dimensions." Research on Aging 6: 67-97.

LAWTON, M. P., M. MOSS, M. FULCOMER, and M. H. KLEBAN (1982) "A research and service-oriented multilevel assessment instrument." Journal of Gerontology 37: 91-99.

LAWTON, M. P., M. MOSS, and M. H. KLEBAN (1985) Psychological Well-being, Mastery, and the Social Relationships of Older People. Philadelphia: Philadephia Geriatric Center.

MILLER, G. A., E. GALANTER, and K. H. PRIBRAM (1960) Plans and the Structure of Behavior. New York: Holt, Rinehart & Winston.

MITCHELL, J. C. (1969) "Concept and use of social networks," in J. C. Mitchell (ed.) Social Networks in Urban Situations. Manchester, England: Manchester University Press.

MURRAY, H. A. (1938) Explorations in Personality. New York: Oxford University Press.

PEARLIN, L. I. and C. SCHOOLER (1978) "The structure of coping." Journal of Health and Social Behavior 19: 2-21.

QUINN, W. H. (1983) "Personal and family adjustment in later life." Journal of Marriage and the Family 45: 57-73.

ROBINSON, I. M., W. C. BAER, T. K. BANERJEE, and P. G. FLACHSBART (1975) "Trade-off games," pp.79-118 in W. Michelson (ed.) Behavioral Methods in Environmental Design. Stroudsburg, PA: Dowden, Hutchinson, and Ross.

ROOK, K. S. (1984) "The negative side of social interaction: Impact on psychological well-being." Journal of Personality and Social Psychology 46: 1097-1108.

RUSSELL, D. and C. CUTRONA (1984) "The provisions of social relationships and adaptation to stress." Presented at the annual meeting of the American Psychological Association, Toronto.

SCHACHTER, S. (1959) The Psychology of Affiliation. Stanford, CA: Stanford University Press.

SIMMEL, G. (1949) "The sociology of sociability." American Journal of Sociology 55: 254-261.

SOLOMON, R. L. (1980) "The opponent-process theory of acquired motivation: the cost of pleasure and the benefits of pain." American Psychologist 35: 691-712.

THOITS, P. A. (1982) "Conceptual, methodological, and theoretical problems in studying social support as a buffer against life stress." Journal of Health and Social Behavior 23: 145-159.

WARD, R. A. (1985) "Informal networks and well-being in later life: a research agenda." The Gerontologist 25: 55-61.

WECHSLER, D. (1958) The Measurement and Appraisal of Adult Intelligence. Baltimore: Williams and Wilkins.

WEISS, R. S. (1974) "The provisions of social relationships," pp.17-26 in Z. Rubin (ed.) Doing Unto Others. Englewood Cliffs, NJ: Prentice-Hall.

WELLMAN, B. (1981) "Applying network analysis to the study of support," pp. 171-200 in B. H. Gottlieb (ed.) Social Networks and Social Support. Newbury Park, CA: Sage.

WHITE, R. W. (1959) "Motivation reconsidered: the concept of competence." Psychological Review 66: 297-333.

WOOD, V. and J. ROBERTSON (1978) "Friendship and kinship interaction: differential effects on the morale of the elderly." Journal of Marriage and the Family 40: 367-375.

Introduction to Chapter 5

Retirement is a twentieth-century phenomenon that has been studied extensively over the past 30 years. Investigators have been particularly interested in factors affecting attitudes toward retirement and adjustment to retirement. Knowledge of these factors is important for the development of policy in a number of arenas. Perhaps the most immediate application is in the development of pre-retirement programs that will enhance the well-being of retired workers. The implications of research on retirement are, however, potentially far broader than pre-retirement programs. If well-being and adjustment in retirement are to be viewed as desirable goals for individuals, then it would follow that policy should attempt to influence those elements of an individual's life that are related to adjustment to retirement. Among the many factors that have consistently been identified as correlates of adjustment and attitudes toward retirement are income, health, occupational status, and patterns of social interaction. Hence, policy concerned with retirement must also focus on health care, housing, income, pension plans, and other services directed toward the elderly. Futhermore, if there are consistent differences between segments of the labor force—for example, between men and women or persons of different occupational status—then policies might take these elements into consideration.

While it is clear that research on retirement is likely to have implications for a wide range of policy issues, in this chapter Hatch identifies numerous conceptual and methodological limitations of past research that have led to inconsistent and inconclusive findings. The chapter gives special attention to studies concerned with sex differences and notes the implications for policy development of inappropriately attributing differences to gender rather than other situational factors. It is clear from the chapter that well-designed studies of retirement are critical to the development of public policy in a number of arenas.

By limiting her discussion to studies concerned with attitudes, Hatch has also limited her attention to the consequences of retirement for individuals. While this is of interest to public policy, a broader perspective of retirement and its implications for society is also of interest. By focusing on individual costs and benefits, researchers have often failed to address questions about the ability of a society as a whole to support a growing number of dependents, regardless of the source of financial support. In conjunction with the needs of individuals, policymakers might raise questions about the capability of the society. As policymakers and analysts raise questions about the timing and financing of retirement, they need to consider both individual and societal costs and benefits.

5

Research on Men's and Women's Retirement Attitudes

Implications for Retirement Policy

LAURIE RUSSELL HATCH

Many studies of retirement attitudes have been conducted during the past thirty years. Differences in the attitudes held by males and females have been noted frequently in the literature. Most research, and particularly research conducted prior to the 1980s, has reported that men are more reluctant to retire than women, and that men are less satisfied with life in retirement (e.g., Tuckman and Lorge, 1953; Kutner et al., 1956; Palmore 1965, 1971; Kline, 1975; Lowenthal et al., 1976). Early writers argued that retirement was not important for women because their primary roles were located in the home rather than in the labor force (Cumming and Henry, 1961; Donahue et al., 1960; Palmore, 1965, 1971).

Recommendations made by these early writers for pre-retirement planning programs and post-retirement recreational programs often focused on alleviating problems assumed to be associated with the loss of men's occupational identity. For example, Cumming and Henry advocated the development of recreational programs for retired men in which "worklike circumstances" would encourage the men to engage in instrumental activities. The authors described one such recreation center, which

> organized its entire program around men's activities—education tours and constructive projects—while the women are organized as if in

auxiliaries to the men. In such a way it is possible to attract a large number of men to the center (1961: 152).

Cumming and Henry argued that such programs would enable retired men to feel useful, and that the men would thus experience greater satisfaction with their lives in retirement.

Recent studies have indicated, however, that sex differences in retirement attitudes lie in a different direction. Compared to men, women have been found to report greater reluctance to retire and greater dissatisfaction with the retirement experience (e.g., Atchley, 1976a, 1976b, 1982; Levy, 1978, 1980; Newman, 1982). On this basis, it may be considered appropriate to develop retirement programs that focus specifically on the needs of female retirees, as has been advocated by some recent writers (Block, 1982; Kroeger, 1982; Szinovacz, 1982b).

This chapter examines research on retirement attitudes, focusing specifically on studies that have reported sex differences. The examination reveals serious weaknesses in the literature and questions whether the gender of retirees should constitute a specific focus of retirement policy. Although the major purpose of the chapter is to review and critique the literature on sex differences in retirement attitudes, attention is paid to retirement in a broader context. Specifically, the examination of sex differences in retirement raises unsettled questions of defining and operationalizing the term "retirement" and also raises questions concerning the measurement of retirement attitudes. These conceptual and methodological issues will first be discussed. The literature will then be reviewed, and recommendations will be made for future directions in retirement research and policy.

Conceptual and Methodological Issues

Definitions of Retirement

Women's patterns of labor force participation have been more varied than those of men, and it has been suggested that the continuing predominance of all-male samples in retirement research may be due to the problem of operationalizing occupational retirement for women (Fox, 1977). Can a woman who has worked in the home most or all of her adult years be considered retired upon the completion of family tasks, such as when children leave home? Or can she be considered retired on the basis of when her husband retires from work in the labor force? In everyday usage, retirement means separation from paid employment (Donahue et al., 1960). But how long and how continuously must one have worked to be able to "retire?"

A clear definition of retirement is difficult to obtain even for men, who typically have longer, more continuous patterns of labor force participation during their lives (Rosenfeld, 1979; Block, 1982; O'Rand and Landerman, 1984). Writers have long cited the lack of clarity of the term "retirement" (Donahue et al., 1960; Palmore, 1965; Koller, 1968; Fox, 1977), and there is still no single, agreed upon definition or measure of occupational retirement. Retirement is treated variously as (1) an act or event (e.g., Spengler, 1966; Maddox, 1968; Atchley and Robinson, 1982; (2) a process (e.g., Atchley, 1972, 1982; Shanas, 1972; Kosloski et al., 1984); (3) a condition or status (e.g., Donahue et al., 1960; Back and Guptill, 1966; Strauss et al., 1976), and (4) a role (e.g., Cavan, 1962; Peretti and Wilson, 1975; Kroeger, 1982; Wan and Odell, 1983). The focus of research will differ depending upon which criterion of retirement is used.

(1) Treating retirement as an act or event refers to the "giving up of work"[1] and signals the beginning of a life in which leisure, rather than labor force participation, predominates (Shanas, 1972). Maddox refers to retirement as a rite of passage, usually informal, "between productive maturity and nonproductive old age" (1968: 357). Retirement as an event has social as well as personal importance and implies that the depature from the world of work is a permanent one (Maddox, 1968). Treating retirement as an act or event focuses attention on the point of separation from work, but this delineation is not always clear-cut (Atchley, 1972). Some people may begin a new job after "retiring" from a previous one; others may continue to work part-time.

(2) Because retirement is usually not an "all or nothing phenomenon," Atchley (1972: 156) and others (e.g., Carp, 1972; Ekerdt et al., 1985) prefer to view retirement as a process. In addition, as Shanas (1972) notes, the treatment of retirement as a special kind of event indicates a critical period in an individual's life. Retirement has often been viewed as representing a "crisis" or at least as an event to which the individual must adjust or adapt. As such, temporal meaning is added. The focus of research on retirement as a process includes attention to preparations for retirement, attitudes toward retirement, the conditions leading to retirement, as well as personal adjustment to retirement (Atchley, 1972).

(3) Retirement is also treated as a social status or condition. Referring to an individual as "retired" indicates a stage of life rather

than an event or process of adjustment (Shanas, 1972). Retirement is often viewed as representing a status loss due to its association with economically nonproductive activities and with aging (e.g., Tuckman and Lorge, 1953; Strauss et al., 1976).

(4) Social statuses are associated with *roles,* or the rights and duties that occupants of particular statuses are expected to perform. The focus on retirement as a role has generally led to the conclusion that retirement results in a "roleless role" about which there is little societal agreement or normative support concerning its specification (Parsons, 1954; Burgess, 1960; Sheppard, 1976). Research following from this approach examines the consequences of the change in roles from worker to retiree (Atchley, 1972).

The term "retirement" thus has a number of different meanings, each of which focuses research in different areas of concern. The way in which retirement is operationalized also has important effects on research. Those individuals who are considered retired will differ according to the measure of retirement used.

Measures of Retirement

A measure often used, especially by economists (see Shanas, 1972), is the number of hours worked during a specified period of time (e.g., Epstein and Murray, 1968; Hardy, 1982). But persons considered retired will vary depending upon the unit of time employed. Numbers of retired individuals differ according to whether, for example, retirement is measured as not working full-time all year or as not working at all during the year. In addition, persons who have never been employed may be excluded from the base. This would affect women's retirement rates more that it would affect men's rates (Palmore, 1965).

The number of hours worked, as well as other objective measures such as length of time spent in the labor force and eligibility for pensions or social security can be problematic methods of classifying certain types of individuals as retired or not retired. Examples of such individuals include those who work at home without pay and persons who no longer receive wages or salary but pursue work such as consulting or lecturing. Other problems of identification include those who "retire" from one career, say from a career in the military, to begin another career. These persons could be considered retired when one measure is used (e.g., they may receive a pension) but would not be considered retired with a different measure (e.g., number of hours worked during the past year).

A measure of retirement status widely used in the literature is that of self-identification (Fox, 1977; Block, 1982; Beck, 1983; Ekerdt et al., 1985). This allows individuals to report whether or not they consider themselves to be retired and thus allows for easy categorization. There are some problems associated with this subjective measure as well, however. Persons who are effectively retired may refuse to consider themselves as such. Others who see themselves as retired may be so only temporarily (Donahue et al., 1960).

It is therefore difficult to operationalize occupational retirement unambiguously, and both objective and subjective measures are subject to methodological criticisms. An advantage of using objective measures, such as the number of hours or weeks worked during a specified period of time, is that retirement may then be measured as an interval-level variable. This measure allows the researcher to treat retirement in terms of gradation or *degrees* of retirement. Murray (1979) advocates using the objective measure of number of hours worked per week because it avoids dichotomizing retirement and also because it corresponds fairly well to subjective measures of retirement. Some researchers have used multiple measures of retirement status in response to the different problems posed by subjective and objective measures (Bell, 1978; Fillenbaum et al., 1985).

Groups of individuals considered retired thus vary across studies due to different methods of defining and operationalizing retirement. In addition, the composition of the "retired" category within a single study will be relatively homogeneous or heterogeneous on certain dimensions, depending upon the measures used. One such dimension is labor force participation. Measures such as eligibility for pensions require participation in the labor force for a given number of years in order for individuals to be categorized as retired. Other measures (e.g., number of hours worked for a given time period and self-identification) do not require a history of labor force participation: An individual who has participated continuously in the labor force for 40 years may not be distinguished analytically from someone who has entered the labor force only recently, or who has never participated in the labor force. A second dimension of relative homogeneity or heterogeneity in studies of retirement concerns whether individuals have retired voluntarily or nonvoluntarily. Voluntary retirees are those persons who choose to retire or who believe that the retirement decision was made voluntarily. Nonvoluntary retirees, in contrast, are those who retire for reasons such as poor health or disability, a mandatory retirement age, or pressure from superiors. Voluntary and nonvoluntary retirees have been found to differ in their attitudes toward retirement and satisfaction with retired life in the few studies where such a distinction has been made (e.g., Peretti and Wilson, 1975; Kimmel et al., 1978).

Thus, studies of retirement vary on a number of important dimensions. The focus of research varies according to whether retirement is conceptualized as an act or event, a process, a status, or a role. Definitions and measures of occupational retirement vary across studies and result in differing groups of individuals who are categorized as retired. In addition, the measure of retirement chosen for use in a particular study results in the relative homogeneity or heterogeneity of the sample population. These alternative methods of considering individuals as retired or not retired have important effects on classifying women as retirees. The use of measures such as eligibility for pensions or length of time employed will exclude many women who have not participated in the labor force or who have had discontinuous patterns of labor force participation.

Whether considered as labor force participants or retirees, men and women have usually reported different attitudes toward retirement— or, in the absence of empirical data have usually been presumed to hold differing attitudes. When examined with empirical data, retirement attitudes, like retirement, have been measured in a variety of ways.

Measurement of Attitudes Toward Retirement

One approach used to measure retirement attitudes is to examine the expressed willingness of individuals to retire (e.g., Streib and Schneider, 1971; Jacobson, 1974; Levy, 1978). In these studies respondents are asked, for example, the age at which they expect to retire (Streib and Schneider, 1971); the age at which they would prefer to retire (Streib and Schneider, 1971); the retirement age they consider ideal (Jacobson, 1974); or whether they want to retire at all (Levy, 1978). Kasl (1980) warns that the use of what may seem to be similar measures of dependent variables may instead represent different constructs. These constructs may have different correlates or determinants. An example he provides is that of respondents' preferences for early retirement (conventionally defined as retirement prior to age 65) versus their plans or intentions for early retirement. Different factors are likely to be associated with these dependent variables.

A second approach used to study attitudes toward retirement is to examine whether retirement is viewed in positive or negative terms. This approach is most often used in studies of post-retirement attitudes (e.g., Atchley, 1976a; Barfield and Morgan, 1978b) but is also used in studies of individuals' attitudes prior to retirement (e.g., Skoglund, 1980). Some researchers employ multiple items with fixed responses to measure these attitudes (Goudy et al., 1980; Skoglund, 1980; Atchley, 1982; Jewson, 1982). For example, Goudy et al. (1980) used items such as "Retirement is a goal for which most people are willing to sacrifice and work hard" and "It is better not to think about retirement." Atchley (1982) used a semantic differential with 16 bipolar adjective pairs by which respondents rated their lives in retirement. The pairs included good/bad, full/empty, busy/idle, happy/sad (Atchley, 1982; see also Atchley and Robinson, 1982). Single-item measures of retirement attitudes are also commonly used (e.g., Kerckhoff, 1966; Barfield and Morgan, 1978b). Examples of single-item measures include "Generally speaking, how do you feel about your life since retirement?" (Barfield and Morgan, 1978b) and "Did you look forward to your retirement?" (Kerckhoff, 1966). Citing evidence from Atchley's 1974 study in which attitudes toward retirement were found to make up four factors, Atchley and Robinson (1982) argue that single items measuring attitudes toward retirement are unreliable because retirement attitudes are multidimensional.

It is important to distinguish between attitudes toward retirement as measured by willingness to retire versus anticipations or perceptions of life in retirement. Within this latter category, distinctions must also be made as to whether respondents are asked to evaluate more or less *stereotypical* dimensions of retired life (e.g., Goudy's item described above, "Retirement is a goal for which most people are willing to sacrifice and work hard") versus the respondents' evaluations of their *own* lives in retirement. Different processes will be tapped depending upon which type of measure is used. A review of the literature shows that few studies have used the same measure of attitudes toward retirement. Comparability between the studies is therefore problematic, particularly where the measures are not described explicitly (e.g., Crook and Heinstein, 1958; Lehr and Dreher, 1969; Quadagno, 1978; Newman et al., 1982).

The Relationship Between Attitudes Toward Retirement and Adjustment to Retirement

A further methodological and conceptual issue concerns the relationship between retirement attitudes and adjustment or adaptation to retirement. "Adjustment to retirement" is a commonly investigated dependent variable in retirement research (MacBride, 1976), but like research on "attitudes toward retirement," it is difficult to compare the results of studies due to measurement inconsistencies. Attitudes toward retired life, along with other measures of reported psychological well-being, such as life satisfaction and personal happiness, are commonly used as indicators of an individual's adjustment to retirement (e.g., Thompson et al., 1960; Beck, 1982; Szinovacz, 1982b). The extent and degree of a retiree's activities and social participation (Friedmann and Orbach, 1974; Fox, 1977; Levy, 1978, 1980) are also used as measures of retirement adjustment. Some researchers use attitudes toward retirement as one component of retirement adjustment (Thompson, 1958, Shanas, 1972; Beck, 1982); other researchers rely on different dimensions of adjustment and do not include retirement attitudes (Thompson et al., 1960; Heidbreder, 1972; George and Maddox, 1977; Levy, 1978, 1980).

The literature on retirement attitudes and on retirement adjustment therefore overlaps to some degree. Although some writers do not appear to distinguish analytically between them (Donahue et al., 1960; Shanas, 1970; Block, 1982), retirement "attitudes" and "adjustment" are conceptually distinct categories of phenomena. While retirement attitudes represent evaluations individuals make about retirement at a given point in time, including whether they are willing to retire as well as how they feel about retired life, adjustment to retirement implies a *process*. A number of explanatory frameworks have been advanced to account for how individuals adjust to retirement, usually considered as part of the larger process of adjustment to aging (see Atchley, 1975; Kosloski et al., 1984). Although attitudes often change over time—and research indicates that attitudes toward retirement are not static (Streib and Schneider, 1971; Ekerdt et al., 1980), they alone cannot be used to represent processes of adjustment or adaptation to retirement.

Women and men have long been thought to differ in their adjustment to retirement. Examination of the literature shows that the major focus of such differentiation has been on retirement attitudes rather than on differential processes of adjustment. Drawing on both empirical and theoretical writings in the field, the direction of sex differences in retirement attitudes as well as the reasons offered by writers for such differences are examined here.[2]

Sex Differences in Retirement:
A Review of the Literature

The Early Literature: Sex Differences in
Retirement Attitudes Due to Male
and Female Primary Roles

Although some writers of the 1950s and 1960s believed sex differences in retirement attitudes were due in part to differential labor
force experiences (Kutner et al., 1956; Lehr and Dreher, 1969), most
assumed that men and women would experience retirement differently
and would hold different attitudes toward retirement due to salient
characteristics of the male and female primary roles. Early studies of
retirement concluded that the withdrawal from working life brings
about a serious crisis for men due to the male's traditional role as
breadwinner (Lehr and Dreher, 1969; Beck, 1982). Turner (1970) is
representative of these writers when he states,

> In American society it is well-nigh impossible to be a man without having
> an occupation, and how much of a man and what kind of a man one
> is are to be measured largely by the nature of the occupation and the
> success with which it is pursued [1970: 255].

The work role is critical to a man because it is likely to be the major
source of influence on his self-identity (Cavan, 1962). Occupations
tie men to the larger social structure and place them in status hierar-
chies in the larger society and in their communities (Parsons, 1954).
Occupations also link men to their family roles of husband and father
due to their activities as economic providers (Turner, 1970). Withdrawal
from the labor force is thus seen as a severe loss for a man since his
identity and his status are defined by work.

The loss of the worker role has been thought to be greatly exacer-
bated by the fact that society has not clearly defined the parameters
for the role of retiree. Writing in 1960, Donahue et al. contrast retirement with other role changes an individual typically undergoes in our
society. They claim that many other stages of social life are delineated
by fairly clear social rules and behavioral expectations and have gradual
transitions with formal and informal preparation for other new roles.
This is not true for retirement. Retirement, they say, is a new form
of social life that has yet to achieve any specific institutional integration. The "challenge of retirement" for contemporary society is

to successfully create and clearly define a meaningful social role for the retired which will provide the individual with a sense of function and value and to integrate this role into the fabric of our industrial civilization [Donahue et al., 1960: 336].

The ambiguity and lack of clarity characterizing the retirement role is a problem that has been cited by various writers for over 30 years (Parsons, 1954; Burgess, 1960; Blau, 1973; Sheppard, 1976; Kroeger, 1982). Role ambiguity has been linked to negative retirement attitudes and to problems of adjustment on the part of the male retiree, who is likely to be beset by feelings of uncertainty and insecurity.

Thus the general consensus in the early retirement literature is that the average, healthy, American male will perceive retirement as aversive and hence will resist it because of the meanings retirement has acquired for men in our society. Retirement deprives a man of the status and identity which are integral parts of the male role. There are no clear-cut expectations available for the retirement role that may replace those of the worker role. Problems associated with relinquishing the worker role have long been thought to result in decreased physical and mental health for males (Barron et al., 1952; Martin and Doran, 1966; Ekerdt and Bosse', 1982).

The negative consequences early writers associated with retirement were said to be more profound for men with a strong commitment to work (see Atchley, 1971). Greater identification with the work role produced a greater resistance to retirement and poorer adjustment to it (Donahue et al., 1960; Fillenbaum, 1971). A distinction was made by some writers, however, between commitment to work based on *intrinsic* versus *extrinsic* attributes of the job. Men who stress intrinsic rewards of work such as identity and self-esteem were considered to fare more poorly than men who stress the extrinsic rewards of status and prestige (see Quadagno, 1978). Men in higher-status occupations (i.e., professional and upper white-collar workers) were expected to develop a strong commitment to work and to stress intrinsic meanings of their work. These men were therefore also expected to resist retirement and to express negative attitudes toward retired life. This assumption appears to have been borne out by findings reported in a number of early studies that men in higher-status occupations are more reluctant to retire and are more likely to express negative attitudes toward retirement than are men in other occupational categories (e.g., Simpson et al., 1966a; Stokes and Maddox, 1967).

The distinctions made among men by some early writers based on commitment to work and occupational status are not as sharp as the distinctions made between men and women. The experience of retirement has not been considered a threat to the identity or the status of the female retiree. Consequently, retirement has been viewed as considerably more benign for women than for men.

The assumption in the retirement literature has been that women experience a great deal less retirement stress than men experience because of the salient characteristics of the female role. Paid employment has been thought to have little significance for women due to their greater involvement in the family (Donahue et al., 1960; Cumming and Henry, 1961; Palmore, 1965; Blau, 1973). A statement made by Cumming and Henry (1961: 144) underscores this notion: "Retirement is not an important problem for women because...working seems to make little difference to them. It is as though they add work to their lives, the way they would add a club membership." Since the primary female roles were considered those of wife and mother, women were expected to work only temporarily and to willingly give up work in the labor force (Donahue et al., 1960; Palmore, 1965). Whereas retirement deprives men of their central source of identity and self-esteem and offers instead an ambiguous role devoid of meaningful content, it has been thought to have little impact on women because society offers them an equally acceptable, if not a more acceptable, role in the position of full-time housewife (Szinovacz, 1982a).

Also, in contrast to the abrupt changes that retirement brings to a man (Blau, 1973), this transition is considered to be more gradual for a woman, "cushioned by the necessity to continue with her household routine and accustomed responsibilities" (Heyman and Jeffers, 1968: 488). Although women have usually already experienced a type of retirement with regard to their familial roles when the children leave home, their household duties, albeit diminished, still continue. Women's roles have been thought to remain essentially unchanged from girlhood to death (Cumming and Henry, 1961) and this continuity, according to the early writers, makes retirement from the labor force easier for them. Retirement from paid labor therefore does not result in a loss of self-identity for women. It also does not result in a loss of status for women since they can continue to perform their "primary" roles and since they derive social status from their husbands (Parsons, 1954). Women were therefore thought to hold positive or neutral views toward retirement and to be affected minimally, if at all, by withdrawal from work in the labor force.

The distinctions made among men based on occupational status and commitment to work were not made among women in the early literature (see Price-Bonham and Johnson, 1982). Some writers, however, distinguished between women who had careers and those who did not (Cumming and Henry, 1961; Palmore, 1965; Gysbers and Johnston, 1968). Palmore notes that career women "to whom work is more important than any other role" represent an exception to the basic principle that the roles of wife, mother, and housewife were women's primary roles (1965: 7). And the work role was thought to be considerably more important for women who did not, in fact, occupy the roles of wife or mother (Palmore, 1965). Based on their review of literature, Keating and Jeffrey (1983) state that most women who are now approaching retirement age viewed work primarily as a means to fill the time between leaving their family of orientation and entering a family of procreation. "For some, this gap became a lifelong pattern, and the never married spinster was then expected to commit herself seriously to work in lieu of a family" (1983: 417). However, the case of the noncareer, married woman was assumed in early arguments concerning how women and men are differentially affected by retirement.

If the assumption that women retain their primary identity when they leave paid employment is—or was—true, it is easy to understand why the negative consequences thought to pertain to males upon retirement have not been thought to apply to females. The arguments made in the early retirement work concerning sex differences follow logically from assumptions drawn from role theory. As with any theoretically informed argument, however, they must be supported by empirical verification. The following section examines the early assumptions concerning retirement and its differential effects on the attitudes and experiences of men and women in light of recent empirical research.

The Recent Retirement Literature: Toward a Revision of Early Views

Two general conclusions can be drawn from the recent retirement research. First, retirement is not so deleterious for men nor so benign for women today as was portrayed in the early retirement literature. And second, situational and structural elements are far more important in influencing attitudes toward retirement for both female and male retirees than was previously considered by most early writers. Much of the contemporary retirement research therefore does not accord with the arguments made in the early work.

Differences in findings reported between early and more recent literature are due in part to changing attitudes in our society toward work and retirement (Friedmann and Orbach, 1974; Glamser, 1976) and to changing gender roles (see Jacobson, 1974). Friedmann and Orbach (1974) review the literature to find increasingly positive views of retirement since the 1940s. They argue that the strong opposition to retirement reported in the 1940s and early 1950s was due primarily to financial concerns. The expansion of private pensions and social security coverage during the 1950s and 1960s provided financial support for most labor force retirees, and by the middle of the 1960s American workers were reporting more favorable attitudes toward retirement. In addition, some writers associate changes in women's attitudes toward work and retirement with increased numbers of women participating in the labor force (Kahn-Hut et al., 1982; Newman et al., 1982).

Changes over time in attitudes toward work and retirement on the part of men and women are difficult to assess, however. Comparability between early and more recent research is problematic because assumptions made in the early work were often based solely on theory or intuition. For example, the importance of the male worker role was often assumed but rarely tested (e.g., Parsons, 1954; Donahue et al., 1960; Turner, 1970). And literature showing negative effects of retirement on physical and mental health was based more often on impressionistic or clinical evidence than on consideration of objective evidence (Martin and Doran, 1966; Friedmann and Orbach, 1974; MacBride, 1976; Skoglund, 1979). Recent writers have charged that the stress placed upon the meaning of work for males was likely due to an upper-middle-class orientation toward work on the part of social scientists (e.g., Glamser, 1976). Others have pointed to the lack of empirical research on female retirees (Quadagno, 1978; Prentis, 1980; Price-Bonham and Johnson, 1982; Szinovacz, 1982c). Statements made by a number of writers concerning sex differences in retirement have been—and continue to be— made in the absence of adequate empirical verification (e.g., Parsons, 1954; Cavan, 1962; Kline, 1975; Bradford, 1979). It is clear, however, that while the early writings may have had some validity with respect to differential meanings of work and retirement for American women and men in past decades, the assumptions they were based on are not valid for many women and men today.

The central assumption concerning men in the early retirement literature was that the work role is so integral to the male's self-identity and status that men resist retirement and suffer negative effects when they must exchange the role of worker for the ambiguous role of retiree. Recent research has not borne out this assumption. Studies have consistently documented that most retirees indicate positive attitudes toward retirement (e.g., Atchley, 1975, 1982; Atchley and Robinson, 1977; Barfield and Morgan, 1978b; Jewson, 1982), that they look forward to retirement (McPherson and Guppy, 1979), and that most are satisfied with retired life (see Sheppard, 1976; Beck, 1982). Research has shown minimal effects of retirment on mental health and well-being (Streib and Schneider, 1971; Kasl, 1980).

In addition, the presumed negative effects of retirement on physical health have not been substantiated. Physical health is related to retirement in that poor health may cause an individual to retire (Thompson and Streib, 1958; Shanas, 1970; Streib and Schneider, 1971). Declining health is also oftentimes a correlate of retirement, since both declining health and "traditional" retirement (occurring at or near age 65) are associated with the aging process. Physical health has not been found to decline as a result of retirement per se. This is true for those who retire "involuntarily" (persons who do not wish to retire but do so for reasons such as a mandatory retirement age or pressure from superiors) as well as for those who retire voluntarily. In fact, some researchers have reported *increased* physical health following retirement (Thompson and Streib, 1958; Martin and Doran, 1966). And studies in which possible effects of retirement on mortality have been analyzed show that retirement is not associated with elevated mortality (McMahan and Ford, 1955; Haynes et al., 1977, 1978).[3]

The "crisis of retirement" has not been documented even for those men strongly committed to their work. Atchley (1971) reports that a high degree of work orientation does not carry over into retirement. Other researchers also have failed to document a relationship between commitment to work, attitudes toward work, and attitudes toward retirement (Fillenbaum, 1971; Goudy et al., 1975; Glamser, 1976; Bell, 1978; McGee et al., 1979).

Men occupying higher-status occupations were described in the traditional literature as those most strongly committed to their work and therefore more likely to resist retirement and to experience negative effects of retirement. While "commitment to work" has been found to be largely unrelated to retirement attitudes and reactions, the impact of occupational status is unclear. Some studies have shown an *inverse* relationship between occupational status and retirement attitudes. These reseachers have reported that men in high-status occupations are more reluctant to retire and anticipate more retirement problems (Friedmann and Havighurst, 1954; Stokes and Maddox, 1967). A suggestion made by some authors is that workers of higher-status occupations are more reluctant to retire but that once retired, they report higher levels of satisfaction than retirees who occupied lower-status occupations (Loether, 1967; Stokes and Maddox, 1967). Other reports indicate a *curvilinear* relationship between occupational status and retirement attitudes, with men occupying either high- or low-status occupations expressing greater reluctance to retire (Simpson et al., 1966a; see also Freidmann and Orbach, 1974; Kasl, 1980). But researchers such as Streib and Schneider (1971), Atchley (1982), and McPherson and Guppy (1979) have found a *positive* relationship between occupational status and retirement attitudes. They have reported that higher occupational status is associated with a more positive orientation toward retirement, including plans for early retirement. Many writers contend that occupational status is an important factor to consider when examining retirement attitudes and experiences (e.g., Stokes and Maddox, 1967; Streib and Schneider, 1971; Levy, 1978), but the literature in this area is complex and does not provide clear evidence for the direction of these relationships.

It is difficult to disentangle occupational status from income, which is a consistent and strong predictor of retirement attitudes. The vast majority of studies show a positive relationship between income and attitudes toward retirement (see Thompson and Streib, 1958; Shanas, 1970; Atchley, 1975; Glamser, 1976; Atchley and Robinson, 1982; Beck, 1983). Studies comparing men of differing income levels have consistently demonstrated more negative evaluations of retired life on the part of lower-income men both prior to and following their retirement. Research has also shown that when individuals expect an adequate retirement income, they will choose to retire early (Shanas, 1972; see also Glamser, 1976).

Health is another situational variable that has emerged consistently in the literature as an important correlate of retirement attitudes. Individuals with poor health have been found by many researchers to express more negative attitudes toward retirement and to report more problems in retirement (see Kasl, 1980; Atchley and Robinson, 1982). Health considerations thus affect the circumstances under which retirement will be experienced (Sheppard, 1976; Szinovacz, 1982c). Other situational factors reported as correlates of retirement attitudes and experiences include levels and patterns of formal and informal social interaction. These do not emerge strongly or consistently in the literature, however (Block, 1982; see also Riddick, 1982).

The importance of situational elements as predictors of the retirement experience was recognized by a number of early writers (Kutner et al., 1956; Thompson, 1958; Thompson and Streib, 1958). But this recognition was eclipsed in much of the early work by the stress placed upon the meaning of the worker role and the problems assumed to be associated with the withdrawal of that role. The relationship of income, health, and other situational factors with pre- and post-retirement attitudes indicates that such attitudes may be "better viewed as resulting from the worker's realistic appraisal of the type of retirement experience which he can expect than as part of a general value orientation stressing the worker role" (Glamser, 1976: 104).

Seen from this perspective, retirement does not represent an experience vastly different from other life experiences. Factors that are important in determining satisfaction or happiness in one's life prior to retirement continue in importance following withdrawal from the labor force (see Beck, 1982). A number of researchers conclude that income, health, occupational status, and levels and type of social interaction predict satisfaction with life in general (see Spreitzer and Snyder, 1974). The notion of such continuity is supported by the finding reported in many studies that an individual's pre-retirement attitudes and activities are strong predictors of his or her attitudes and activities in retirement (Thompson, 1958; Roman and Taietz, 1965; Streib and Schneider, 1971; McPherson and Guppy, 1979).

Continuity of attitudes and activities into retirement has been documented for women as well as for men. In addition, situational factors have been shown to be important elements in the retirement experience for workers of both sexes. But studies comparing male and female retirees continue to report sex differences in retirement attitudes and experiences even after controlling for these factors (Atchley, 1976b, 1982; Newman et al., 1982).

Some researchers report that women express more positive attitudes toward retirement and fewer problems following withdrawal from the labor force (e.g., Atchley, 1982; Jewson, 1982). Their findings are consistent with predictions made in the early retirement literature. But a growing consensus among researchers in the field is that sex differences in retirement lie in the opposite direction. A number of studies comparing male and female retirees have found that women indicate more problems in retirement than men and also report more negative expectations and attitudes toward that experience (Atchley, 1976a, 1982; Jacobson, 1974; Thurnher, 1974; Barfield and Morgan, 1978b; Newman et al., 1982).[4]

The reasons offered by current writers for such sex differences are more varied than those proposed by earlier writers. Those who report more positive attitudes and fewer problems of adjustment on the part of women tend to use a role-based argument, although they do not claim that retirement is less important to women due to their presumed primary roles of wife and mother. Instead, these writers argue that women are likely to have an easier time in retirement due to greater role flexibility (e.g., Kline, 1975). The assumption here is that women experience a number of roles and transitions throughout their lives and therefore can adjust more easily than men to a retirement role.

Explanations have also been offered to account for the more frequent finding that, compared to men, women express greater reluctance to retire and anticipate and report having more problems in retirement. Some writers suggest that because women live longer than men and therefore face more years of retired life, they *should* indicate more negative retirement attitudes (Newman, et al., 1982). These writers do not take into consideration the converse of this argument: Men should fear retirement due to its association with the end of life.

Atchley (1976a) discusses the possibility that sex differences reported prior to and following retirement may be due to women's greater willingness to admit to problems. He does not subscribe to this view, however, and cites a study conducted by Clancy and Gove (1974) who examined the effects of various forms of response bias on respondents' reports of psychiatric symptoms. They found that when these response biases are controlled for, sex differences *increase* rather than diminish.

More tenable explanations for women's negative attitudes focus on possible effects of labor force participation patterns. Since many women have shorter and more discontinuous patterns of labor force participation during their lives as compared to men, they have less time to attain personal career goals (Newman et al., 1982; Szinovacz, 1982a). Negative retirement attitudes expressed by women are also likely to reflect the loss of resources that may accompany retirement. Women may be particularly vulnerable to economic losses associated with retirement (Szinovacz, 1982a). Retirement income is based on length of time on the job and on the level of pre-retirement income. Since the income attached to jobs women hold is, on average, lower than for jobs held by men and since women are likely to be employed in jobs offering fewer retirement benefits (Campbell, 1979; Block, 1982), women's income in retirement compared to men's may be even lower than it was prior to retirement.

In addition, Szinovacz argues that the loss of contacts with coworkers may represent a greater problem for women than for men "since women's emotional well-being seems to be more contingent than men's on the maintenance of social contacts outside the family" (1982a: 19). The research Szinovacz cites for this contention (Candy, 1977) is not strong, but it is true that women are more likely than men to be unmarried at the time of retirement: Widowhood is a more common experience for women, and divorced or widowed women are less likely to remarry than are their male counterparts (Campbell, 1976; see also Uhlenberg, 1979). Therefore, losses in social contacts as well as in income may be especially problematic for women at the time of retirement.

Although most of the early and recent writers agree that retirement affects women and men differently, they do not agree on the reasons why these differences in retirement attitudes and experiences might exist or on the direction of such differences. Most of the empirically based research indicates differences in the direction of more negative attitudes and more problems on the part of women. However, it is difficult to evaluate conclusively such a relationship or the reasons why it may exist on the basis of available evidence.

Some Limitations of Studies Comparing Female and Male Retirees

Most empirical studies of retirement in which women have been included as respondents suffer from one or more methodological problems. Small samples characterize many of the studies in which female and male retirees are compared (e.g., Tuckman and Lorge, 1953; Kutner et al., 1956; Thurnher, 1974; Lowenthal et al., 1976; Quadagno, 1978; Jewson, 1982). Jewson (1982) examined three small subsamples of men and women in retirement: 32 retired professional women, 16 retired professional men and 14 retired nonprofessional women. Quadagno's study (1978) of older physicians was based on 20 females and 20 males. And while Tuckman and Lorge (1953) employed a reasonably sized subsample for retired males they used a very small one for retired females: 216 men were compared with 24 women. The use of such small samples greatly limits the generalizability of findings reported in the studies.

The use of nonrepresentative samples is often associated with small sample size and also limits generalizability. Many studies are based on samples not considered representative of workers or retirees in the population (e.g., Kutner et al., 1956; Crook and Heinstein, 1958; Thurnher, 1974; Lowenthal et al., 1976; Levy, 1978, 1981; Jewson, 1982; Keith, 1982). Highly specialized subgroups such as physicians (Quadagno, 1978), aerospace engineers (Kasschau, 1976) and university faculty (Newman et al., 1982) are often used. In addition, some studies are based on nonrandomly selected samples (e.g., Tuckman and Lorge, 1953; Jewson, 1982).

A more serious methodological problem for studies of potential sex differences is the use of noncomparable subsamples of men and women (e.g., Tuckman and Lorge, 1953; Kutner et al., 1956; Streib and Schneider, 1971; Jacobson, 1974; Thurnher, 1974; Lowenthal et al., 1976; Newman et al., 1982). Many researchers who have found sex differences in retirement attitudes and "adjustment" have compared groups of men and women who differ on multiple dimensions in addition to sex. These include length and continuity of participation in the labor force, occupational status, income, age, and marital status. Comparison groups of men and women often differ from one another in their patterns of labor force participation. For example, Lowenthal et al. (1976) compared 30 men and 30 women as "preretirees." While all the men except one were currently working full-time, only half of the women were participating full-time in the labor force. Of the remaining 15 women, 3 were working part-time and 12 were not working outside of the home at all.[5] While many of the studies are based on samples of men and women who *have* participated or are currently participating in the labor force, it is rarely known how long or how continuously these individuals have worked (e.g., Crook and Heinstein, 1958; Palmore, 1965, 1971; Back, 1974; Kasschau, 1976; Barfield and Morgan, 1978b; Levy, 1981; Atchley and Robinson, 1982).

Subsamples of men and women are also commonly differentiated by the income they earn and the occupations they hold (e.g., Jacobson, 1974; Atchley, 1982; O'Rand and Landerman, 1984). Given that income and occupational status have been found to differentiate groups of male retirees and that many males and females occupy different positions in the occupational structure, it is not surprising that sex differences should be found when comparing men and women prior to or following their retirement. Newman et al. (1982) provide an illustrative study. They compared male and female university faculty members and found sex differences in attitudes toward retirement. The authors note, however, that occupational position seems to play a major role in their findings: More women than men in the sample occupied the lower-paid position of "nonteaching professional." Comparing a sample of female nonteaching professionals with a sample of male nonteaching professionals (or comparing samples of female and male teaching professionals) would provide a more appropriate basis of comparison.

It is likely that men and women in the general population do differ in their retirement attitudes and experiences. Research based on large, national samples has indicated sex differences in retirement attitudes as well as in other variables such as the timing of the retirement decision and the problems reported by retirees (Palmore 1965, 1971; Barfield and Morgan 1978a, 1978b). But the fact that samples of men and women often differ on a number of dimensions known to be important predictors of these dependent variables raises questions as to *why* these sex differences are being found. Are the differences due to dimensions such as income or occupational status, or to other, usually unmeasured differences such as the possibility that women require greater social contact outside the family than do men as per Szinovacz's suggestion?

Atchley (1976b) addresses this problem explicitly. Citing a review of sex comparisons conducted by Riley and Foner (1968), he notes that few studies have controlled for alternative causes of sex differences. To address this problem Atchley controls statistically for age, marital status, education, and income adequacy (see also Atchley, 1976b; 1982). After implementing these controls, persisting differences are presumed to be due to "real" sex differences. Statistical controls will be inadequate, however, if one does not identify the true cause of differences between the groups but rather controls for a correlate of the differences. Furthermore, the identification of sources of true differences does not imply the specification of *all* sources of differences. Thus persisting differences may be due to sex differences or to inadequate specification of covariates. Both interpretations remain viable.[6]

In order to determine whether sex differences in such factors as occupational status and income are, in fact, responsible for measured differences in retirement attitudes, it is necessary to compare men and women who occupy equivalent positions on the key variables. If groups of men and women who are equivalent on these variables continue to indicate dissimilar attitudes prior to or following retirement, then other factors would seem to be at work. However, such comparability may not be easily accomplished. Producing samples equivalent on such variables as age and marital status is a straightforward task, but obtaining groups of men and women who are exactly comparable with regard to their position in the occupational structure is difficult given persistent sex segregation in occupations (Howe, 1977; Quadagno, 1978; Kahn-Hut et al., 1982). In addition, as Agassi (1979) has noted in her research, it can be difficult to compare men and women within the same occupational category because men tend to perform more prestigious work and may be paid more than women.

While there is as yet no visible research that can comprehensively address the problem of comparing equivalent groups of women and men, a study conducted by Quadagno (1978) adresses several issues raised here. The sample on which Quadagno based her research is very small (N = 20 males and 20 females) and highly specialized (physicians aged 55 to 72). Some problems of subsample comparability are reduced, however, because her sample is composed of persons in a single occupational category. In addition, patterns of labor force participation are similar for her subsamples: The female physicians did not have more career interruptions than the males, and although the women had spent longer periods of time away from work, this difference is small. (We do not know, however, how the subsamples may differ on other dimensions such as income, age, and marital status.) As the author notes, the findings of this study are limited; they cannot be generalized to all physicians, much less to individuals in other occupations. However, Quadagno is one of the few researchers who has examined groups of men and women with comparable labor force histories. She is also one of the few researchers who has not reported sex differences in attitudes toward work and retirement.

Studies Comparing Types of Female Retirees

A few, usually quite recent studies have examined women who differ on the basis of occupation, employment status, and other factors that have been found to differentiate groups of men. Studies in which different groups of women have been compared show that access to resources such as income, occupational status and education are important predictors of retirement attitudes (e.g., Jaslow, 1976; Fox, 1977; Riddick, 1982). This is in line with findings reported by researchers who have examined different groups of men (e.g., Thompson and Streib, 1958; Glamser, 1976; Beck, 1982) and emphasizes that distinctions between differing types of female workers and retirees must also be made.

It is important to note that these studies are characterized by methodological problems similar to those discussed above for studies in which groups of men and women have been compared. Many are based on small, nonrepresentative samples (see Szinovacz, 1982a). Also, comparability between studies is extremely limited because of the different dependent variables involved: These range from perceptions of the effect retirement will have on the respondents' lives (Price-Bonham and Johnson, 1982) and whether respondents look forward to retirement (Prentis, 1980), to life satisfaction (Riddick, 1982), well-being (Fox, 1977; Keith, 1982); and morale (Jaslow, 1976).

Some of these researchers have examined the effect of women's employment status. For example, Fox (1977) compared groups of women drawn from the second Duke Longitudinal Study of Aging. Female retirees ($N = 56$) were compared with female labor force participants ($N = 87$) and housewives ($N = 69$). The retirees had the lowest income, were least likely to currently have spouses, and were on average older than the other women. Retirees in this study were found to have lower well-being and also to possess fewer resources. A similar study was conducted by Riddick (1982). She examined life satisfaction among older women who were drawn from five different national samples (total $N = 753$). Respondents were either employed or retired from the labor force and were 65 years of age or older. Riddick argues that retired women are triply disadvantaged because (1) retirees had lower life satisfaction than employed women; (2) retirees had lower income; and (3) retirees had lower levels of leisure activity.

Jaslow (1976) also examined the effect of employment status. He used a subsample ($N = 2,398$) drawn from a multistage area probability sample. The comparison groups used were (1) women currently employed; (2) women who had never participated in the labor force; and (3) female retirees. The employed women were found to have higher morale than the retirees; women who had never worked outside the home were found to have the lowest morale. "Small but statistically significant differences" between the groups remained after controlling for the effects of age, income, and health. This indicated that the group differences stemmed in part from the fact that the working women tended to be the youngest, the healthiest, and financially better off, while the women who had never worked tended to be the oldest, poorest, and in the worst health. Jaslow believes his findings indicate that work is a significant factor in the lives of older women—and, compared to a study of men conducted by Thompson (1973) drawn from the same parent sample, shows that work may be more important for older women than for men. However, it is not known how the women in Jaslow's subsample compare to the men in Thompson's subsample with regard to health, age, and other background variables or resources.

Occupational differences also have been observed. Using a sample of 1,235 white-collar working women employed in a midwestern state, Prentis (1980) investigated whether perceptions of retirement would vary by type of occupation. Two subgroups were included: (1) professionals, including nurses, and (2) those in "general employment." The professional group had higher education compared to female white-collar workers in the nation, and both groups had substantially higher incomes than white-collar women in the labor force. Prentis found that most women said they looked forward to retirement; most said they were confident about making a satisfactory adjustment to retirement. Greater interest in retirement was expressed by those in general employment, however. In addition, professionals more often than those in general employment said they would miss their work when retired.

Price-Bonham and Johnson (1982) also compared professional and nonprofessional women and attitudes toward retirement. An earlier sample of 59 (see Johnson and Price-Bonham, 1980) was expanded to 100 women, including 52 classified as professional and 48 as nonprofessional (e.g., clerical and sales workers). Subjects were currently employed and ranged in age from 55 to 63 years. The sample was restricted to married women in order to examine the relevance of the work role as compared to other roles. Although no significant differences in the women's attitude toward retirement emerged (both groups expressed positive attitudes), the predictors of these attitudes differed by group. For example, for women in professional occupations, a negative retirement view was associated with strong commitment to work and a lack of continuation of work activities after retirement. For the women in nonprofessional occupations, a negative retirement attitude was associated with greater current life satisfaction.

These results are analogous to those reported by Keith (1982) who found that although groups of retired women and homemakers did not differ in their "evaluations of life," the sources of their satisfaction were somewhat different.

Similarly, Block (1982) did not find group differences on the dependent variable she used in her study, but she does not discuss whether different predictor variables may be associated with the groups. In an effort to unravel the effects of different work histories on the retirement attitudes held by professional women, Block compared professional women with continuous work histories (N = 150) with those who had intermittent work histories (N = 29). Comparison of these groups showed no differences in these women's attitudes toward retirement. The subsamples also did not differ on the basis of social interaction networks, health, education, and pre-retirement income. Block's subsamples are each composed of generally privileged women, with higher occupational status, educational levels, and financial status as compared with women in the general population. An inference that may be drawn from this research is that women's work histories may be important only to the extent that they influence the individual's current situation.

As has been concluded for research on men and retirement, women's willingness to retire and their views of retired life (as well as various measures of psychological well-being) may be best seen in light of the individual's evaluation of her life in retirement (see Glamser, 1976; McGee et al., 1979). To the extent that women's situations are less advantageous, they may be expected to evaluate their lives in retirement less positively than do men. It is therefore likely that sex differences in retirement attitudes will persist as long as women enter retirement with fewer economic and social resources, including being more likely to be single due to widowhood or divorce.

Conclusions

While it is easy to call for additional research, questions concerning sex differences in retirement attitudes truly require further work. Much groundwork has been laid, but it is difficult to make progress when research questions have been defined and operationalized in so many different ways. As a consequence, the ability to make comparisons across studies is severely limited.

This chapter has called for the use of equivalent comparison groups of women and men in order to investigate more comprehensively questions of sex differences. The groups should be equivalent on the key variables known to be important correlates of attitudes toward retirement and related factors. These key variables include age, health, marital status, education, occupational status, and income. The issue can be made explicit by noting that secretaries and airline pilots, who have quite different educations, incomes, styles of life, and so on, can be compared. But comparison of these persons may be like describing the differences between apples and pineapples. If there are *sex* differences, then comparisons of male and female secretaries, or male and female airline pilots, would be the issue. Otherwise, the comparisons really cannot determine whether there is a sex difference. A main thrust of research requires that equivalence be a central, if not *the* central consideration in making comparisons.

While most of the variation in group differences may be explained by comparing groups (selected by stratified random sampling, for example) that are comparable on the basis of such things as current marital status, occupational status, current income and expected retirement income, it is unlikely that comparison groups could ever be exactly equivalent. Societies are structured so that men and women differ in various life chances, including life expectancy and the potential for remarriage. In this way, they *do* represent "distinctive subgroups of retirees" (Atchley, 1982).

However, comparing groups of men and women who are equivalent, to the degree that that is possible, can help us to understand *why* such differences may exist. If the comparison groups are equivalent on the key variables listed above, but sex differences continue to be observed, then the next step is to explore how and why the groups may differ on other dimensions. Hypotheses such as sex differences in role flexibility or the importance attached to social interaction may then be appropriate to test.

The early and more recent literature can be contrasted not only on the direction of presumed sex differences. These studies also differ with regard to their grounding in theory. While the early work emphasized theory and neglected empirical research, the converse may be said about the more recent work. But theorizing is limited to the degree that we do not measure or take into consideration *how* men and women may differ from one another.

It is important for reasons of social policy, as well as for the development of theory, to understand clearly how and why men and women may differ in their retirement attitudes. The need for pre-retirement planning programs that adequately prepare workers for their lives in retirement will become increasingly important as our population ages and proportionately more people occupy the category of retired. However, the nature of such programs—and their effectiveness—may differ according to how the results of recent studies on retirement attitudes are interpreted. If sex differences in retirement attitudes are thought to be due to sex per se—to different orientations held by all women as compared to all men—then pre-retirement planning programs may be developed that focus on the interests and needs presumed to hold for members of one sex but not the other. For example, following from the notion expressed by some writers that women are reluctant to terminate the social contact provided by coworkers (Jacobson, 1974; Fox, 1977; Levy, 1980; Szinovacz, 1982a), special programs for female retirees might focus on ways in which social interaction may be augmented in retirement. On the other hand, if sex differences in retirement attitudes are thought to be due to structural differences in the labor force experiences of men and women, then pre-retirement planning programs for women would be more likely to concentrate on financial rather than social issues.

Further, if research indicates that men and women who occupy similar positions in the occupational structure also tend to hold similar attitudes toward retirement, then a focus on gender in retirement policy seems unwarranted. It is important to recognize that on average, women continue to earn lower incomes than men and are less likely to be covered by pensions (Block, 1982; Kahn-Hut et al., 1982). Special efforts may well be required to make pre-retirement planning programs available to women (see Block, 1982; Kroeger, 1982; Szinovacz, 1982b). The "special needs" of many female retirees may be shared, however, by men in similar occupational circumstances.

NOTES

1. The term "work" is used here in a restricted sense of paid employment in the labor force.

2. The conceptual orientation of many "early" writers (1950s through early 1970s) toward sex differences in retirement can be differentiated from the orientations of more

recent writers. While exceptions to these general trends do exist and will be noted, the categorization on the following sections reflects these differences in orientation.

3. In his review of the literature on health, mortality, and retirement, Kasl (1980) states that the studies are each subject to methodological criticisms. He believes, however, that although the studies are flawed, the consistency of findings reported in them is difficult to dismiss. Kasl concludes that retirement does not lead to decreased physical health or to increased mortality.

4. A few early writers such as Lehr and Dreher (1969) and Streib and Schneider (1971) reported that female retirees may be more reluctant to retire and may experience more problems in retired life as compared to men.

5. Lowenthal's results have been converted from percentages.

6. A number of methodological problems are associated with using statistical controls to account for preexisting differences in comparison groups. See Nunnally (1975) for a detailed discussion of this issue.

References

AGASSI, J. B. (1979) Comparing the Work Attitudes of Women and Men. Lexington, MA: Lexington Books.

ATCHLEY, R. C. (1971) "Retirement and work orientation." The Gerontologist 11 (Spring): 29-32.

ATCHLEY, R. C. (1972) The Social Forces in Later Life. Belmont, CA: Wadsworth.

ATCHLEY, R. C. (1975) "Adjustment to loss of job at retirement." International Journal of Aging and Human Development 6(1): 17-27.

ATCHLEY, R. C. (1976a) "Selected social and psychological differences between men and women in later life." Journal of Gerontology 31(2): 204-211.

ATCHLEY, R. C. (1976b) "Orientation toward the job and retirement adjustment among women," pp. 199-208 in J. F. Gubrium (ed.) Time, Roles, and Self in Old Age. New York: Human Sciences Press.

ATCHLEY, R. C. (1982) "The process of retirement: comparing women and men," pp. 153-168 in M. Szinovacz (ed.) Women's Retirement: Policy Implications for Recent Research. Newbury Park, CA: Sage.

ATCHLEY, R. C. and J. L. ROBINSON (1982) "Attitudes toward retirement and distance from the event." Research on Aging 4(3): 299-313.

BACK, K. W. (1974) "Transitions to aging and the self-image," pp. 207-216 in E. Palmore (ed.) Normal Aging II: Reports from the Duke Longitudinal Studies, 1970-1973. Durham, NC: Duke University Press.

BACK, K. W. and C. S. GUPTILL (1966) "Retirement and self-ratings," pp. 120-129 in I. H. Simpson and J. C. McKinney (eds.) Social Aspects of Aging. Durham, NC: Duke University Press.

BARFIELD, R. E. and J. N. MORGAN (1978a) "Trends in planned early retirement." The Gerontologist 18(1): 13-18.

BARFIELD, R. E. and J. N. MORGAN (1978b) "Trends in Satisfaction with retirement." The Gerontologist 18(1): 19-23.

BARRON, M. L., G. STREIB, and E. A. SUCHMAN (1952) "Research on the social disorganization of retirement." American Sociological Review 17: 479-482.

BECK, S. H. (1982) "Adjustment to and satisfaction with retirement." Journal of Gerontology 37(5): 616-624.

BECK, S. E. (1983) "Position in the economic structure and unexpected retirement." Research on Aging 5, 2: 197-216.

BELL, B. D. (1978) "Life satisfaction and occupational retirement: beyond the impact year." International Journal of Aging and Human Development 9, 1: 31-50.

BLAU, Z. S. (1973) Old Age in a Changing Society. New York: New Viewpoints.

BLOCK, M. R. (1982) "Professional women: work pattern as a correlate of retirement satisfaction," pp. 183-194 in M. Szinovacz (ed.) Women's Retirement: Policy Implications for Recent Research. Newbury Park, CA: Sage.

BRADFORD, L. P. (1979) "Emotional problems in retirement and what can be done." Group and Organization Studies 4, 4: 424-429.

BURGESS, E. L. (1960) "Family structure and relationships," in E. W. Burgess (ed.) Aging in Western Societies. Chicago: University of Chicago Press.

CAMPBELL, A., P. E. CONVERSE, and W. L. RODGERS (1976) The Quality of American Life. New York: Russell Sage Foundation.

CAMPBELL, S. (1979) "Delayed mandatory retirement and the working woman." The Gerontologist 19, 3: 257-263.

CANDY, S.E.G. (1977) "What do women use friends for?" pp. 106-111 in L. E. Troll et al. (eds.) Looking Ahead. Englewood Cliffs, NJ: Prentice-Hall.

CARP, F. M. (1972) "Retirement as a transitional life stage," pp. 1-27 in F. M. Carp (ed.) Retirement. New York: Behavioral Publications.

CAVAN, R. S. (1962) "Self and role in adjustment during old age," pp. 526-536 in A. M. Rose (ed.) Human Behavior and Social Processes. Boston: Houghton Mifflin.

CLANCY, K. and W. GOVE (1974) "Sex differences in mental illness: an analysis of response bias in self-reports." American Journal of Sociology 80, 1: 205-216.

CROOK, G. H. and M. HEINSTEIN (1958) The Older Worker in Industry. Berkeley: Institute of Industrial Relations, University of California.

CUMMING, E. and W. E. HENRY (1961) Growing Old. New York: Basic Books.

DONAHUE, W., H. L. ORBACH, and O. POLLAK (1960) "Retirement: the emerging social pattern," pp. 330-406 in C. Tibbits (ed.), Handbook of Social Gerontology. Chicago: University of Chicago Press.

EKERDT, D. J. and R. BOSSE' (1982) "Change in self-reported health with retirement." International Journal of Aging and Human Development 15, 3: 213-223.

EKERDT, D. J., R. BOSSE', and S. LEVKOFF (1985) "An empirical test for phases of retirement: findings from the normative aging study." Journal of Gerontology 40, 1: 95-101.

EKERDT, D. J., R. BOSSE', and J. M. MOGEY (1980) "Concurrent change in planned and preferred age for retirement." Journal of Gerontology 35, 2: 232-240.

EPSTEIN, L. A. and J. H. MURRAY (1968) "Employment and retirement," pp. 354-356 in B. L. Neugarten (ed.) Middle Age and Aging. Chicago: University of Chicago Press.

FILLENBAUM, G. C. (1971) "On the relation between attitude to work and attitude to retirement." Journal of Gerontology 26, 2: 244-248.

FILLENBAUM, G. C., L. K. GEORGE, and E. B. PALMORE (1985) "Determinants and consequences of retirement among men of different races and economic levels." Journal of Gerontology 40, 1: 85-94.

FOX, J. H. (1977) "Effects of retirement and former work life on women's adaptation in old age." Journal of Gerontology 32, 2: 196-202.

FRIEDMANN, E. A. and R. J. HAVIGHURST (1954) The Meaning of Work and Retirement. Chicago: University of Chicago Press.

FRIEDMANN, E. A. and H. L. ORBACH (1974) "Adjustment to retirement," pp. 611-645 in A. Silvana (ed.) American Handbook of Psychiatry, Vol. 1: The Foundations of Psychiatry. New York: Basic Books.

GEORGE, L. K. and G. L. MADDOX (1977) "Subjective adaptation to loss of the work role: a longitudinal study." Journal of Gerontology 33, 4: 456-462.

GLAMSER, F. D. (1976) "Determinants of a positve attitude toward retirement." Journal of Gerontology 31, 1: 104-107.

GOUDY, W. J., E. A. POWERS, and P. KEITH (1975) "Work and retirement: a test of attitudinal relationships." Journal of Gerontology 30, 2: 193-198.

GOUDY, W. J., E. A. POWERS, P. KEITH, and R. A. REGER (1980) "Changes in attitudes toward retirement: evidence from a panel study of older males." Journal of Gerontology 35, 6: 942-948.

GYSBERS, N. C. and J. A. JOHNSTON (1968) "Characteristics of homemaker- and career-oriented women." Journal of Counseling Psychology 15, 6: 541-546.

HARDY, M. A. (1982) "Social policy and determinants of retirement: a longitudinal analysis of older white males, 1969-75." Social Forces 60, 4: 1103-1122.

HAYNES, S. G., A. J. McMICHAEL, and H. A. TYROLER (1977) "The relationship of normal, involuntary retirement to early mortality among U.S. rubber workers." Social Science and Medicine, 11: 105-114.

HAYNES, S. G., A. J. McMICHAEL, and H. A. TYROLER (1978) "Survival after early and normal retirement." Journal of Gerontology 33, 2: 269-278.

HEIDBREDER, E. M. (1972) "Factors in retirement adjustment: white-collar/blue-collar experience." Industrial Gerontology 12: 69-79.

HEYMAN, D. K. and F. C. JEFFERS (1968) "Wives and retirement: a pilot study." Journal of Gerontology 23: 488-496.

HOWE, L. K. (1977) Pink-Collar Workers: Inside the World of Women's Work. New York: Avon.

JACOBSON, D. (1974) "Rejection of the retiree role: a study of female industrial workers in their 50's." Human Relations 27, 5: 477-492.

JASLOW, P. (1976) "Employment, retirement, and morale among older women." Journal of Gerontology 31, 2: 212-218.

JEWSON, R. H. (1982) "After retirement: an exploratory study of the professional woman," pp. 169-181 in M. Szinovacz (ed.) Women's Retirement: Policy Implications for Recent Research. Newbury Park, CA: Sage.

JOHNSON, C. K. and S. PRICE-BONHAM (1980) "Women and retirement: a study and implications." Family Relations 29: 380-385.

KAHN-HUT, R., A. K. DANIELS, and R. COLVARD (1982) Women and Work: Problems and Perspectives. New York: Oxford University Press.

KASL, S. V. (1980) "The impact of retirement," pp. 135-196 in C. I. Cooper and R. Payne (eds.) Current Concerns in Occupational Stress. New York: Wiley.

KASSCHAU, P. L. (1976) "Perceived age discrimination in a sample of aerospace engineers." The Gerontologist 16, 2: 166-173.

KEATING, N. and B. JEFFREY (1983) "Work careers of ever married and never married retired women." The Gerontologist 23, 4: 416-421.

KEITH, P. M. (1982) "Working women versus homemakers: retirement resources and correlates of well-being," pp. 77-91 in M. Szinovacz (ed.) Women's Retirement: Policy Implications of Recent Research. Newbury Park, CA: Sage.

KERCKHOFF, A. C. (1966) "Husband-wife expectations and reactions to retirement," pp. 510-516 in I. Simpson and J. C. McKinney (eds.) Social Aspects of Aging. Durham, NC: Duke University Press.

KIMMEL, D. C., K. F. PRICE, and J. W. WALKER (1978) "Retirement choice and retirement satisfaction." Journal of Gerontology 33, 4: 575-585.

KLINE, C. (1975) "The socialization process of women: implications for a theory of successful aging." The Gerontologist 15, 6: 486-492.

KOLLER, M. R. (1968) Social Gerontology. New York: Random House.

KOSLOSKI, K., G. GINSBURG, and C. W. BACKMAN (1984) "Retirement as a process of active role transition," pp. 331-341 in V. L. Allen and E. van de Vliert (eds.) Role Transitions: Explorations and Explanations. New York: Plenum Press.

KROEGER, N. (1982) "Preretirement preparation: sex differences in access, sources, and use," pp. 77-91 in M. Szinovacz (ed.) Women's Retirement: Policy Implications of Recent Research. Newbury Park, CA: Sage.

KUTNER, B., D. FANSHEL, A. M. TOGO, and T. S. LANGNER (1956) Five Hundred Over Sixty: A Community Survey on Aging. New York: Russell Sage Foundation.

LEHR, U. and G. DREHER (1969) "Determinants of attitudes towards retirement," pp. 116-137 in R. J. Havighurst et al. (ed.) Adjustment to Retirement: A Cross-National Study. Assen, The Netherlands: Koninklijke Van Gorcum & Comp.

LEVY, S. M. (1978) "Some determinants of temporal experience in the retired and its correlates." Genetic Psychology Monographs 98: 181-202.

LEVY, S. M. (1980) "The adjustment of the older woman: effects of chronic ill health and attitudes toward retirement." International Journal of Aging and Human Development 12, 2: 93-110.

LOETHER, H. J. (1967) Problems of Aging. Belmont, CA: Dickenson Publishing.

LOWENTHAL, M. F., M. THURNER, D. CHIRIBOGA et al. (1976) Four Stages of Life. San Francisco: Jossey-Bass.

MacBRIDE, A. (1976) "Retirement as a life crisis: myth or reality?" Canadian Psychiatric Association Journal 21, 8: 547-556.

MADDOX, G. L. (1968) "Retirement as a social event in the United States," pp. 357-365 in B. L. Neugarten (ed.) Middle Age and Aging. Chicago: University of Chicago Press.

MARTIN, J. and A. DORAN (1966) "Evidence concerning the relationship between health and retirement." Sociological Review 14: 329-343.

McGEE, M. G., J. HALL, III, and C.J.L. LUTES-DUNCKLEY (1979) "Factors influencing attitude towards retirement." Journal of Psychology 101: 15-18.

McMAHAN, C. A. and T. R. FORD (1955) "Surviving the first five years of retirement." Journal of Gerontology 10: 212-215.

McPHERSON, B. and N. GUPPY (1979) "Pre-retirement life-style and the degree of planning for retirement." Journal of Gerontology 34, 2: 254-263.

MURRAY, J. (1979) "Subjective retirement." Social Security Bulletin 42(November): 20-25.

NEWMAN, E. S., S. R. SHERMAN, and C. E. HIGGINS (1982) "Retirement expectations and plans: a comparison of professional men and women," pp. 113-122 in

M. Szinovacz (ed.) Women's Retirement: Policy Implications of Recent Research. Newbury Park, CA: Sage.

NUNNALLY, J. C. (1975) "The study of change in evaluation research: principles concerning measurement, experimental design, and analysis," in E. L. Struening and M. Guttentag (eds.) Handbook of Evaluation Research. Newbury Park, CA: Sage.

O'RAND, A. M. and R. LANDERMAN (1984) "Women's and men's retirement income status: early family role effects." Research on Aging 6, 1: 25-44.

PALMORE, E. B. (1965) "Differences in the retirement patterns of men and women." The Gerontologist 5: 4-8.

PALMORE, E. (1971) "Why do people retire? Aging and Human Development 2: 269-283.

PARSONS, T. (1954) Essays in Sociological Theory. New York: Free Press.

PERETTI, P. O. and C. WILSON (1975) "Voluntary and involuntary retirement of aged males and their effect on emotional satisfaction, usefulness, self-image, emotional stability, and interpersonal relationships." International Journal of Aging and Human Development 6, 2: 131-138.

PRENTIS, R. S. (1980) "White-collar working women's perception of retirement," The Gerontologist 20, 1: 90-95.

PRICE-BONHAM, S. and C. K. JOHNSON (1982) "Attitudes towards retirement: a comparison of professional and nonprofessional married woman," pp. 123-138 in M. Szinovacz (ed.) Women's Retirement: Policy Implications for Recent Research. Newbury Park, CA: Sage.

QUADAGNO, J. S. (1978) "Career continuity and retirement plans of men and women physicians: the meaning of disorderly careers." Sociology of Work and Occupations 5, 1: 55-74.

RIDDICK, C. C. (1982) "Life satisfaction among aging women: a causal model," pp. 45-59 in M. Szinovacz (ed.) Women's Retirement: Policy Implications of Recent Research. Newbury Park, CA: Sage.

ROMAN, P. and P. TAIETZ (1965) "Organizational structure and disengagement: the emeritus professor." The Gerontologist 7: 147-152.

ROSENFELD, R. A. (1979) "Women's occupational careers: individual and structural explanations." Sociology of Work and Occupations 6, 3: 283-311.

SHANAS, E. (1970) "Health and adjustment in retirement." The Gerontologist 10(Spring): 19-21.

SHANAS, E. (1972) "Adjustment to retirement: substitution or accommodation?" pp. 219-243 in F. M. Carp (ed.), Retirement. New York: Behavioral Publications.

SHEPPARD, H. L. (1976) "Work and retirement," pp. 286-309 in R. H. Binstock and E. Shanas (eds.) Handbook of Aging and the Social Sciences. New York: Van Nostrand.

SIMPSON, I. H., K. W. BACK, and J. C. McKINNEY (1966) "Orientation toward work and retirement, and self-evaluation in retirement," pp. 75-89 in I. H. Simpson and J. C. McKinney (eds.) Social Aspects of Aging. Durham, NC: Duke University Press.

SKOGLUND, J. (1979) "Job deprivation in retirement: anticipated and experienced feelings." Research on Aging 1, 4: 481-493.

SKOGLUND, J. (1980) "Attitudes toward work and retirement in Sweden: a multigroup, multivariate analysis." International Journal of Aging and Human Development 11, 2: 147-162.

SPENGLER, J. J. (1966) "Some economic and related determinants affecting the older worker's occupational role," pp. 3-41 in I. H. Simpson and J. C. McKinney (eds.) Social Aspects of Aging. Durham, NC: Duke University Press.

SPREITZER, E. and E. E. SNYDER (1974) "Correlates of life satisfaction among the aged." Journal of Gerontology 29, 4: 454-458.

STOKES, R. G. and G. L. MADDOX (1967) "Some social factors on retirement adaptation." Journal of Gerontology 22: 329-344.

STRAUSS, H., B. W. ALDRICH, and A. LIPMAN (1976) "Retirement and perceived status loss: an inquiry into some objective and subjective problems produced by aging," pp. 220-234 in J. F. Gubrium (ed.) Times, Roles, and Self in Old Age. New York: Human Sciences Press.

STREIB, G. F. and C. J. SCHNEIDER (1971) Retirement in American Society: Impact and Process. Ithaca, NY: Cornell Univ. Press.

SZINOVACZ, M. (1982a) "Research on women's retirement," pp. 13-21 in M. Szinovacz (ed.) Women's Retirement: Policy Implications of Recent Research. Newbury Park, CA: Sage.

SZINOVACZ, M. (1982b) "Retirement plans and retirement adjustment," pp. 139-152 in M. Szinovacz (ed.) Women's Retirement: Policy Implications for Recent Research. Newbury Park, CA: Sage.

SZINOVACZ, M. (1982c) "Service needs of women retirees," pp. 221-223 in M. Szinovacz (ed.) Women's Retirement: Policy Implications for Recent Research. Newbury Park, CA: Sage.

THOMPSON, G. B. (1973) "Work versus leisure roles: an investigation of morale among employed and retired men." Journal of Gerontology 28, 3: 339-344.

THOMPSON, W. E. (1958) "Pre-retirement anticipation and adjustment in retirement." Journal of Social Issues 14, 2: 35-45.

THOMPSON, W. E. and G. F. STREIB (1958) "Situational determinants: health and economic deprivation in retirement." Journal of Social Issues 14, 2: 18-34.

THOMPSON, W. E., G. F. STREIB, and J. KOSA (1960) "The effect of retirement on personal adjustment: a panel analysis." Journal of Gerontology 15: 165-169.

THURNHER, M. (1974) "Goals, values, and life evaluations at the preretirement stage." Journal of Gerontology 29, 1: 85-96.

TUCKMAN, J. and I. LORGE (1953) Retirement and the Industrial Worker: Prospect and Reality. New York: Columbia University.

TURNER, R. H. (1970) Family Interaction. New York: Wiley.

UHLENBERG, P. (1979) "Older women: the growing challenge to design constructive roles." The Gerontologist 19, 3: 236-241.

WAN, T.T.H. and B. G. ODELL (1983) "Major role losses and social participation of older males." Research on Aging 5, 2: 173-196.

Introduction to Chapter 6

The role of the family in providing care for dependent elderly persons has attracted the attention of researchers, policy analysts, and policy-makers over the past decade. Much attention has been given to documenting the prevalence and importance of family members as caregivers, describing the characteristics of family members assuming the role of caregivers, and investigating the consequences of the role. In fact, a large literature has developed that concludes that the family is the major source of long-term care and, as such, must be considered a central element affecting future long-term care services.

Despite this recognition of the importance of the family as a critical element of the health care system, the availability of family members and resources to support the dependent elderly has not been system-atically studied. Research has focused on units in which caregivers already exist rather than on family structures and potential caregivers. Factors affecting current availability of family members as long-term care resources have not been systematically studied, nor has the rela-tionship of these factors to demographic and social trends been investigated. Without this critical information, planning for long-term care that capitalizes on the availability of family caregivers cannot be meaningful. Policy that is advanced, for example, on the assumption that there will be many caregivers available will lead to a serious mismatching of services and needs if there are in fact few available caregivers.

This critical gap between knowledge and public policy is the focus of this chapter. With a firm grasp of the issues, the authors identify the systematic data necessary for policy development and describe a research process that can be used to generate critical information that can lead to the development of informed public policy in the area of long-term care.

6

Dependency, Family Extension, and Long-Term Care Policy

RHONDA J. V. MONTGOMERY, LAURIE RUSSELL HATCH,
THOMAS PULLUM, DONALD E. STULL,
and EDGAR F. BORGATTA

In recent years policy analysts have recognized the importance of the family in providing care to the frail or disabled elderly. This recognition has led some analysts to advocate services to enhance the family's role in the provision of care, while others have expressed concern that government aid will supplant the family and in the long run incur greater public costs (see Horowitz, 1985). Both of these viewpoints are based largely on speculation, however, because currently little is known about the supply of informal caregiving. This chapter identifies the research process that is necessary to generate systematic data on the levels and patterns of family caregiving that now exist, and the levels and patterns that are likely in future. Because the level of public resources necessary for long-term care of the elderly is related to the extent of family resources devoted to their care (Callahan et al., 1980; Soldo, 1982; Stoller, 1985), the availability of such systematic data will enable policymakers to plan for the future needs of the elderly.

The Current State of Knowledge

As Soldo (1982: 3) notes, the lack of knowledge about the supply aspects of informal care in part stems from "difficulties in conceptualizing and measuring 'supply' or the availability of informal care services.'' One approach to measuring supply has been to locate a population of elders in need of care and to ask them the source of their support (Soldo, 1982, 1983; Johnson, 1983; Stoller and Earl, 1983). This method provides some insight into the relative balance between formal and informal supports, but it does not provide information about the "potential" amount of informal support. For example, it is not clear from these studies what proportion of kin who are "potential" caregivers are currently providing care for those in need. For dependent persons who have caregivers, there is no knowledge of the caregiving potential in terms of replacement or substitutes. While a principle of substitution has been recognized (Shanas, 1979), the conditions under which family members step in to substitute are unknown, as is the prevalence of available substitutes. Similarly, when the study population is confined to those elderly currently receiving care, it is not known how many elders "need" care. It is also not known what proportion of elderly who could be in need in the future have informal resources available to them. Finally, when availability of informal support is measured by asking persons to name the sources of their current support, there is no basis for taking into account demographic and social changes and using them to project future patterns of informal support.

A second approach to measuring the availability of informal resources has been to inventory the kin structure of elderly persons and to derive an indicator of the availability of informal supports. The simplest indicator of availability of supports using this method is the presence or absence of kin, regardless of location (Wan and Weissert, 1981; Branch and Jette, 1983). This approach yields the most liberal estimate of availability of supports, or what might be termed the *maximum potential* of informal support for the study population. This indicator of supply has been refined in a number of different ways. Soldo (1983) focused only on kin who reside with the dependent elder. Others have elicited information only about kin with whom the respondent has the most contact (Kivett, 1985; Scott, 1983) or with whom the respondent is engaged in various activities or exchanges of aid (Fischer, 1985). While these alternate measures yield more conservative estimates of supply, they still do not measure the amount of informal resources available. Refinements of these indices need to take into account the fact that not all potential caregivers currently provide care or may ever provide care, nor do all elderly actually need care at the point of data collection or beyond that point.

Furthermore, not all caregivers provide the same types or amounts of support. A sizable literature has developed that indicates that type, intensity, and duration of caregiving varies by the relationship and proximity of the potential caregiver to the receiver (Troll, 1971; Horowitz, 1981, 1982; Soldo and Myllyluoma, 1983; Fischer, 1985; Kivett, 1985; Montgomery and Borgatta, 1985). In addition, caregiving orientations and behaviors have been found to differ by race and social class (Lieberman, 1978; Soldo, 1982; Mitchell and Register, 1984). When estimating the availability of informal resources to support the elderly, attention must be given to these variations in caregiving patterns.

In addition to the measurement issues discussed above, past research has been characterized by conceptual and methodological limitations. First, most studies that have measured the types of services or resources provided by a family caregiver have focused on the primary caregiver and the care receiver, and have collected little information about other kin in the support system (e.g., Cantor, 1980; Crossman et al., 1981; Johnson, 1983; Lang and Brody, 1983; Poulshock and Deimling, 1984). Second, previous studies often have been limited to samples that are nonrandom or generated from clinical populations (e.g., Robinson and Thurnher, 1979; Brody, 1981; Johnson, 1983; Johnson and Catalano, 1983; Lang and Brody, 1983; Poulshock and Deimling, 1984).

Perhaps the biggest barrier to the study of family caregiving patterns is the failure of researchers to appreciate the complexity of the issue. A recent study conducted by Soldo (1985) represents an exception to this observation. Her research examines multiple determinants of formal service utilization, including demographic factors, health care needs, living arrangements, income, and informal service usage. The probability of using formal services is shown to vary directly with the severity of health care needs and indirectly with the availability of informal caregivers. This approach can help us to understand the dynamics of service utilization. The data on which this research was based (the Home Care supplement to the 1979 National Health Interview Survey) do not, however, provide information needed concerning the location of kin living outside of the household and the aid exchanged by family members.

Despite wide acknowledgment of the importance of the role of the family in caring for dependent elders, studies concerned with informal caregiving have not provided the data needed to describe adequately the current situation in the population. Thus there is no basis from which to make projections for the foreseeable future. In the following section a research process is identified for the systematic study of family support for the elderly.

Conceptual Framework

Figure 6.1 illustrates a conceptual framework that identifies the numerous variables that interact to determine the extent of family resources available to support dependent elders. The intent of the diagram is to identify the key variables and to depict the way in which they are assumed to be related. *The figure is provisional and is not intended to be a causal model to be tested at this time.*

The key variable of interest for any given time period and any given population is the AMOUNT OF KIN SUPPORT PROVIDED for elderly persons. Previous research would suggest that the AMOUNT OF SUPPORT PROVIDED is determined by the NUMBER OF PERSONS NEEDING HELP and the AMOUNT OF KIN SUPPORT AVAILABLE. Recognizing that need is a relative term, one arbitrary definition of NEED FOR HELP could be the health status of the elderly. The AVAILABILITY OF KIN SUPPORT is assumed to be determined by the FAMILY STRUCTURE of the dependent elderly and the PROXIMITY OF KIN. FAMILY STRUCTURE encompasses both the number and type of relatives available. It is assumed that the type and amount of resources available to an elder from his or her kin depend upon the number of kin, their proximity, and the type of relationship (e.g., parent, sibling, spouse).

For any given time period, knowledge of these key variables should provide an adequate description of kin support. To move beyond current patterns to make projections for future populations, it is necessary to recognize the influence of DEMOGRAPHIC VARIABLES and SOCIAL NORMS. Morbidity and mortality rates will affect the NUMBER OF PERSONS IN NEED. These two factors, along with birth, marriage, divorce, and mobility rates, will affect FAMILY STRUCTURE AND PROXIMITY. In addition, SOCIAL VALUES will affect FAMILY STRUCTURE, PROXIMITY, and the AMOUNT OF KIN RESOURCES AVAILABLE. Any attempt to

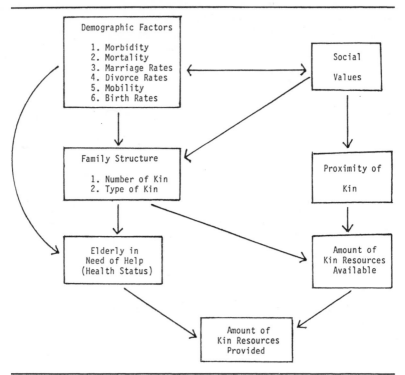

Figure 6.1 Conceptual Framework for Describing Current and Future Patterns of Kin Support for Elderly

project future patterns of kin support must be able to take into account changes in demographic patterns and social norms.

Requisite Data

It is clear from the conceptual framework that an adequate description of the current situation will require the collection and integration of a diverse set of data. The outside limit or maximum potential of family members to care for the elderly is defined by population and household family characteristics. The three pieces of information necessary to describe the "potential" supply of informal services are

(1) the age and sex distributions of the population (by geographic areas);
(2) information on how the population is structured into households with particular reference to family membership (kinship); and
(3) information on the geographical distribution of family members outside of the household under consideration (i.e., the physical proximity of potential caregivers).

Two additional pieces of information are necessary to describe the current supply of informal services:

(4) knowledge of the extent of care needed by the elderly—that is, the incidence and prevalence of disability; and
(5) knowledge of the extent of care provided by family members. This includes information on different types of supports such as financial aid, assistance with grooming, assistance with household chores, and so forth.

Together these five pieces of information would generate an accurate description of the family resources currently available for supporting the elderly.

Having identified the information required to assess current patterns of family support, the next step is to obtain the necessary data. The pragmatic approach would be to use existing data sets. In the next section we review several data bases that might be advanced as plausible sources for this information.

Existing Data Sets

Census Data

A major source of information on households is the census, which collects data on family and nonfamily households. Using Public Use Microdata from the 1980 census, the distribution of family types by age and sex of head of household can be estimated. This data base includes household- and individual-level information from the census "long form." Normally these files are hierarchical in structure. That is, the household record is followed by a variable number of person records, one record for each person in the household. Designations are made for subfamilies within these records.

For the purpose at hand, a rectangular file could be created of cases composed of household information for each household, followed by the person record for each related person in the household. The largest household size would set the limit. (In the Washington state sample the limit was 12.) Thus families with fewer than the maximum related members living in the household would have blanks inserted for those additional records. This file structure would allow the identification of various family structures as defined by designated criteria (e.g., age of the head of the household, sex of the head of the household, presence or absence of a spouse or other relatives). The prevalence of each type of family structure can also be determined.

While these census data are useful in determining household family structures within various subgroups, they do not provide information on the extent of family structures outside the household. In addition, information is not available on aid exchanged by family members within or outside the household.

The Myth and Reality of Aging

The Myth and Reality of Aging surveys, sponsored by the National Council on Aging, provide information on household and family composition, frequency of contact with various kin, and family support networks. These surveys do not, however, indicate the geographic location of family members living outside the household nor do they include information concerning the functional capacity of respondents.

The National Survey of the Aged

The National Survey of the Aged (NSA) is a national probability data set. It includes information on various tasks with which respondents indicate they need help, as well as information about the person or persons who help with these tasks. Information is available about persons who *could* help with these tasks if the respondent does not indicate a current need for help. Respondents were also asked about the aid they provide to family members, including financial aid, as well as aid they receive. Numbers of living parents, siblings, children, and grandchildren are recorded for each respondent.

This data set thus provides rather extensive information on the kinds of aid given and received. Unfortunately, not all types of family members who may be involved in these exchanges were included.

Response categories for relatives who provide aid or could provide aid to the respondent include (1) spouses, (2) children, (3) relatives who live within the household, and (4) relatives who live outside the household. The relatives included in categories 3 and 4 are not specifically identified. Information on help given and received from children is available, but exchange patterns with other types of relatives (such as siblings and parents) are not included. In addition, information is not available on the geographic location of family members living outside of the household, except for an item that asked how long it would take for children not living with the respondent to visit "by the usual way."

The National Health Interview Surveys (NHIS)

The NHIS (1970, 1975, 1977, 1978, 1979, 1980) represent a series of national probability samples of the resident, civilian, noninstitutionalized population. Indicators of functional capacity and the sources of assistance for basic activities of daily living (ADL) and instrumental activities of daily living (IADL) for older family members are included in the Home Care supplementary data. However, as discussed previously, the data set is quite limited for the proposed purpose due to the lack of information on (1) the geographic location of family members living outside of the household and (2) aid exchanged by family members.

The Retirement History Study

The longitudinal Retirement History Study (RHS) was initiated in 1969 by the Social Security Administration. A multistage area probability sample was selected from members of households in 19 discontinued rotation groups of the Current Population Survey. The initial sample consisted of 11,153 persons aged 58 to 63 years. Blacks were sampled proportionally to their representation in the population. Women who were married and living with their husbands at the time of the survey were not included as primary respondents, but were asked a subset of questions (women were included as primary respondents only if they were never married, widowed, divorced or separated). Data were collected every other year through 1979 from the original respondent or, in the case of married men, the surviving spouse.

The RHS contains information on household composition, including the sex, marital status, and relationship to the head of household of each family member. Since this information was collected in every wave, change over time in household structure can be documented.

While the RHS includes fairly complete information on the existence of various types of family members and whether they live within the household, it is a limited source of other information that is needed. The RHS does not indicate the proximity of family members who live outside of the household (the single exception to this is found in the 1975 wave when respondents were asked about the proximity of children living outside of the household). Although respondents were asked about frequency of interaction with kin living outside of the household, the questions pooled the information of physically visiting those persons with talking with them on the telephone. The data set is further limited in that questions about exchanges of aid were confined to financial exchanges. Also, the amount of information about the disability of the respondents and their spouses is limited. Finally, the questions of disability are only asked at the time of retirement. Thus the data are available only for a group of persons that includes the young-old rather than the old-old, who have a much greater probability of needing assistance.

In summary, our review of the literature and possible national data sets indicates that, currently, a data base that describes the geographical distribution of family members does not exist. Furthermore, there is no data set that includes information on the distribution of family characteristics, along with information on the level of need of elders and the exchange of resources between family members. A data set containing this combination of information is necessary to permit the construction of a cumulative descriptive model that would then permit projections, given certain parameters. The development of projections of household and family characteristics in the future will only be achieved when information is systematically collected so that it can be analyzed for cohorts.

Research Questions

As is true for any data collection efforts, specific research questions are required to organize and guide the process. The following research questions can be used for the issue at hand: to provide comprehensive information on current patterns of aid exchanged by family members and to be able to project future patterns of such aid. (Reference is to the population of the United States.)

(1) What is the distribution of family members for persons 45 years of age and older?
　(a) What is the geographic distribution (that is, the possible availability) of primary or close family members (i.e., parents, spouse, siblings, children) for persons specified by age and sex, and by other characteristics such as rural/urban, region, etc.?
　(b) For persons of a given age and sex (and other characteristics that are of interest), what percentage have family (support) resources available?
　(c) For persons of a given age and sex (and other characteristics), what is the distribution of disabilities and dependency?

(2) Given the current population distribution of persons 45 years of age and older and *assuming no changes in patterns of dependency* or in patterns of allocation of available family resources, what will be the characteristics of the population in the future?
　(a) Assuming continuation of current patterns, what will be the distribution and geographic location of primary relatives for persons by age and sex (and other characteristics)?
　(b) Assuming continuation of current patterns of need for assistance (dependency) and of current patterns of family resource allocation, what is the distribution of family support for persons by age and sex (and other characteristics)?

(3) Given the current population distribution of persons 45 years of age and older and *assumptions that current patterns of disability and patterns of family mobility and resource allocation will change,* what will be the distribution of family resources allocated to supporting older persons in the future?
　(a) Assuming changes in patterns of family mobility, what will be the distribution of primary relatives for persons by age and sex (and other characteristics)?
　(b) Assuming changes in patterns of disability and dependency and in patterns of family resource allocation, what will be the distribution of family support for persons by age and sex (and other characteristics)?

The Need For a Cumulative Model

While the collection of appropriate data is essential to an adequate understanding of family support for the elderly, the method of analysis may be even more critical. Too often investigators are tempted by inappropriate techniques. In this case, measures of association and multiple regression techniques will have the potential of diluting the usefulness of the data collected. Such analyses will not yield the level of detail that is required for making projections. What is needed is a model that can integrate large amounts of data and provide summary information about the characteristics of the population by household and by family. By summary information we are referring to a cumulative model based on characteristics of the population. For example, the most useful model would generate the proportion of people of a given age and sex who have persons available to them who could potentially provide care. Given assumptions about caregiving and exchange, the model could then generate information on the proportion of people that are likely to need care, and the proportion that would be likely to obtain care from their family members.

The model should be capable of manipulation with regard to conditions of dependency for persons by age and sex, as well as family structure. Experience indicates that the family member who is most likely to provide care is the spouse, and usually the female. The nature of support systems that involve members beyond the marital dyad requires additional considerations. These relationships commonly involve adult children and, secondarily, siblings and other relatives such as in-laws. In addition to providing summary information on current caregiver relationships, the model must generate data on the potential for a second or a substitute caregiver. This information will provide some realistic basis for understanding the complex process by which family members become caregivers.

Ideally, a computer model would be developed that could divide or decompose the population of interest into discrete segments and then accumulate these segments to produce summary information to correspond to the defined population of interest. The procedure would be a sorting procedure best described through an illustration. Assume information is desired about males between the ages of 70 and 74. When applied to a set of empirical data, the model would first identify all cases (from survey data) that are males between the ages of 70 and 74. The model would then sort these cases according to the number and type of relations, creating a subset of discrete groupings. For example, all individuals having a spouse only would be placed in one group; cases having one child only would be placed in a second group; cases having a spouse and child available would be placed in a third group. This sorting procedure would continue until all males between the ages of 70 and 74 have been allocated to groups. Individuals in each segment then would be further divided into groups according to other relevant variables such as the proximity of the relatives. Thus, the group of males from 70 to 74 years old who have one child would be further divided into groups on the basis of the child's proximity. There would be a group with the child residing in their home, a group with a child residing within a 10-minute drive, a group with a child residing within an hour's drive, and so on, until all cases have been exhausted. This process would continue until the population had been divided according to all characteristics of interest, including such variables as disability and dependency status, the actual transfer of specified resources and the like.

After the population has been decomposed according to all characteristics of interest, the computer model would then summarize across groups to provide summary information about *any* segment of the total population of interest. In this manner, the model would generate information about any group of persons with particular characteristics.

Application of the Model to Project Future Trends

The model should also be able to project future summary information for any defined population. To make projections, the model must be able to manipulate the probabilities that, given available family members, the members would provide care. The model should also be able to manipulate simultaneously expectations that any person is likely to have particular family members living.

These manipulations can be accomplished through altering the information in the model at the level of the decomposed segments. Alterations would correspond to changes in population characteristics when extended into the future, or according to other assumptions of change. The summary statements from these altered decomposed segments thus create the projections for the future according to the desired specifications.

For example, a 20-year projection of the availability of kin for 65 to 69-year-olds would be an extrapolation of the findings for 45 to 49-year-olds in the survey. The objective here would not be to project the *number* of 65 to 69-year-olds; population projections are available from the Bureau of the Census. Rather, the objective would be to project the number of available kin for those persons who do survive to that age range.

These projections would then be bounded by certain parameters. For example, since virtually no women, and few men, have children after age 45, one can reasonably ignore fertility in these projections. Only two kinds of rates would be relevant: (1) mortality, as it applies to both the respondent and his or her kin, and (2) the propensity of kin to live nearby and to be available for support. In the example above, one would first project the expected number of living children that a woman aged 45 to 49 at the time of the survey would still have by the time she is 65 to 69, 20 years after the survey. Second, one would then project the proportion of those children who would be available for support.

Both schedules of rates can be pushed forward, in their own right, on several alternative trajectories. For example, the first of four hypothesized trajectories of mortality could come from an assumption of *no change* from 1986 levels. The second trajectory can be based on the assumption that mortality rates will become more favorable during the coming decades, continuing the trend of past decades. The data for this trajectory can come from the interpolation (across time periods) of projected life tables for the United States, which have already been published by the Social Security Administration (1983). The third trajectory can be halfway between the first and the second; the fourth trajectory can be 50 percent above the second. The fourth projection is thus based on an assumption of accelerated improvements in mortality. Additional modifications could be based on analysis of the disease-specific death rates and age-specific death rates that appear to be changing.

Projections for the propensity to be available (i.e., of the probability that a specific type of relative will live within an accessible distance) are somewhat more difficult to establish. Given a cross-sectional design, only the empirical estimates of propensity at the time of data collection would be available, and therefore no direct evidence of the direction or intensity of any changes. Initially, two trajectories of propensity could be established (arbitrarily) on the basis of the empirically observed propensities in both the cohort being projected and in the age group to which the projection is being made. Some existing data (for example, the Social Security Administration's Retirement History Study) could provide part of this information, which might aid in setting parameters for some of the trajectories.

Thus by considering different trajectories for mortality and the availability of kin, plausible projections for future caregiving patterns can be made. Projections can also take into consideration the context of changing values and the apparent contradictory pressures in society. For example, government entitlements historically have been *individual* entitlements, but the current emphasis among policymakers is on *family* responsibility. Hence, family characteristics become important when considering future allocations of public resources.

Conclusions

It can be seen from the discussion above that systematic data collection and the development of a model are two critical and integral steps toward rational policymaking. This systematic process must provide data on (1) distributions of the population by age and sex; (2) the structure of households; (3) the geographic distribution of kin living outside the household; (4) the extent of care needed by the elderly; and (5) the extent of care provided by family members. Taken together, this information can describe the current levels of family resources available to support the elderly, as well as elders' current levels of dependency. With a model that can cumulate this data, projections of future patterns of resource allocation and levels of dependency can be made. Both a clear picture of the current situation and the ability to make projections into the future are needed for informed policy on family-based long-term care.

References

BRANCH, L. G. and A. M. JETTE (1983) "Elders' use of informal long-term care assistance." The Gerontologist 23, 1: 51-56.

BRODY, E. M. (1981) " 'Women in the middle' and family help to older people." The Gerontologist 21, 5: 471-479.

CALLAHAN, J., L. D. DIAMOND, J. Z. GIELE, and R. MORRIS (1980) "Responsibility of families for their severely disabled elders." Health Care Financing Review 1, 3: 29-48.

CANTOR, M. H. (1980) "Caring for the frail elderly: impact on family, friends, and neighbors." Presented at the thirty-third Annual Meeting of the Gerontological Society of America, San Diego.

CROSSMAN, L., C. LONDON, and C. BARRY (1981) "Older women caring for disabled spouses: a model for supportive services." The Gerontologist 21, 5: 464-470.

FISCHER, C. (1985) "The dispersion of kinship ties in modern societies: contemporary data and historical speculation," pp. 443-465 in B. C. Miller and D. H. Olson (eds.) Family Studies Review Yearbook. Newbury Park, CA: Sage.

HOROWITZ, A. (1981) "Sons and daughters as caregivers to older parents: differences in role performance and consequences." Presented at the annual meeting of the Gerontological Society, Toronto.

HOROWITZ, A. (1982) The Role of Families in Providing Long-Term Care to the Frail and Chronically Ill Elderly Living in the Community. Final Report submitted to the Health Care Financing Administration, Department of Health and Human Services.

HOROWITZ, A. (1985) "Family caregiving to the frail elderly," pp. 194-246 in M. P. Lawton and G. L. Maddox (eds.) Annual Review of Gerontology and Geriatrics. New York: Springer.

JOHNSON, C. L. (1983) "Dyadic family relations and social support." The Gerontologist 23: 377-383.

JOHNSON, C. L. and D. J. CATALANO (1983) "A longitudinal study of family supports to impaired elderly." The Gerontologist 23, 6: 612-618.

KIVETT, V. R. (1985) "Consanguinity and kin level: their relative importance to the helping network of older adults." The Gerontologist 42, 2: 228-234.

LANG, A. M. and E. M. BRODY (1983) "Characteristics of middle-aged daughters and help to their elderly mothers." Journal of Marriage and the Family (February): 193-202.

LIEBERMAN, G. L. (1978) "Children of the elderly as natural helpers: some demographic differences." American Journal of Community Psychology 6, 5: 489-498.

MITCHELL, J. and J. C. REGISTER (1984) "An exploration of family interaction with the elderly by race, socioeconomic status, and residence." The Gerontologist 24, 1: 48-54.

MONTGOMERY, R.J.V. and E. F. BORGATTA (1985) Family Support Project. Final report submitted to Administration on Aging, Dept. of Health and Human Services.

National Center for Health Statistics. Health Interview Survey (1970) Ann Arbor: Inter-University Consortium for Political and Social Research and NCHS.

National Center for Health Statistics. Health Interview Survey (1975) Ann Arbor: Inter-University Consortium for Political and Social Research and NCHS.

National Center for Health Statistics. Health Interview Survey (1977) Ann Arbor: Inter-University Consortium for Political and Social Research and NCHS.

National Center for Health Statistics. Health Interview Survey (1978) Ann Arbor: Inter-University Consortium for Political and Social Research and NCHS.

National Center for Health Statistics. Health Interview Survey (1979) Ann Arbor: Inter-University Consortium for Political and Social Research and NCHS.

National Center for Health Statistics. Health Interview Survey (1980) Ann Arbor: Inter-University Consortium for Political and Social Research and NCHS.

POULSHOCK, S. W. and G. T. DEIMLING (1984) "Families caring for elders in residence: issues in the measurement of burden." Journal of Gerontology 39, 2: 230-239.

ROBINSON, B. and M. THURNHER (1979) "Taking care of aged parents: a family cycle transition." The Gerontologist 19, 6: 586-593.

SCOTT, J. P. (1983) "Siblings and other kin," pp. 47-62 in T. H. Brubaker (ed.) Family Relationships in Later Life. Newbury Park, CA: Sage.

SHANAS, E. (1979) "The family as a social support system in old age." The Gerontologist 19: 169-175.

SOLDO, B. J. (1982) "Supply of informal care services: variations and effects on service utilization patterns." Working Paper, The Urban Institute, Washington, D.C.

SOLDO, B. J. (1983) "A national perspective on the home care population." Presented at the thirty-sixth Annual Meeting of the Gerontological Society of America, November.

SOLDO, B. J. (1985) "In-home services for the dependent elderly: determinants of current use and implications for future demand." Research on Aging 7, 2: 281-304.

SOLDO, B. J. and J. MYLLYLUOMA (1983) "Caregivers who live with dependent elderly." The Gerontologist 23, 6: 605-611.

STOLLER, E. P. (1985) "Exchange patterns in the informal support networks of the elderly: the impact of reciprocity on morale." Journal of Marriage and the Family 42(5): 335-342.

STOLLER, E. P. and L. L. EARL (1983) "Help with activities of daily living: sources of support for the noninstitutionalized elder." The Gerontologist 23, 1: 64-70.

TROLL, L. E. (1971) "The Family of Later Life: A Decade Review." Journal of Marriage and the Family 3(2): 240-256.

WAN, T. H. and W. G. WEISSERT (1981) "Social support networks, patient status and institutionalization." Research on Aging 3, 2: 240-256.

Introduction to Chapter 7

As Wister and Burch note, there has been a sharp increase in the proportion of older persons living alone in modern Western countries. This phenomenon, which began around 1950 in Canada and the United States, has major implications not only for policy related to housing but also for the development of social and health services within the community. While it is clear that the majority of the current cohort of elderly prefer independent living in individual units, this trend should prompt policymakers to raise critical questions about the costs of such housing. When borne by the elderly themselves, the costs are not and probably should not be the concern of public policymakers. However, when the primary source of income for the elderly is through public financing, either by support of pensions or public assistance, questions about the cost of housing, which accounts for an average 20 to 30 percent of an older person's household budget, become relevant. When those elders also suffer from chronic disabilities and limitations that prevent them from self-care and necessitate assistance from others, the implications for policy become even more obvious. Not only must questions about the cost-efficiency of assisting the elderly be considered, but also questions about the efficient design and delivery of health and maintenance services.

Wister and Burch investigate the process by which elders arrive at their choice of living arrangements. Drawing upon data from a stratified random sample of 454 elderly persons living in London, Ontario, the authors explore the factors that contribute to older persons' decisions for a living arrangement. Attention is devoted to perceptions of thresholds, views of alternatives, time horizons, preferences and normative factors, health status, domestic competence, and the influence of other persons as constraints. The authors pay particular attention to the potential influence of specific cohort experiences and appropriately raise questions about future trends that may diverge from current trends as a result of different historical experiences.

In addition to providing a critical analysis to guide future policy, this discussion of dimensions related to choice of living arrangement has immediate implications for targeting and marketing housing as well as community and social services.

7

Values, Perceptions, and Choice in Living Arrangements of the Elderly

ANDREW V. WISTER and THOMAS K. BURCH

The recent growth of social gerontological research has generated theoretical work from a variety of disciplines. A common thread running through this research is an interest in decision-making processes and the application of appropriate decision-making models. Older people's decisions about residence location, dwelling type, living arrangements, and utilization of health and social services represent key life concerns where decision-making approaches have been adopted for explanatory purposes (see, for example, Wister, 1984; Ermisch, 1981; Lagory and Pipkin, 1981; Struyk, 1980; Anderson and Newman, 1973). Investigation of the dynamics of such choices provides a fuller understanding of the behavior in question. In addition, the identification of decision-making traits that may be characteristic of older people has relevance for the development, implementation, and targeting of community and social services for the elderly.

The focus of this chapter is the choice of living arrangement among the elderly, a topic that is of special interest due to the sharp increase over the past three decades in the proportion of older persons in

AUTHORS' NOTE: We wish to thank Dr. Neena Chappel and Cheryl Deviane for their comments on an earlier draft of this chapter. This research was supported, in part, by a Manitoba Health Research Council Post-doctoral Fellowship. Data for the analysis were collected and analyzed with a grant from the Social Sciences and Humanities Research Council of Canada (#492-82-0034).

Western countries who live alone. An understanding of the causes and consequences of this trend is important since it has implications for families, for community and social services, as well as for housing policy.

The primary tasks of this chapter are (1) to explore the decision-making process and to identify general components of the process for investigation; (2) to investigate the decision-making dimensions that have been identified as relevant to older persons' choices for living arrangement; and (3) to discuss the significance of these dimensions for social policy and future research.

Empirical data have been drawn from personal interviews with 454 elderly persons (65 and over) living in London, Ontario, selected by means of a stratified random sample by age and sex. Although the main purpose of the study was to analyze determinants of choices for living arrangement, some data were collected that relate to characteristics of the decision-making process. In addition, field notes compiled by the principal author during 120 interviews provide valuable qualitative data to assist in the identification of attributes that might typify decision-making behavior among the elderly.

In sociology, the decision-making perspective originates from the proponents of exchange theory, borrowing from psychology and economics (see especially Homans, 1974; and Blau, 1964), where decisions about social interaction or exchange are based on human desires to achieve joint satisfaction through the transfer and mutual experience of rewards and punishments. These rewards may be social, increasing status; psychic gaining, (love); or physical, receiving money (Bagozzi and Van Loo, 1980: 99). In its simplest form, the decision-making perspective views individuals as rational decision makers who consciously weigh the perceived costs and benefits associated with various options.

In the study of demographic behavior, decison-making models have been successfully applied to fertility, migration, marriage and divorce, and household formation.[1] These have been instrumental in advancing theoretical developments in decision models of behavior. Furthermore, this multidisciplinary research on decision making has direct application to other forms of behavior and to specific subgroups (Burch, 1980).

Age as associated with life-cycle change represents an indicator of various alterations in physical, sociological, psychological, and economic conditions. Viewing people in the later stages of the life cycle as a group whose experiences, past and present, have been and are substantially different than those associated with other ages suggests that certain dimensions of their decision-making may be distinctive. While this remains an empirical question, it may be advantageous to develop a conceptual framework from which testable propositions can be extracted involving relevant parameters of decisons.

A General Model of Decision-Making

At the heart of decision-making theory is the assumption that perceived rewards and costs are assessed rationally. The term "rational" has numerous connotations, but its technical meaning here involves the maximization of expected value (Meeker, 1980: 30). Different disciplines applying decision-making theory do not assume that the process involves purposeful and cumulative aspects to the same degree. Economics clearly builds the strongest case for continual and long-term maximizing behavior while sociology, anthropology, and psychology lean toward a less rigorous assumption about the ordering of objectives and goals, which are not necessarily cumulative or additive (Robinson and Harbison, 1980). It is argued here that rationality in decision making can be thought of as a subjective process whereby individuals select and interpret information in a variety of ways with an underlying motive of maximizing their welfare in the face of various constraining factors. In this way it is recognized that "a complex web of cultural knowledge and symbolism surrounds all decisions" (Hull, 1981: 6) and that a primary goal is to analyze the *nature* of the decision as it is shaped through interactions with normative and preference factors, constraints, and individual perceptions. Similarly, Tversky and Kahneman (1981) use the term "decision frame" to refer to the decision maker's conception of the acts, outcomes, and contingencies associated with a particular choice. They state that "the adopted decision frame is controlled partly by the formulation of the problem and partly by the norms, habits, and personal characteristics of the decision-maker" (1981: 453).

The general decision-making components to be investigated are aligned in a provisional path diagram in Figure 7.1. Within this framework decisions are considered to be the result of a subjective evaluation of costs and benefits associated with various alternatives. This evaluation, however, is a product of several interrelated components:

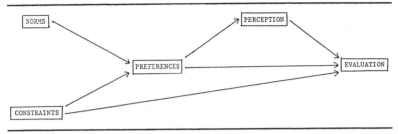

Figure 7.1   A Path Diagram of Decision-Making Components

individual perceptions, constraints on choice, social norms, and personal preferences.

It is argued here that social norms work through personal preferences in affecting evluations underlying decision outcomes. Constraints on choice may be viewed as affecting preferences as well as exerting a direct effect on evaluations. While perceptions may, in part, be the result of personal preferences, both can be seen as influencing decision-making.

It is important to emphasize that the causal components within this general model are dynamic in nature. Social norms surrounding decisions are continually changing; constraints, such as those imposed by health-related or economic factors, change over time and vary across ages; and individual perceptions (which may be affected by the former two) also are a function of age, period, and cohort temporal effects.

Drawing from this general model and the demographic and social gerontological literature on which it is based, the following dimensions of the decision process were assessed in the context of older persons' living arrangement decisions: (1) perceptions of thresholds, (2) viewing alternatives, (3) perceptions of time horizons, (4) norms and preferences, (5) constraints on choice, and (6) individual versus joint decision-making. Although these areas of interest are discussed separately, it will be apparent that there is substantial interaction among them.

Perceptions of Thresholds

It is generally recognized that residential and household decision-making among the elderly, as well as other decision concerns, may often involve large elements of passivity and inertia rather than decisiveness (Burch, 1981). Rather than invest time and energy to change, which entails continous decision problems, individuals *appear* to refrain from making a decision to alter their physical environment. However, this can be seen as at least a partial indicator that their present circumstances make acceptance the least negative decision (Hull, 1981), and may be a reflection of accumulated wisdom rather than tacit acceptance.

Liebenstein (1981) has contributed to the development of decision-making theory in his distinction between active and passive decision-making.[2] He begins by distinguishing passive decision-making as the more frequent form, usually involving routine behavior. Liebenstein argues that this routine behavior can be viewed as behavior "within a holding pattern" and that only if an event is potent enough that it results in significant impact will one realize that an active decision is called for. Active decisions may result in no change, but they invariably involve weighing alternatives. It should also be understood that passive decision-making can be viewed as one form of maximizing behavior; a product of accumulated knowledge and satisfaction with one's present situation.

Data from the living arrangement study show that when respondents were asked about the amount of time spent thinking about change, only 4.2 percent of the sample said "a fair amount or a lot;" 28 percent said "very little," and the remaining 68 percent devoted no time whatsoever to such considerations. This suggests that routine decision-making is overwhelmingly the norm. Among those who spent a fair amount or a lot of time thinking about a change in their living arrangement, the most common reasons were health problems and loneliness. Furthermore, support was found for a general satisfaction of living arrangements, with only 6 percent of the sample expressing dissatisfaction with their present situation.

Work by Wolpert (1965) and Speare (1974) attempts to fit residential mobility and migration into a decision-making framework. These behaviors are considered to be responses to evaluations about a wide range of social and economic variables. However, search behavior is not activated until a *threshold* level is reached, where a negative evaluation or lack of satisfaction (Speare, 1974) is of sufficient strength. Speare (1974) shows that the satisfaction index (reflecting feelings about one's household environment) intervenes between personal and environmental factors and that it has the strongest impact on the wish to move. Perhaps the transition from routine behavior to active decision-making can be understood as resulting from crossing a threshold level of dissatisfaction with present living conditions.

In a recent survey report prepared by the London Coalition for Seniors Organization, it was shown that elderly people can be very accepting of their circumstances and that their ideas concerning acceptable standards of living appear to be very different from what their grandchildren want for them. This suggests that the threshold level needed to stimulate active decision-making or their minimum level of acceptable living standards may be quite distinct from—and generally lower than—that of other age groups.

Our data indicate that elderly individuals view "younger people" as frivolous in their spending habits and inclined to take too many risks in financing material items. The younger generations simply want "too much too soon," in the eyes of older generations. When asked if a person's children are apt to be so different when they grow up (in terms of income, moral values, recreational interests and hobbies, etc.) that it's hard to share day-to-day living with them in the same household, 66.8 percent of the sample of elderly either agreed or strongly agreed, 10 percent were uncertain, and only 23.2 percent disagreed or strongly disagreed. Furthermore, elderly respondents tended to emphasize the "irresponsible spending habits of younger people" as well as their "self-centered approach to life" in conversations with the interviewer.

Past histories (such as experiencing a world war or the Great Depression) may have contributed to age or cohort differentiation (Elder, 1974), and may be an influential force in the apparent deviation in the decision-making behavior of older people. Easterlin's (1978) discussion of changes in acceptable levels of living due to relative deprivation appears to shed light on this decision-making characteristic common to current older people. According to Easterlin's hypothesis, the expectations of today's elderly were developed through comparisons with their own early life experiences and what their parents experienced. The relative advances that many elderly believe they have enjoyed due to social security policies and substantial increases in standard of living when compared to the lives of their parents, or themselves in earlier years, may contribute to a low level of perceived relative deprivation. In this sense, many of today's seniors may have fairly low expectations for what constitutes a minimum acceptable living standard.

This perspective is supported by the informal discussions with elderly respondents. Many stated informally their satisfaction with the benefits that they currently receive. In addition, 67.3 percent of the total sample agreed or strongly agreed with the statement, "In this age of pensions and welfare, it isn't necessary anymore for older persons to be taken care of by their adult children." Only 20.8 percent disagreed or strongly disagreed, while 11.9 percent were uncertain.

Of course, future cohorts of elderly may have much higher expectations for what constitutes a minimum acceptable living standard. This would be expected particularly for cohorts who enjoyed the benefits of the 1960s rapid economic progress during their teenage and early adult years, at which time they would have been developing such standards.

Viewing Alternatives

It has been stated that the most irrational aspect of the decision-making process is probably the limited number of behavioral options that individuals perceive (Meeker, 1980). This appears to be consistent with the previous discussion concerning the propensity toward a routine or passive style of decision-making, where individuals avoid stressful and time-consuming evaluations of various alternatives for as long as possible. In this sense, the routine decision-making stage allows an individual to procrastinate or even ignore the calculative psychological process involved in active decision-making. This is because, at the very least, a minimum amount of effort is required to select information and organize it in a way that allows one to perceive and assess the implications of various options. Furthermore, personal preferences and individual personalities affect the framing of decision problems and the choice of whether *all* relevant elements are to be considered.

For elderly persons today, for example, the idea of sharing accommodations with nonrelatives is not usually considered as an option to living alone. Responses were gathered to the question, "From time to time, it often happens that people change their living arrangements (whom they live with) due to changes in health, finances, and so on. If you should have occasion to do so, what alternative living arrangements do you visualize?" Respondents were allowed up to three possibilities. Regarding the first option, only 1.8 percent visualized living with friends as a possibility, while almost 50 percent did not visualize any alternative. Similarly, among those stating a second alternative 1.1 percent stated friends as a possible living arrangement option, while 87 percent did not view a second alternative. Of those who gave three alternatives, no one chose living with friends as the third option.

In response to the question, "Overall, how do you feel about living with one or more friends?" 5.2 percent stated that it would be, or is, preferable or slightly preferable; 8.6 percent were neutral; and 86.2 percent saw this arrangement as not preferable. These data suggest that while some elderly individuals are dissatisfied with separate living many do not see viable alternatives. Moreover, few see living with friends as a possibility even though this type of arrangement may be beneficial to those elderly living alone who suffer from financial problems, loneliness, and the lack of interaction with others of their generation. The idea of residing with a friend or even with a stranger (a service which several agencies across Canada are presently attempting to provide for single elderly) may never be considered by most elderly.

The perception of potential living arrangement alternatives appears to be affected by past histories, which may be linked to the development of such factors as personal tastes and preferences, social norms, and social roles. Research that isolates the influence of specific cohort-related experiences or attitude formation would therefore be valuable. For example, future cohorts of older women will probably display changes in attitudes, linked to past histories, by viewing some of these alternative forms of living arrangements as more acceptable or perhaps even desirable. The experience of cohabitation among today's college students may affect later decisions regarding living styles at the latter stages of the life cycle. This cohort-related heterogeneity suggests the need for a greater range of alternatives in living environments made available for future elderly. Furthermore, there is a necessity for further development of work done by Easterlin (1978) that attempts to account for changes in social and economic expectations over time and across cohorts and the effect that these expectations may exert on various behavioral patterns.

Time Horizons and Age

An important dimension of decision-making among the elderly at a general level is the notion of perceived time horizons—the view that there is limited time remaining to enjoy the benefits of change. Objectively, an older person has on average fewer years of remaining life than does a younger person. The next question is that of perceptions on the subjective experience of this fact. Research has shown that older people underestimate time intervals associated with temporal experience in the social milieu (Levy, 1979). This, coupled with the possibility of death, becomes an influential factor in the organization of time (Ward, 1982). For example, these perceptions may affect threshold levels associated with minimal standards of acceptance. Thus the very old may be expected to view moving as too costly due to their perception of the time left for them to enjoy the benefits of a change in living arrangements (Sjaastead, 1962).

Based on this rationale, the research tested the hypothesis that among the elderly, age will be positively associated with perceptions involving the effect of limited time horizons on major changes. Perceptions of time horizons were measured using the attitude item, "When you reach my age, it isn't worth the trouble required to make major changes like moving, establishing new relationships, and so on." The cross-tabulation of time horizons and three categories of age resulted in a chi-square = 22.5, p = .01. The probability of agreement with this statement increases about 20 percent (from 44.2 percent to 64.8 percent) when comparing the young-old and the old-old.

While the effect of limited time horizons is most pronounced at the older ages, there is still a large portion of people aged 64 to 69 years (44 percent) who agreed with this statement. This suggests that the elderly as a group exhibit distinctive decision-making traits. The onset of age, therefore, tends to magnify perceptions of limited time horizons. The effect is that the costs of a decision to alter living environments tend to be perceived as greater (at least in relation to an expected stream of future benefits) by the elderly than by younger age groups. This perception of limited time may also inhibit other decisions, such as utilization of medical or other formal services. There is another general possibility, namely, that scarcity of remaining years would make them appear more valuable such that considerable costs in the present would be justified in order to make them as rewarding as possible. Which of these reactions to a limited future lifetime occurs is presumably a function of personality, social context, and the decision content.

Preferences, Norms, and Decisions

As is apparent from the previous discussion, personal preferences and social norms play a primary role in living arrangement decisions. These may not only influence the way in which people view alternative living styles but may directly affect the desirability of particular options.

A study by Jirovec (1977), investigating the connotative meaning of the residential environment, found that the elderly preferred affective qualities including friendliness, quietness, neatness, and aesthetic value. This cluster of qualities was nearly unique to the elderly when compared to younger age groups, suggesting that preference structures may, at times, be age-related or cohort-specific.

It has been argued that the changing structure of the family in industrial societies has partly been due to greater emphasis on separateness. Thus young adults tend to leave home earlier to set up their own households and elderly parents are reluctant to co-reside with adult children or other kin (Abu-Laban, 1980). These preferences for privacy and independence and their implications for autonomy in decision-making may, in part, be the result of normative forces in society.

An individual may prefer living alone because other options are not viewed as proper. Social norms involving the expected separateness of the elderly, age segregation or differentiation, and expectations involving family obligations and ties have been found to be significant predictors of seniors' living arrangements (Wister, 1984). Moreover, of all the independent variables investigated, the preference for privacy/independence arose as the best discriminating factor, where "living alone," "with spouse only," or "with others," represent the three living arrangement categories.[3] It was concluded that normative and preference factors persist as strong determinants even after controlling for other key variables. The increased separateness in living style among the elderly appears to be mostly the result of a preference for independence—that is, for being able to do what one wants when one wants—as well as a preference for privacy. The propensity to live separately is also, to a lesser degree, the result of age differences in lifestyle across generations. Rapid social change and the distinct life experiences connected with different age cohorts seem to have affected the desirability of certain options. It is once again apparent that past histories can be significant in the decision-making tendencies of people. However, the development and relationship between social norms and personal preferences requires further attention.

Health Status and Domestic Competence
as Constraints on Choice

The domain of significant constraints within decision-making models depends on the type of decision being made. They affect the *feasibility* and *availability* of various options, thereby shaping perceptions of viable alternatives. For the elderly, two interrelated constraints are of particular importance since they have bearing upon a host of life-shaping decisions, including living arrangement selection. These are health status and domestic competence.

For an older person with chronic or acute illness and limited functional ability, options are usually limited to either living with kin, institutionalization, or having a nursemaid. Good health, on the other hand, creates the opportunity to live alone, if one so desires. For older persons who are currently married, health problems may not be a constraining pressure on living arrangements if the spouse can maintain the household and look after his or her marriage partner. In this sense, the presence of adequate informal or formal social support determines whether health status and limited functional ability act as constraints on household choice.

Partly related to health status is the notion of domestic competence (which is viewed here as analogous to functional capacity). With regard to living arrangement choice, inability to meet a minimum level of domestic competence will result in reliance on one or more household members for assistance unless frequent visits from a nearby helper (probably an adult child) can satisfy these requirements.

Our analysis found that measures of health status and domestic competence[4] display statistically significant associations with the three category living arrangement variable (chi-square = 26.5 and 15.2, respectively, p = .001), suggesting that these factors represent important constraints on decisions involving living arrangements of the elderly.

Health status and domestic competence do not exhaust all possible constraints on living arrangement decisions. Past fertility as an indicator of availability of kin with whom one might co-reside represents a powerful demographic constraint on living arrangement decisions (Wister and Burch, 1983). In addition, economic resources affect the feasibility of certain options. However, the constraining effect of health status and domestic competence tends to be more specific to the aging process, with the latter also being tied to cohort experience, such as socialization into historically specific sex roles. This is not to say that these are the only constraints but that they represent two important ones of the many that may be operational in the decision-making situation.

Individual Versus Joint Decision Making

The conceptualization of an individual's decision-making becomes more complex once it is broadened to include other persons. Looking beyond the individual necessitates the inclusion of intrafamily conflict and power as elements in conflict resolution. An elderly individual or couple actively deciding whether to live with a kin member or separately may need to consider these elements. The question arises, Should the decision process be based on the needs of a single individual or include information concerning other members of the household or kin network?

In studying household choices among the elderly, it makes sense to view these decisions as affected by other individuals both within and outside of the household. For example, when a married couple is making a living arrangement decision, both parties help determine the outcome. Outside the household, adult children may directly shape their parents' decisions by exerting influence, which at times can be quite forceful; or even by affecting the supply of alternative living arrangements because of their own preferences. Other significant others and reference groups may also have bearing upon these decisions, sometimes less directly, through imposing norms or expectations on behavior. For example, having a circle of friends who feel that living with adult children or other relatives is not proper behavior for a widow may exert a strong normative proscription on behavior.

The fact that the psychological state of certain subgroups of the elderly is often typified by characteristics of alienation and passivity (Ward, 1984) suggests that consideration of significant others in the dynamics of decision-making may be productive. Future research may benefit from the inclusion of data on norms, preferences, and beliefs elicited directly from family and friends surrounding the elderly decision-maker, in addition to information on the extent to which they actually intervene.

Before discussing policy implications, a word of caution is warranted concerning the tentativeness of some of the conclusions. They are viewed here as plausible and based on partly verified hypotheses, but not without frequent uncertainty about the extent to which something is due to age or period effect.

Significance for Social Policy

A number of significant implications for social policy can be drawn from the previous discussions. First, the lower standards or expectations held by older residents regarding what constitues acceptable living conditions suggests that the elderly, in general, may be more content than their circumstances would lead us to believe. This is not to say that there are not target populations with specific unmet needs but that, overall, social service and policy planners often interpret need according to a different set of standards than those used by the intended recipients. A 1983 study report released by the London Coalition for Seniors based on 770 seniors living in London, Ontario, concluded that most seniors are satisfied with the way they live. Furthermore, 65 percent of those surveyed were not able to list one outstanding need. The identification of social problems related to the elderly (e.g., the adequacy of pension benefits) should attempt to focus on specific groups—for example, older widows living alone—to minimize distorted perceptions of social need and the development of rigid stereotypes. Awareness of older people's tolerance, acceptance, and contentment with conditions that younger cohorts may view as unacceptable may assist in the accurate delineation of relevant and necessary social policy.

Second, the widespread preponderance of preferences involving privacy and independence in living style coupled with the general adherence to norms of separateness and age segregation suggests that, for the most part, today's older people prefer to enjoy the later stages of life autonomously, with little outside interference. Programs set up to improve the lives of elderly individuals should be aware of this attitude when organizing strategies to reach seniors. Innovative and tactful dissemination of information on available social and community services is therefore a prerequisite for prompting effective utilization of these services for specific populations. The family and friendship network may play a central role in achieving this goal. In addition, those attributes noted as characteristic of elderly decision-makers point toward the potential usefulness of self-help groups containing elderly professionals, workers, and volunteers. While social interaction with young people appears to be preferred by seniors in some instances, there is no doubt that age homogeneity may overcome age-related social barriers in attempts to provide certain services to those in need.

Third, the existence and potency of limited perceived time horizons contribute to elders' emphasis on the costs of various options. Often changes may appear too costly in the face of limited remaining time to enjoy the benefits of such change. Such perceptions have direct impact on any decision to utilize services developed for improving one's physical or environmental condition. For example, efficient utilization of medical and other formal care agencies may be hampered by internalized time constraints. Service organizations may benefit by directing their advertising strategies at the modification of this attitude. Again, informal networks may be able to limit the influence of time horizons on decisions involving the utilization of services targeting such groups.

Finally, the relevance of past histories and the development of personal expectations indicates that future cohorts of elderly may hold very different values, norms, and expectations surrounding various forms of behavior and underlying personal satisfaction and well-being. Realizing that these factors are dynamic and age-related emphasizes the necessity to alert social researchers and practitioners to the importance of cohort life experiences when forecasting into the future.

Summary

Several aspects of the decision-making process have been investigated in the context of the selection of living arrangements among older persons. Their identification has been based on the introduction of a general model grounded in literature from demographic, economic, and social gerontological sources. Underlying this framework is the assumption that costs and benefits associated with various options are assessed rationally in such a way as to maximize personal welfare. Decisions are shaped by the dynamics of normative and preference factors, constraints on choice, and individual perceptions.

A family of factors affecting individual perceptions has been found relevant in the choice of living arrangement among elderly persons. Our research suggests that low levels of relative deprivation among cohorts comprising today's elderly may have developed out of comparisons with earlier life experiences (especially the Depression and

World War II years). The consequences of these experiences appear to magnify age differentials and transform expectations of acceptable living standards in such a way as to inflate threshold or tolerance levels associated with living environments or other aspects of quality of life. Past histories may also mold perceptions of viable alternatives. In particular, although shared living among nonfamily peers of a similar age may at some point represent one option to living alone, few present-day elders seriously consider this possibility. Finally, perceptions of limited time horizons and their influence on the organization of time also enter into decision-making processes. The cost of change seems to be inflated by older individuals' mental cognizance of temporal boundaries, which appear to inhibit positive evaluations of change.

The choice of living arrangements, as well as other significant decisions, must be made in the face of constraining factors. By exerting their influence on coping ability, the constraining forces of health status and domestic competence affect the feasibility of various living alternatives. In addition to these factors, economic feasibility and the demographic availability of kin for co-residence also act as constraints on living arrangement choice.

A widespread preference for privacy and independence has been noted among today's elderly, and reflects a propensity towards autonomous decision-making. It has been suggested that these personal preferences may be a product of the adherence to certain social norms in society. Furthermore, empirical evidence displays support for the salience of social norms encompassing the expected separateness of older persons, significant age differences across generations, and the relevance of family obligations and ties within the context of living arrangement selection. Mirrored in these normative and preference factors are historical transitions in family relationships, which have been characterized, in the past, by a gradual decline in instrumental kinship support and the concomitant rise in government and community support. The significance of social change and its effect on the development of social norms and personal preferences underlying decision processes requires greater attention by social researchers.

NOTES

1. For specific applications of decision-making theory to these areas see Bagozzi and Van Loo (1980) for fertility; Bach and Smith (1977) for migration; Wolfe (1977)

and Becker, Landes, and Michael (1977) for marriage, divorce, and remarriage; and Ermisch (1981) for household formation.

2. He notes that these terms are altered from their more common meaning referring to the extent to which an individual participates in family decision-making.

3. This multivariate analysis included hierarchical and stepwise discriminant analysis, where the independent variables included preferences for privacy and independence; social norms of expected separateness; social norms depicting age segregation and kinship obligations and ties; strength and mobility; domestic competence, fertility, ethnicity, income, education, age, and sex.

4. Health status was measured using the question, Would you describe your physical strength and ability to get around as (1) excellent; (2) good; (3) fair; or (4) poor? A domestic competence scale was computed using five dimensions of household tasks. These included (1) preparing meals, (2) laundry and sewing, (3) household cleaning, (4) cooking for self and others during minor illness, and (5) financial responsibilities. This provided an additive domestic competence scale ranging from 0 to 5.

References

ABU-LABAN, S. M. (1980) "The family life of older Canadians," pp. 125-134 in V. Marshall (ed.) Aging in Canada: Social Perspectives. Toronto: Fitzhenry and Whiteside.

ANDERSON, R. and J. R. NEWMAN (1973) "Societal and individual determinants of medical care utilization in the United States." Health and Society 51, 1: 95-124.

BACH, R. L. and J. SMITH (1977) "Community satisfaction, expectations of moving, and migration." Demography 14, 2: 147-167.

BAGOZZI, R. P. and M. F. VAN LOO (1980) "Decision-making and fertility: a theory of exchange in the family," in T. K. Burch (ed.) Demographic Behavior: Interdisciplinary Perspectives on Decision-making. Boulder, CO: Westview.

BECKER, G. S. (1976) The Economic Approach to Human Behavior. Chicago: University of Chicago Press.

BECKER, G. S., E. M. LANDES, and R. T. MICHAEL (1977) "An economic analysis of marital instability." Journal of Political Economy 85: 1141-1187.

BLAU, P. (1964) Exchange and Power in Social Life. New York: Wiley.

BULTENA, G. and V. WOOD (1969) "Normative attitudes toward the aged role among migrant and non-migrant retirees." The Gerontologist 9: 204-208.

BURCH, T. K. (1980) "Decision-making theories in demography: an introduction," in T. K. Burch (ed.) Demographic Behavior: Interdisciplinary Perspectives on Decision-making. Boulder, CO: Westview.

BURCH, T. K. (1981) "Interactive decision-making in the determination of residence patterns and family relations." Solicited papers: International Population Conference, Manila, Vol. 1, pp. 451-461.

CARLINER, G. (1975) "Determinants of household headship." Journal of Marriage and the Family 37: 28-38.

CHEVAN, A. and J. H. KORSON (1972) "The widowed who live alone: an examination of social and demographic factors." Social Forces 51: 45-53.

DIXON, R. B. (1978) "Late marriage and non-marriage as demographic responses: are they similar?" Population Studies 25, 2: 215-234.

EASTERLIN, R. A. (1978) "What will 1984 be like?" Socio economic implications of recent twists in age structure." Demography 15, 4: 397-421.

EASTERLIN, R. A., R. A. POLLOCK, and M. L. WACHTER (1980) "Towards a more general model of fertility determination," pp. 81-149 in R. A. Easterlin (ed.) Population and Economic Change in Developing Countries. Chicago: University of Chicago Press.

ELDER, G. H. (1974) Children of the Great Depression. Chicago: University of Chicago Press.

ERMISCH, J. F. (1981) "An economic theory of household formation: theory and evidence from the general household survey." Scottish Journal of Political Economy 28: 1-19.

FLETCHER, S. and L. O. STONE (1980) "Living arrangements of Canada's older women and their implications for access to support services." Statistics Canada, Ottawa. (unpublished)

HAREVEN, T. K. (1981) "Historical changes in the timing of family transitions: their impact on generational relations." pp. 143-165 in R. Fogel et al. (eds.) Aging: Stability and Change in the Family. New York: Academic Press.

HARRISON, B. R. (1980) "Living alone in Canada: demographic and economic perspectives." Ottawa: Statistics Canada.

HILL, D. H. and M. S. HILL (1976) "Older children splitting off," pp. 117-153 in G. J. Duncan and J. N. Morgan (eds.) Five Thousand Families: Patterns of Economic Progress, Vol. 4: Family Composition and Change and Other Analysis of the First Seven Years of the Panel Study of Income Dynamics. Ann Arbor: University of Michigan Institute for Social Research, Survey Research Center.

HOMANS, G. (1974) Social Behavior: Its Elementary Forms. New York: Harcourt Brace Jovanovich.

HULL, T. H. (1981) "Cultural influences on decision style in fertility decision-making." Washington, DC: National Academy of Sciences.

JIROVEC, R. L. (1977) "Optimum residential environments across the life span." Presented at the annual meeting of the Gerontological Society, San Francisco, November.

KOBRIN, F. E. (1981) "Family extension and the elderly: economic, demographic and family cycle factors." Journal of Gerontology 36: 370-372.

KOBRIN, F. E. and C. GOLDSCHEIDER (1982) "Family extension or non-family living: life cycle, economic, and ethnic factors." Western Sociological Review 13, 1: 103-118.

LAGORY, M. and J. PIPKIN (1981) Urban Social Space. Belmont, CA: Wadsworth.

LAWTON, M. P. (1980) Enviromment and Aging. Belmont, CA: Wadsworth.

LAWTON, M. P. and S. L. HOOVER (1981) Community Housing Choices for Older Americans. New York: Springer.

LEIBENSTEIN, H. (1981) "Economic decision theory and human fertility behavior: a speculative essay." Population and Development Review 7, 3: 381-400.

LEVY, S. M. (1979) "Temporal experience in the aged: body integrety and the social milieu." Aging and Human Development 9: 313-344.

MEEKER, B. F. (1980) "Rational decision-making models in interpersonal behavior," pp. 23-42 in T. K. Burch (ed.) Demographic Behavior: Interdisciplinary Perspectives on Decision-making. Boulder, CO: Westview.

MICHAEL, R. T., V. R. FUCHS, and S. R. SCOTT (1980) "Changes in the propensity to live alone: 1950-1976." Demography 17, 1: 39-53.

PAMPEL, F. C. (1983) "Changes in the propensity to live alone: evidence from consecutive cross-sectional surveys." Demography 20, 4: 433-447.

RITCHEY, P. N. (1976) "Explanation of migration." Annual Review of Sociology 2: 363-404.

ROBINSON, W. C. and S. F. HARBINSON (1980) "Toward a unified theory of fertility," pp. 201-235 in T. K. Burch (ed.) Demographic Behavior: Interdisciplinary Perspectives on Decision-making. Boulder, CO: Westview.

SHANAS, E. (1962) The Health of Older People: A Social Survey. Cambridge, MA: Harvard University Press.

SHANAS, E. (1969) "Living arrangements and housing of old people," pp. 129-150 in E. W. Busse and E. Pfeiffer (eds.) Behavior and Adaptation in Later Life. Boston: Little, Brown.

SJAASTAD, L. A. (1962) "The costs and returns of human migration." Journal of Political Economy 70: 80-93.

SMITH, D. (1981) "Historical change in the household structure of the elderly in developed countries," pp. 91-114 in R. Fogel et al. (eds.) Aging: Stability and Change in the Family. New York: Academic Press.

SOLDO, B. J. (1981) "The living arrangements of the elderly in the near future," pp. 491-512 in S. Kiesler et al. (eds.) Aging: Social Change. New York: Academic Press.

SOLDO, B. J. and H. BROTMAN (1981) "Housing whom," pp. 36-55 in M. P. Lawton and S. Hoover (eds.) Community Housing Choices for Older Americans. New York: Springer.

SPEARE, A., Jr. (1974) "Residential satisfaction as an intervening variable in residential mobility." Demography 11: 173-188.

STRUYK, R. J. (1980) "Housing adjustments of relocating elderly households." The Gerontologist 20: 45-55.

STRUYK, R. J. (1981) "The changing housing and neighbourhood environment of the elderly: a look at the year 2000," pp. 513-542 in S. Kiesler et al. (eds.) Aging: Social Change. New York: Academic Press.

SUSSMAN, M. B. (1976) "The family life of old people," pp. 218-243 in R. H. Binstock and E. Shanas (eds.) Handbook of Aging and the Social Sciences. New York: Van Nostrand.

THOMAS, K. and A. V. WISTER (1984) "Living arrangements of older women: the ethnic dimension." Journal of Marriage and the Family 46, 2: 301-311.

TVERSKY, A. and D. KAHNEMAN (1981) "The framing of decisions and the psychology of choice." Science 211, 30: 453-458.

WAKE, S. B. and M. SPORAKOWSKI (1972) "An intergenerational comparison of attitudes towards supporting aged parents." Journal of Marriage and the Family 34: 42-48.

WARD, R. A. (1982) "Aging, the use of time, and social change." Aging and Human Development 14: 177-187.

WARD, R. A. (1984) The Aging Experience. New York: Harper & Row.

WISEMAN, R. E. (1980) "Why older people move." Research on Aging, 2: 141-154.

WISTER, A. V. (1984) "Living arrangement choices of the elderly: a decision-making approach." Ph.D. thesis, University of Western Ontario.

WISTER, A. V. and T. K. BURCH (1983) "Fertility and household status of older women in Canada." Canadian Studies in Population 10: 1-13.

WOLFE, D. A. (1977) "Income maintenance, labor supply, and family stability." Ph.D. thesis, University of Pennsylvania.

WOLK, S. and S. TELLEEN (1976) "Psychological and social correlates of life satisfaction as a function of residential constraint." Journal of Gerontology 31: 89-98.

WOLPERT, J. (1965) "Behavioral aspects of the decision to migrate." Papers for the Regional Science Association. 15: 159-169.

Introduction to Chapter 8

The emergence of senior centers in the 1950s was the beginning of a long trend in the development of programs specifically for the elderly. Because senior centers were among the first programs to be established, other social and health services directed at the elderly have often been developed and/or administered in connection with centers. As Ralston notes, however, senior centers have not developed in a uniform manner nor have all centers been established to meet the same goals or needs.

Despite this long history and perhaps because of the diversity among centers, the relative merits of senior centers continue to be debated. Much of this debate has been uninformed by empirical data. Given the growing trend to designate senior centers as service delivery organizations, Ralston's review of the issues and of research findings is critical. At a minimum, informed judgments about the merits of senior centers require careful definition and descriptions of senior centers, knowledge of the goals of centers, and data to help determine the correspondence between goals and achievements. In this review Ralston has addressed each of these issues, identified gaps in the current knowledge and provided suggestions for further research.

Certainly this chapter represents a first step in the development of informed policy. There are, however, several issues of importance not addressed by the chapter that deserve attention. First, the diversity of goals for senior centers reflect differences in values. While an assessment of the correspondence between the goals and achievements of a senior center is necessary for any evaluation, it is also necessary to raise questions about the appropriateness of the goals. In the same vein, while it is important to compare the relative success of different models in achieving different goals, questions must be raised about the values that underly the different goals. Comparisons between senior centers and alternative programs and delivery systems may be more important than comparisons between types of senior centers. Even if senior centers are found to meet desired goals, it does not follow that they are the most appropriate means.

It is almost alarming to realize that after 30 years of development and public funding so little is known about the relative merits of senior centers. This chapter provides a starting point for using knowledge and identifying values to inform public policy concerning senior centers in particular, but also for the delivery of services to the elderly.

8

Senior Center Research

Policy from Knowledge?

PENNY A. RALSTON

Over the past 20 years there has been a consistent theme in the literature regarding what senior centers do with and for older people. For
example, senior centers are said to provide socially enriching experiences that (1) help preserve the dignity of older people and enhance
their self-worth (Maxwell, 1962); (2) compensate for decrements of
aging process (National Institute of Senior Centers [NISC], 1978); (3)
ward off loneliness (Frankel, 1966; Maxwell, 1962); and (4) provide
outlets for stimulation and self-expression (Frankel, 1966). In an
opposing view, however, Matthews (1979) argues that senior centers
promote "postadulthood," or a social image of old age that is based
on incompetency. Matthew states,

> Adult members of society may have unmet needs, but are generally
> thought capable of dealing with them unless for some other reason they
> are viewed as incompetent....The old, however, simply because of their
> age, are deemed incapable. In essence, they are assumed to be "post
> adults...". [W]orkers in senior centers in order to justify their posi-

AUTHOR'S NOTE: This chapter originally appeared as Journal Paper 338 of the Home
Economics Research Institute, College of Home Economics, Iowa State University, Ames,
Iowa. An earlier version of this chapter was presented at the Thirty-Seventh Annual
Scientific Meeting of the Gerontological Society of America, San Antonio, Texas, in
November, 1984.

tions, must see the aged as post adults and in doing their jobs, promote a view of the aged as post adults [1979: 152-153].

With these contrasting views of senior centers, there is a need to synthesize available empirical research to either support or refute the generalizations in the literature. In addition, due to the growing numbers of senior centers and the policy implications regarding their designation as service delivery models, there is a need for a review of research findings on senior centers to identify gaps and provide direction for future research.

The purpose of this chapter is to review our present knowledge of senior centers. Specifically, the chapter will address the concept of senior center, programs in senior centers, and utilization of senior centers. The concept of senior center will be discussed in terms of definitions and models of senior centers. Programs or activities and services in senior centers will be discussed in terms of quantity of programs (e.g., growth in number of programs and how number may vary according to organization, staff, budget, and hours open) and quality of programs. Finally, utilization of senior centers will be discussed in terms of reasons for attending or not attending senior centers and correlates of senior center utilization.

Concept of Senior Center

Definitions

A question that has continuously plagued researchers, policymakers, and practitioners is, What is a senior center? However, there appears to be some consistency in the definitions of senior centers over the past 20 years. As shown in Table 8.1, five major definitions of senior centers have been developed since 1962. Maxwell's (1962) definition evolved from the work of the National Council on Aging (NCOA) and was used in one of the classic guidebooks on senior centers. Frankel's (1966) definition resulted from the work of the senior center committee of the President's Council on the Aging. A definition for multipurpose senior centers was included in the 1973 amendments to the Older Americans Act. Leanse and Wagner's (1975) definition was used as a basis for NCOA's *Directory of Senior Centers* and their comprehensive study of senior center programs. Finally, the NISC's definition

TABLE 8.1

Definitions of Senior Centers

Maxwell, J. (1962)[1]:

A program of services offered in a designated physical facility in which older people meet at least two days or more each week, under the guidance of paid leaders performing professional tasks.

The senior center may be a single purpose or multi-purpose agency established as a result of community planning based on the unmet needs of older people in a given community.

The basic purpose of such centers is to provide older people with social enriching experiences which would help preserve their dignity as human beings and enhance their feelings of self-worth. (p. 7)

Frankel, G. (1966)[2]:

A senior center is a physical facility open to senior citizens at least five days a week and four hours a day, year-round, and operated by a public agency or a nonprofit organization with community planning which provides under the direction of paid professional leadership three or more of the services for senior citizens listed below:

1. Recreation
2. Adult education
3. Health services
4. Counseling and other social services
5. Information and referral services
6. Community and voluntary services

Older Americans Act, Title V,
Section 501(c), 1973:

The term 'multipurpose senior center,' means a community facility for the organization and provision of a broad spectrum of services (including provision of health, social and educational services and provision of facilities for recreational activities) for older persons.

(Continued)

203

TABLE 8.1 (Continued)

Leanse, J., and Wagner, S. (1975)[3]:

A program directed to older adults, meetings at least once weekly on a regularly scheduled basis and providing some form of educational, recreation or social activity.

National Institute of Senior Centers (1978):

A senior center is a community focal point on aging where older persons as individuals or groups come together for services and activities which enhance their dignity, support their independence, and encourage their involvement in and with the community.

As a part of a comprehensive community strategy to meet the needs of older persons, senior center programs take place within and emanate from a facility. These programs consist of a variety of services and activities in such areas as education, creative arts, recreation, advocacy, leadership development, employment, health, nutrition, social work and other supportive services.

The center also serves as a community resource for information on aging, for training professional and lay leadership and for developing new approaches to aging programs.

	Maxwell	Frankel	OAA	NCOA	NISC	
	✓	✓	✓		✓	Community planning
		✓	✓	✓	✓	Broad spectrum of services and activities
					✓	Purpose of senior centers
	✓	✓				Paid professional staff
	✓	✓		✓		Regular schedule
	✓	✓	✓		✓	Physical facility

1. Result of Advisory Committee—Consultation on Senior Centers. Purdue University, September 1959.
2. Senior Center Committee of the President's Council on Aging.
3. Operational definition used for *Directory of Senior Centers and Clubs: A National Resource.* Washington, D.C.: NCOA, 1974.

was used in NCOA's 1978 publication, *Senior Center Standards.*

The definitions appear to be relatively consistent in three areas. First, most of the definitions suggest that senior centers should develop as a result of community planning, that they should operate from a designated physical facility, and that they should offer a broad spectrum of activities and services. There is less agreement among the definitions in terms of inclusion of professional staff, regularity of scheduling, and the outcomes or impact that senior centers should seek. The staffing and scheduling components were included in the earlier definitions by Maxwell (1962) and Frankel (1966) and might reflect the initial attempts to differentiate senior centers from senior clubs. Interestingly, by 1978, the NISC definition was broad enough to include senior clubs as well as single-purpose senior centers.

Models

Three types of models for senior centers appear in the literature: (1) models based on physical facilities; (2) models based on programs (activities and services); and (3) models based on senior center participants. Each has received only limited attention in the literature.

Jordan (1978) outlines four different models of senior centers based on physical facilities: donated facilities (occupying space in an existing facility such as an abandoned restaurant or school that has received little or no alterations); shared facilities (occupying space in a large, multigenerational facility such as a community center); renovated facilities (occupying space in an existing building that has been altered and renovated); and new facilities (occupying space in a new building that has been specially designed for the particular needs of senior center programs). Although research is not available concerning these types of facilities, Carp (1976) did find that a senior center within a public housing complex was highly satisfactory and frequently used by tenants. However, elderly who did not reside in the housing complex seldom utilized the center.

Models based on programs have been proposed by three authors. Maxwell (1962) suggested that there were single-service centers, which have a single purpose or function (such as recreation, education, or serving as a drop-in center), and multiservice centers, which provide a wide range of individual and group activities and services. Leanse and Wagner (1975) expanded this framework to also include senior clubs and clubs for elderly in larger organizations. Ralston (1982) proposed and tested a classification of senior centers including senior clubs, nutrition sites, and multipurpose senior centers. These models of senior centers based on programs suggest that there are levels of senior centers and that programming within centers is more exclusive (limited to one or two activities and services) at lower levels and becomes more inclusive (several activities and services) at higher levels.

Models based on senior center participants have been addressed in two studies. Taietz (1976) examined the extent to which the characteristics of senior center users are consistent with a conception of the senior center as a social agency as opposed to a voluntary organization. In a sample of 920 older adults in New York state, he investigated community attachment, formal voluntary organization participation, income, age identification, and preference for type of organization. Based upon the findings that senior center users tend to have stronger attachments to the community and have lifestyles that reflect organizational participation, he concluded that the voluntary organization model more appropriately describes the senior center than does the social agency model. Schneider et al. (1985), in a panel study of 500 older people in two rural Arkansas counties, proposed that Taietz's model could be viewed in sequential stages. That is, a center might first seek to direct services to priority groups of elderly persons (e.g., "old-old", poor, functionally disabled, and those who live alone), reflecting the social agency model. Later, the center might reflect the voluntary organization model by trying to improve the quality of life of participants through increased social activity, diet, or use of related social services. Findings of the study showed little evidence that programs were specifically targeting the most needy. Moreover, the study showed that some variables (e.g., church attendance) associated with participation lend support to Taietz's earlier findings of senior centers being more representative of the voluntary organization model.

Although these models do provide an initial framework for studying senior centers, a major limitation is that there are few data to support their validity. Until these gaps are addressed, few generalizations can be made about senior center models.

Programs

Quantity of Programs

Programs or the activities and services offered in senior centers often have been used as the criteria for determining the value of these agencies. There has been the consistent message in the literature that senior centers began as narrowly conceptualized social clubs with the potential for growth and sophistication of programs (Anderson, as cited in Leanse and Wagner, 1975; Frankel, 1966). Thus the assumption appears to be that the more programs provided by senior centers, the more worthy the agency is and the better the needs of older people will be met.

Although the message is clear, there have been few comprehensive attempts to determine the number of activities and services provided by senior centers. However, three studies are helpful in at least providing some data in this area. In a 1969 national study, Anderson (as cited in Leanse and Wagner, 1975) projected that 300 to 400 senior centers of the 2,000 then identified would be expected to expand and provide at least 3 services. In comparison, Leanse and Wagner (1975), in their national study of senior centers for NCOA, found that of the 4,706 senior group programs identified, 2,739 (58 percent) had at least 3 basic services (e.g., education, recreation, and information/referral or counseling). Of this number, 31 percent had 4 services and 21 percent had 5 services. Krout (1983b), in a recent national study of senior centers, found that the 755 senior centers studied offered a mean of 11.1 activities and 17.6 services. These data point out in general the growth of senior center programs and in particular the growth in the number of activities and services provided by these programs.

Another aspect of quantity of programs in senior centers is how the number of activities and services varies with regard to factors such as number of participants, type of senior center organization, staff, budget, and number of hours the center is open. Leanse and Wagner (1975) found that number of programs varied by type of senior center organization. Of the multipurpose senior centers sampled 40 percent had 5 or more services compared to 22 percent for senior centers, 15 percent for clubs for elderly in larger organizations, and 7 percent for senior clubs. In a study of senior group programs in Iowa, Ralston (1982) found that the number of activities and services increased as the level of program (e.g., senior club, nutrition site, or multipurpose senior center) increased. Leanse and Wagner (1975) also found that more varied services and activities were available in more densely populated areas and at programs with larger numbers participating, with facilities open more often, and with directors receiving higher salaries. Thus it appears that the quantity of programs does vary according to the characteristics of the senior center.

Quality of Programs

Documentation regarding the quantity of programs may be some-what limited, but there is almost *no* empirical research documenting the quality of activities and services in senior centers. Most studies addressing programs in senior centers have explored only whether or not an activity or service is available, without addressing effectiveness. The few studies available that focus on the qualitative aspects of programs in senior centers suggest that their effectiveness is limited. An example would be in the area of education, which is mentioned in four of the five senior center definitions as one of the main programs provided in senior centers (see Table 8.1). Four studies were found that focused on the effectiveness of education programs within senior centers.

Jones (1976) analyzed adult education programs in five senior centers in Rhode Island to determine factors affecting participation of older adults in these programs. He attributed the fact that education was only a marginal activity to tight budgets, the high priority placed on social activities, and the fact that directors were not devoting time and energy to this area. Jacobs (1982), in investigating the educational goals of senior centers as perceived by senior center staff, board members, and participants, concluded that education was not a primary consideration for these constituent groups. They were more concerned about service delivery, the environment, and personal growth than about the acquisition of skills and knowledge. In another study investigating goals of senior centers as perceived by participants, Meredith and Amor (1976) found that the highest priority goals were "to promote fellowship and welfare of members" and "to generate harmony, love and compassion for everyone." In contrast, one of the goals receiving the lowest endorsement was "to learn new skills and hobbies." Finally, in a community study, Ralston (1981) investigated the relationship of educational needs and activities of older adults to senior center programs. Of the five centers studied, most were not providing adequate educational programming in personal development, problems of aging, and home and family concerns, areas in which a representative sample of community older adults clearly were involved.

Other studies also point out the general weakness of programs in senior centers. In a national survey of 70 senior centers, Guttmann and Miller (1972) examined the provision of health, financial, housing, and employment services. Although services provided ranged from 40 percent to 63 percent in the centers surveyed, the authors concluded that the social services offered by senior centers were significantly inadequate. Daum and Dobrof (1983) surveyed 162 senior center directors in New York state to determine the extent to which senior centers were able to meet the seasonal needs of their participants. They found that in cold weather there was an increase in demand for transportation, energy assistance programs, home delivered meals, telephone reassurance, friendly visiting, and escort services. However, the centers were best geared to provide congregate meals and recreation. The researchers noted that "directors expressed willingness to provide additional seasonal supports, but indicated they were already overextended and understaffed, and would require additional resources to do so" (Daum and Dobrof, 1983: 81).

Although the literature has some program success stories regarding political consequences of senior center membership (Trela, 1971) and the integration of nursing home residents into senior centers (Hirsch, 1977), most of the research points out the limitations of programs in senior centers.

Utilization

Reasons for Attending or Not Attending

The motives for older adults to attend or not attend senior centers have received only minimal attention in the literature. Most studies included either a checklist of reasons or an open-ended question. Few attempts have been made to go beyond these listings of reasons in order to determine psychosocial factors and motivational orientations for senior center participation (Sadowski and Schill, 1979).

The data that are available are difficult to summarize because of the different wording used in instruments. However, Table 8.2 indicates that, in attempting to summarize the findings from the four relevant studies, there appears to be some tentative trends. Users of senior centers appear to attend in order to be with existing friends, to make new friends, and to be involved in activities, whether formally through organized activities or through informal visiting and socializing. On the other hand, nonusers are either not interested or are too busy with family, friends, or other activities. Transportation and lack of facilities are not high priority reasons, although these are indicated as more

TABLE 8.2
Ranking of Reasons for Attending
or Not Attending Senior Centers
for Users and Nonusers

	Trela and Simmons (1971)	Harris (1975[1])	Carp (1976)	Krout (1983a)
Reasons of users for attending				
Have companionship/make friends	3	NA	—	3
Participate in activities	1	NA	2	—
Invitation or urging from friends/others	2	NA	—	2
Use facilities for meetings	—	NA	1	—
Utilize leisure time	—	NA	3	1
Reasons of nonusers for not attending				
Not interested	—	1	—	2
Too busy	—	2	—	1
Too "young"	—	3	—	—
Poor health	3	4	—	—
Transportation problems	4	5	1	—
No facilities	—	6	—	—
No information about senior center	—	—	2	—
Competing activities	2	—	—	—
Ambivalence toward senior center activities	1	—	—	—
Not accepted at senior center	—	—	3	—

NOTE: Reasons of nonusers included respondents who were not interested in attending senior centers.

1. Rankings are based on reported percentage of respondents indicating reason for attending or not attending senior center.

important when nonusers who are interested in senior centers are examined (Harris & Associates, 1975). Poor health also does not appear to be a high priority reason for not attending senior centers.

These very sketchy data suggest that senior centers attract older adults interested in social and group involvement, and that those choosing not to attend do so because of lack of interest in such programs and because they have other things to do with their time. The deeper meaning of these reasons, however, has not been explored.

Correlates of Senior Center Utilization

Of the areas addressed in this chapter, correlates of senior center utilization have received the most attention by researchers. Older adults who use senior centers were compared with those who do not in 16 studies; 2 studies compared groups of older adults according to their

TABLE 8.3

Studies Concerning Correlates of Senior Center Utilization

Study	Sampled Population	N	Age Range	Study Design	Utilization factors Investigated	Statistical Analysis	Major Findings
Storey (1962)	Menlo Park and Palo Alto, CA	1582	50+	Attenders of Little House senior center (n = 1132); nonattenders from Menlo Park and Palo Alto communities (n = 450)	Age Marital status Religion Sex Retirement Education Gross income level Occupational classification Health problems Retirement attitudes Leisure time activities Chief need of people 60+	Descriptive	In comparison with community sample, Little House (LH) group had fewer in 50 to 64 age group. More LH men women had been regularly employed outside the home. LH Members were more involved in leisure activities (e.g., hobbies, church, organizations), had more positive attitudes towards retirement, and indicated "satisfying interpersonal relationships" (i.e., having friends, being wanted) as chief need of people 60+.
Tuckman (1967	Philadelphia, PA	138	55+	Three levels of attenders of Adult Health and Recreation Center (within last 3 months): those who had attended 1 to 4 days (n = 58), 5 to 11 days (n = 65), and 12 or more days (n = 65)	Sex Income Race Age Native Born Religion Occupation Relatives Education Marital Status Living arrangement	Chi square	Health (physician's report) and distance from center were the only significant results, with percentage of members classified in good health increasing as attendance

(continued)

TABLE 8.3 Continued

Study	Sampled Population	N	Age Range	Study Design	Utilization factors Investigated	Statistical Analysis	Major Findings
					Source of income Health (self report) Health (physician's report) Church attendance Referral source Reason for joining Length of center membership Distance from center Activities prior to joining		increased and members who lived closer to center more frequently attending than those who lived further away.
Tissue (1971)	Sacramento, CA	286	65+	Old age assistance recipients (n = 256); Members of senior center (n = 30)	Occupation Educational level Social life space Recreational interest Living arrangement Life satisfaction Health	Descriptive	Only 46 OAA recipients had ever attended senior center and only 10 percent had been more than once. OAA recipients differ from SC attenders in SES during middle age (less educated and have worked lower-status jobs), health (poorer health), social life space (fewer contacts with friends and greater social loss), recreational interest (fewer activities), current living ar-

Study	Location	N	Age	Variables	Analysis	Findings
						rangement (more likely to live with children) and life satisfaction (considerably more discouraged and unhappy about their present circumstances).
Trela and Simmons (1971)	Cleveland, OH	320	62+	Reasons for attending/not attending	Descriptive	Majority of both attenders and nonattenders were constrained by competing activities and interests, ambivalence toward organizational activity, poor health and limited access to transportation. Primary factor differentiating samples was poor health. In follow-up study, poor health, competing activities and disenchantment with center were main reasons for attrition.
Hoppa and Roberts (1974)	Snohomish County, WA	542	65+	Loneliness Recreation Sex Worry indicator Mobility indicator Mood tone Age Transportation	Chi-square	Attenders indicated more loneliness than nonattenders; more men in sufficient activity (ISA) attender group compared to sufficient activity (SA) attender group; ISA attender group indicated more

Sample descriptions:
- Attenders (n = 210) and nonattenders (n = 110) of senior center; follow-up study sample included 206 attenders and 107 nonattenders
- Attenders (n = 101); nonattenders (n = 441). Further analyzed by insufficient and sufficient activity attenders/nonattenders

(Continued)

TABLE 8.3 Continued

Study	Sampled Population	N	Age Range	Study Design	Utilization factors Investigated	Statistical Analysis	Major Findings
							loneliness and need for recreation than SA attender group; ISA nonattender group had greater need in transportation, health, worry and recreation areas than SA nonattender group. In general, ISA group felt more unhappiness than SA group.
Louis Harris & Associates (1975)	National	3283	55+		Age Income Educational level Geographical region Race Sex	Descriptive	Senior centers least accessible to black, older people in south and the people in rural areas. Females, blacks, those with lower incomes and those 65+ have higher participation rates than their comparison group.
Rosenzweig (1975)	Philadelphia, PA	90	60+	Jewish Community Center (JCC) participants (n = 30); control groups: subjects living alone (LA); subjects living with family (LWF)	Age Occupation Activities Years of education Satisfaction with work Attitudes towards life Number of friends and relatives Marital Status Present income	Descriptive	JCC's were not well-educated and had blue-collar backgrounds. They obtained social gratification through group activities (were joiners). They had many acquaintances but few close friends whose loss could

					be a threat. The LA and LWF groups were better educated, more successfully financially, and more likely to derive personal satisfaction from their work. They formed closer family attachments and were more vulnerable to loss of home and family.
Leanse and Wagner (1975)	National	728	55+	Users (n = 528); nonusers (n = 200)	Income Marital status Health Use of time Distance from center Membership patterns Education Transportation Loneliness Life satisfaction	Descriptive	Users had lower incomes, had completed fewer years of formal education, were more likely widowed in comparison with nonusers, and had higher life satisfaction scores. Users who knew about a center were more likely to live within a very short distance from center. Nonusers were more likely to indicate cost of transportation as a very serious or somewhat serious problem, and to consider poor health and lack of mobility as very serious problems. Users

(Continued)

TABLE 8.3 Continued

Study	Sampled Population	N	Age Range	Study Design	Utilization factors Investigated	Statistical Analysis	Major Findings
							and nonusers were similar in contact with family and friends and in not perceiving loneliness as a problem. Although some differences between users and nonusers were seen in activity and membership patterns, the researchers cautioned that there was no evidence to suggest that large majority of users are outgoing joiners and "doers."
Taietz (1976)	New York State	920		Attenders; nonattenders (11 percent of sample)	Community attachment Formal voluntary associations Income Age identification Preference for type of organization	Chi-square	Elderly who have strong attachment to community and whose lifestyle is one of organizational participation are more often members of senior centers than those who do not have these characteristics. Senior center members do not differ from nonmembers in age identification, preference for age segregated organizations or income (primarily because

	Location	N	Age	Sample	Variables	Statistics	Findings
							75 percent of members were women with low income).
Trela (1976)	Cleveland, OH	320	62+	Attenders (n = 210); nonattenders (n = 110)	Social class	Chi-square	Middle class were more involved in age graded associations. Lower class were as likely to join as middle class when extensive recruitment strategies were employed. No class differences in level of participation or attrition over the six years following retirement.
Toseland and Sykes (1977)	Dane County, WI	137	55+		Senior center participation as variable in model to determine predictors of life satisfaction. Model included demographic, social interaction and other variables.	Stepwise regression Chi-square	Senior center participation was not a significant predictor of life satisfaction. Both participants and nonparticipants have a homogeneous profile in relation to their life satisfaction score.
Hanssen et al. (1978)	Burbank, CA	129	60+	Users of Joslyn Adult Center (n = 39); users of nutrition site (n =30); former users (n = 30); nonuser (n = 30)	Demographic variables Lifestyle Mood Health Social background	Chi-square ANOVA	No differences between groups on any of demographic variables, (age, income, educational level, marital status, living arrangements, presence of children in metropolitan

(Continued)

TABLE 8.3 Continued

Study	Sampled Population	N	Age Range	Study Design	Utilization factors Investigated	Statistical Analysis	Major Findings
							area, availability of transportation and distance person lived from senior center). Nonusers were least likely to have heard about the center through friends. Health was similar among all groups, but SC users and nonusers had greater walking ability capacity. Senior center and nutrition site users had less feelings of depression. Users reported high levels of social and out-of-home activities and low levels of passive activities while nonusers had highest frequency of engaging in passive activities, and had lowest scores for social and out-of-home activities. Neither group (SC users versus nonusers) had complaints about program. Former participants generally indicated either they were too busy or had health

Study	Location	N	Sample	Variables	Analysis	Findings
						problems that precluded their participation.
Demko (1979)	Detroit, MI	54	High (n = 27) and low (n = 27) frequency users of senior centers	Sex Income Education Age Race Marital status Occupation Social loss Living arrangement Contact with friends & family Number of friends Opportunity for alternative activities Length of senior center membership Membership in other clubs	Chi-square biserial correlation	No differences between groups were found for sex, race, income, marital status, education, occupation or age. Both high and low frequency user groups identified a variety of losses as the contributing factor for joining the center. In comparison with high frequency users, low frequency users tended to live with others, have more contacts with friends and relatives, belong to other clubs, have greater opportunity for alternative activities, have been members of the senior center longer, and reported greater number of friends outside the center.

(Continued)

TABLE 8.3 Continued

Study	Sampled Population	N	Age Range	Study Design	Utilization factors Investigated	Statistical Analysis	Major Findings
Rosen et al. (1982)	Rural counties in southeastern state	169		Sample senior center dropouts who had been members for more than one year. Comparisons were made between those who dropped out for health versus unrelated health reasons and between those who lived in urban versus rural areas.	Health Place of residence Social activities Activity level Attitudes toward senior center Morale	Chi-square ANOVA	In comparison to those who dropped out for health unrelated reasons, those who dropped out for health reasons perceive their health as poorer, take on activities that involve little physical exertion, depend on others for transportation, and are less optimistic about future. However, this group had more positive attitudes toward senior centers. In comparing urban to rural dropouts, rural dropouts have poorer living conditions, poorer health, are less active, more socially isolated, more lonely, unhappy, pessimistic, and have fewer transportation alternatives.
Daum (1982)	National (secondary analysis of	2797	65 +	Comparison between those who had attended senior	Preference for age-homogeneous versus age	Chi-square	Senior center attenders had significantly higher

Author (Year)	Location	n	Age	Sample	Model/Factors	Analysis	Findings
	Harris study)			center in past year to those who had not attended	heterogeneous social interaction		preference for interaction with people of all ages than those who had not attended. Of the nonattending group, those who were not interested had a higher preference for interaction with people of all ages than those who were not interested in attending.
Krout (1983a)	Small urban community in New York	350	60+	Users (n = 125) and nonusers (n = 125) of senior center	Model included four factors: predisposing (age, sex, education, marital status, living arrangement), enabling (income, car ownership, frequency of car use), need (self-perceived health, mobility, number of sick days, and need for transportation), and informal network interaction (visit daily with children, friends, and neighbors).	Multiple regression	Individuals who have lower incomes and levels of education, see their friends more often, and desire more contact with their children are more likely to be senior center participants. (These variables explained 20 percent of variance.) Income was strongest predictor, followed by frequency of contact with friends, education and desire for more contact with children.
Ralston (1984)	Waterloo and Davenport, IA	106	60+	Black elderly attenders (n = 46) and nonattenders	Model included three factors: social (contact with	MANOVA (covariates):	Age, sex, marital status, health and transportation

(Continued)

221

TABLE 8.3 Continued

Study	Sampled Population	N	Age Range	Study Design	Utilization factors Investigated	Statistical Analysis	Major Findings
				(n = 33) of neighborhood senior center; nonattenders (n = 27) in a comparable community	family and friends), attitudes (disengagement potential, acceptability to others, commitment to become involved in senior centers), and knowledge (perception of senior centers).	sex, age, marital status, health, and transportation)	had no significant effect on six variables studied. Differences among three groups were seen in commitment to become involved in senior centers (Waterloo attenders more committed), perception of senior centers (Waterloo attenders and nonattenders more knowledgeable), contact with family and friends (Waterloo attenders and nonattenders had more contact).

222

frequency of senior center use (see Table 8.3). In reviewing the studies, 10 major factors were identified and will be discussed.

Sex. Studies have consistently shown that women have higher rates of senior center participation than men (Harris & Associates, 1975; Krout, 1983a, 1983b), which may reflect the ratio of men to women in the older population and the tendency of widower men to remarry women younger than themselves (Leanse and Wagner, 1975). However, sex does not appear to be a factor that significantly differentiates between users and nonusers (Krout, 1983a) and between users with varying frequency of use (Demko, 1979; Tuckman, 1967).

Age. Some studies indicate that users of senior centers are underrepresented by those in "young-old" age categories. For example, Storey (1962), in comparing Little House (LH) Senior Center participants to community residents, found that the LH group had fewer in the 50 to 64 age group, although differences between users and nonusers 65 years old and older were not significant. In the national study by Harris and Associates (cited in Leanse and Wagner, 1975), 48 percent of the nonusers compared to 28 percent of the users were between 55 and 64 years of age. Several studies, however, indicate no significant differences in age between users and nonusers (Hanssen et al., 1978; Krout, 1983a) and between users with varying frequency of use (Demko, 1979; Tuckman, 1967). These latter studies, however, have been conducted using small samples of older adults in single communities.

Race/ethnicity. Few studies have addressed race or ethnicity in studies of senior center utilization. The few that have show mixed results. Tuckman (1967) and Demko (1979) did not find race a significant factor in distinguishing users with varying frequency of use. However, Harris & Associates (1975) found that blacks (11 percent) were slightly more likely than whites (8 percent) to be senior center users than nonusers. In addition, in the nonuser group, a much larger percentage of blacks (39 percent) than whites (21 percent) indicated they would like to attend a senior center or club.

Lack of transportation, facilities, and relevant programming have traditionally been cited as reasons preventing senior center utilization by black elderly (Harris & Associates, 1975; Vickery, 1972; Downing and Copeland, 1980). A study comparing black elderly attenders and nonattenders in a community with a neighborhood senior center (NSC) with nonattenders in a comparable community without similar facilities found that, with health and transportation controlled in the analysis, the attenders and nonattenders with the NSC were more knowledgeable of and committed to senior centers than the comparison group of nonattenders (Ralston, 1984).

Marital status. In their national study, Leanse and Wagner (1975) found that about equal numbers of senior center users and nonusers were married and living with their spouses (42 percent and 46 percent, respectively), and a larger number of users were widowed (45 percent) compared to nonusers (31 percent). However, other more localized studies show no significant differences in marital status between senior center users and nonusers (Hanssen et al., 1978; Krout, 1983a) and between users with varying frequency of use (Tuckman, 1967; Demko, 1979).

Socioeconomic status. As a correlate of senior center utilization, socioeconomic status will be discussed in terms of education level, occupation, and income. Research regarding educational level and senior center use has had mixed results. Several studies have found that educational level was not a factor distinguishing users from nonusers (Hanssen et al., 1978; Harris & Associates, 1975; Storey, 1962) or users with varying frequency of use (Demko, 1979; Tuckman, 1967). Other studies show that senior center users have lower educational levels in comparison to nonusers (Leanse and Wagner, 1975; Krout, 1983a; Rosenzweig, 1975). In only one study, which compared senior center users with Old Age Assistance recipients, did users have higher educational levels than nonusers (Tissue, 1971).

Similar mixed results were found in relation to occupation, with no differences between senior center users and nonusers (Storey, 1962) and users with varying frequency of use (Demko, 1979; Tuckman, 1967). However, Tissue (1971) and Trela (1976) found users more likely to have white-collar occupations, while Rosenzweig (1975) found users more likely to have blue-collar occupations.

Research regarding income and senior center utilization shows more consistent findings. Although some studies have found no difference in income for senior center users and nonusers (Hanssen et al., 1978; Storey, 1962; Taietz, 1976) and for users varying in frequency of use (Demko, 1979; Tuckman, 1967), several studies, including those that incorporated national samples, showed nonusers had lower income levels than users (Harris & Associates, 1975; Leanse and Wagner, 1975; Rosenzweig, 1975). Moreover, in using a multiple regression analysis, Krout (1983a) found that income was the strongest predictor of senior center use.

Health/mobility. In their national study, Leanse and Wagner (1975) found that while both users and nonusers experienced health problems, these problems were more serious and more limiting to nonusers. These results are supported by Tissue (1971), who found that nonusers had poorer health and by Tuckman (1967), who found, in comparing three levels of users, that the percentage of members classified in good health significantly increased as attendance increased. In comparing senior center users, nonusers, former users, and nutrition site users, Hanssen et al. (1978) found that all groups reported similar health status. However, senior center users and nonusers had greater walking capacity than the other two groups. Only two studies report that health did not have a relationship to senior center utilization (Krout, 1983a; Storey, 1962).

Rosen et al. (1981) compared older adults who dropped out of senior centers for health-related and health-unrelated reasons. They found that those who dropped out for health-related reasons perceived their health as poorer, took on activities that involved little physical exertion, depended on others for transportation and were less optimistic about the future. These and the other data related to health suggest that health may be an important factor in both initiating and discontinuing senior center use, which contrasts with findings related to nonusers' perceived reasons for not attending centers.

Accessibility to center. Accessibility to center will be discussed in terms of proximity to center, availability of transportation, and place of residence. Only three studies have addressed the relationship between proximity to center and senior center utilization. Leanse and Wagner (1975) found that senior center users were more likely than nonusers who knew about a center to live within a relatively short distance from the center. Tuckman (1967) found that older adults who live closer to a center more frequently attended than those who lived further away. Hanssen et al. (1978) found no differences between users and nonusers in proximity to center.

Although availability of transportation has been traditionally mentioned as an inhibitor to senior center use, the few studies including this variable suggest that it may not be as major a problem as previously thought. Leanse and Wagner (1975) found few differences between users and nonusers in their perception of "no public transportation" and "not having a car or being able to drive" as problem areas. However, nonusers (14 percent) were more likely than users (7 percent) to cite cost of public transportation as a "very serious" or "somewhat serious" problem. Hanssen et al. (1978) found no significant differences between users and nonusers in terms of availability of transportation, while Krout (1983a) found that car ownership, frequency of car use, and need for transportation were not significant predictors of senior center use. Thus these studies, although limited in number, suggest that transportation may not be as important as previously thought in differentiating senior center users from nonusers.

Place of residence or whether a person lives in an urban or rural area appears to have a relationship to their accessibility to senior centers. Harris & Associates (1975) found that senior centers were less accessible to the elderly in rural areas compared to those in urban areas. In comparing senior center dropouts from urban and rural areas, Rosen et al. (1981) found that rural dropouts had poorer living conditions and poorer health; were less active; more socially isolated; more lonely, unhappy, pessimistic; and had fewer transportation alternatives. The researchers concluded that, due to the few alternative support systems available in rural areas, rural elderly may attend senior centers until their health prevents them from doing so.

Social contact. The discussion of social contact includes living arrangement and contact with family and friends. From the studies conducted, social contact appears to be a very important variable in differentiating senior center users from nonusers, yet the findings do not show a consistent trend. With regard to living arrangement, some studies suggest that nonusers and low frequency users are more likely to live with others (Demko, 1979; Tissue, 1971), while other studies indicate that this variable was not significant (Hanssen et al., 1978; Krout, 1983a; Tuckman, 1967). Similar mixed results were found regarding contact with family and friends. Some studies show that senior center nonusers and low frequency users were more likely to have contact with family and friends (Demko, 1979; Ralston, 1984; Rosenzweig, 1975), while other studies suggest that users are more "socially minded" and have a need for more frequent contact (Daum, 1982; Krout, 1983a; Tissue, 1971). Krout (1983a) argues that senior center users may have a need for higher-than-average levels of sociability that leads to center involvement. In supporting this view, Storey (1962) found that users were more likely than nonusers to indicate the need for satisfying interpersonal relationships (i.e., to have friends, be loved, wanted) as the chief need of people over 60 years of age. These findings regarding social contact suggest that the population of senior center users may not be monolithic in regard to social contact. Some may come to centers because of the lack of social contact in their lives; other may come to extend their social networks because of their high need for social activity.

Activities. This section incorporates literature concerning leisure time activities and membership patterns in organizations in relation to senior center use. As with social contact, involvement in activities appears to be an important factor distinguishing senior center users from nonusers, and there also appears (for once!) to be some consistent trends in the literature. Almost all of the related studies reviewed showed that users were more likely than nonusers to be involved in group-oriented social activities (Hanssen et al., 1978; Leanse and Wagner, 1975; Rosenzweig, 1975; Storey, 1962; Tissue, 1971) and had a pattern of organizational participation (Leanse and Wagner, 1975; Taietz, 1976). Leanse and Wagner's (1975) research, however, suggests that both senior center users and nonusers may have had similar organization participation patterns early in life but that users may have continued this pattern in later life. Demko's (1979) research, which showed that low frequency users tended more than high frequency users to belong to clubs and have greater opportunities for alternative activities, suggests that there may be a great deal of variability in activity and organizational participation within groups of senior center users. Thus as Leanse and Wagner (1975) argue, there may be a sizeable minority of users who are not "joiners" and "doers."

Well-being. A traditional view of senior centers is that they help ward off loneliness and enhance older people's sense of self-worth (Frankel, 1966; Maxwell, 1962). This statement suggests a causal model that has not been addressed in the design of senior center studies. However, the few studies that have investigated loneliness as a variable in senior center use show that either users were more lonely than nonusers (Hoppa and Roberts, 1974) or that there were no differences between groups (Leanse and Wagner, 1975). These studies, although limited, indicate the possible higher social needs of users and the fact that senior centers do not attract any more "lonely" elderly than would be found in the older population in general.

The studies regarding well-being and senior center use show that, for the most part, users have higher levels of life satisfaction (Leanse and Wagner, 1975; Tissue, 1971) and were less depressed (Hanssen et al., 1978). However, in a more sophisticated analysis, Toseland and Sykes (1977) found that senior center participation was not a significant predictor of life satisfaction. Hoppa and Roberts (1974), in abandoning the senior center user/nonuser dichotomy, found that those with insufficient activity were more unhappy than those with sufficient activity. These findings regarding well-being may suggest that senior centers may be an outlet that *some* elderly choose to maintain feelings of self-worth. Because of this self-selection process, senior center users do appear to have higher levels of life satisfaction than nonusers. However, perhaps in a more global sense, senior centers are just one of many ways that help elderly maintain a positive outlook on life.

Some tentative generalizations about senior centers can be drawn from extant research. First, there appears to be some consistency in how senior centers have been defined over the past 20 years. More recent definitions, however, are more global, allowing for the inclusion of less structured senior center programs. Models of senior centers have been based on physical facilities, programs, and characteristics of participants. Few of the models, however, have been tested in terms of their effectiveness. Programs or activities and services in senior centers appear to be growing in number, and the number appears to vary according to the characteristics of the senior centers, but the existing data point out the general weaknesses particularly in regard to educational programs. Users of senior centers attend for activities and for companionship (seeing and making friends), but nonusers are either not interested or too busy with other activities to attend. Studies concerning correlates of senior center use suggest that there are many relevant factors but, because of the mixed results, few general trends can be seen.

Senior Centers: Past Promises and Future Potential

This review of literature suggests that there may be a "good news/bad news" scenario regarding senior centers. The bad news concerns past promises made about senior centers, while the good news relates to the future potential of senior centers, particularly in terms of populations served.

The past promises of senior centers reflect the high expectations that practitioners and policymakers have had for these organizations. As indicated by Maxwell (1962) and Frankel (1966), from their inception senior centers were designed to help provide a buffer for some of the social, economic, and physical losses suffered by the elderly. The recent

NCOA literature has continued this theme, suggesting that senior centers are viable community organizations with the capacity of having an impact on diverse populations of older people (Jacobs, 1975, 1976; Jacobs and Pflaum, 1982). In an effort to assist practitioners, numerous materials have been developed by NCOA concerning senior center management and program development (see, for example, NISC, 1978; Abbott and Nosbaum, 1982; Leanse et al., 1977).

Policy initiatives over the past decade also demonstrate the high expectations for senior centers and are reflected in the research reviewed here. For example, the establishment of congregate meal programs and movement toward multipurpose senior centers (in 1973 and 1975 amendments to the Older Americans Act) have affected the number of programs in senior centers, as shown in the differentials in data between studies by Leanse and Wagner (1975) and Krout (1983b). Considering the initial sanctioning and eventual funding of multipurpose centers, these findings are not surprising. Also not surprising are the findings regarding "single purpose" centers and clubs as described by Leanse and Wagner (1975) and Ralston (1982). These organizations are often operated by seniors themselves, are locally funded, and are sometimes more resistant to federal mandates. Taken together, both types of centers are institutions that older adults identify as "senior centers," as evidenced by the increasingly global definitions of senior centers (NISC, 1978).

The question becomes whether or not multipurpose or other types of senior centers can deliver what is promised. From the research literature available, there are no clear cut answers. The diversity in size, models, staff, and programming capabilities suggests that not all senior centers are able to deliver on promises. And although senior centers are offering more programs to their clients, there are considerable questions concerning the quality of these programs. For example, education is consistently mentioned as a major purpose in senior centers, and Leanse and Wagner (1975) found that 58 percent of their national sample of senior centers offered it as one of three basic services. Yet the available research on the quality of educational programs in senior centers suggests that programs are weak and that both staff and participants find education to be of only minimal importance (Jacobs, 1982; Jones, 1976; Meredith and Amor, 1976; Ralston, 1981).

Perhaps the quality of programming is related to the image of senior centers that is internalized by both senior center staff and participants.

As argued by Matthews (1979), postadult treatment by senior center staff may cause participants to adopt "doer" or volunteer roles in the center while distancing themselves from center-sponsored activities. Quality of programming may also be related to the ambitious program offerings in senior centers. Krout's (1984) work demonstrated that senior centers are offering an average of 30 activities and services, and he questions whether this reflects a less optimal use of colocation, coordination, and service linkage between agencies. A further question is whether or not senior centers can offer such an array of programs without making tradeoffs in terms of quality. Congregate meals and recreation may still be the programs that senior centers do best (Daum and Dobrof, 1983). Thus senior centers may be focal points for comprehensive service delivery, but only in the sense of offering a smorgasbord of programs that lack depth and development. Much work is needed before senior centers can truly begin to meet the expectations that others have for them. Future policy efforts should concentrate on evaluation and accountability of programming in these agencies.

Although the past promises point out the limitations in senior centers, the future potential of these organizations is encouraging. Perhaps what is most encouraging is that senior centers are serving diverse older populations. Few trends, for example, could be found in the literature regarding correlates of senior center utilization. The mixed results suggest that senior centers are not modal or normative in nature, which is not surprising since they are community-based organizations and should reflect diversity within respective communities. However, of more interest is that senior centers appear to fit both existing conceptual models as proposed by Taietz (1976). Senior centers appear to fit the voluntary organization model by attracting older adults who are married, healthy, and from higher socioeconomic backgrounds; who have high levels of social contact and life satisfaction; and who have had previous organizational participation. On the other hand, senior centers also seem to fit the social agency model by attracting the widowed, less healthy, less financially well-off elderly who may have little previous organizational participation or have discontinued participation. The challenge to service providers is dealing with this diversity in client populations, particularly when it occurs within a single senior center. However, the future potential of senior centers may rest on how the most needy elderly are served.

Directions for Research

This chapter has emphasized throughout that more senior center research is needed. Major areas needing further research are senior center models, utilization, and program effectiveness.

Further exploration of senior center models is necessary in order to have a better grasp of the concept of senior center. Although the models discussed in this chapter provide a conceptual framework for senior centers in terms of facilities, programs, and participants, future research needs to test these and other models to determine how functional they are in fully explaining senior centers.

Senior center utilization also needs attention in future research, even though the majority of studies on senior centers have been done in this area. The sketchy nature of the data on motivation to attend senior centers suggests that more in-depth studies need to be conducted, using psychosocial theoretical constructs. In addition, the mixed results regarding correlates of senior center use suggest that larger, more comprehensive studies are needed where a conceptual framework is developed regarding the factors to be investigated. More rigorous statistical treatments are extremely important because most previous studies have been descriptive (Krout, 1983a). These studies could broaden the user/nonuser groupings to include potential users (i.e., those showing interest) and former users. Also, incorporating these groups into longitudinal designs might not only help to clarify further the factors affecting senior center use, but might also point out the "fluid" nature of senior centers (Demko, 1979). Finally, studies are needed that investigate in more depth those who choose to use senior centers, sorting out the characteristics of users and determining how these characteristics might vary according to frequency of senior center use and types of activities involved in at the center. The work by Cobb and Ferraro (1984) is a good step in this direction.

Considering the high expectations for senior centers and the accompanying funding at the federal, state, and local levels, future research should also focus on evaluation studies that determine program effects. Although the difficulty in conducting and reporting evaluation research for aging programs is well documented (see for example Lawton, 1977; Cain, 1977), these studies, such as the one by Schneider et al. (1985), may help to at least put into perspective the role and contributions of senior centers. Schneider et al. (1985) examined selectivity of participation and program impacts, using a panel of approximately 500 older persons contacted before implementation of senior center programs and again two years later. Findings showed that programs tended to reach socially active elderly who were not high risks for institutionalization. Participation failed to lower rates of institutionalization, to improve health and life outlook, or to increase rates of use of other available government services. Although the researchers were concerned about reporting such negative findings, it is this type of research that may help to pinpoint the actual outcomes, if any, of senior center participation. Moreover, there may be "unintended" outcomes from these programs that are beneficial to older people, which might require the use of other evaluation models (Chen and Rossi, 1980; Scriven, 1972).

Some final comments need to be made regarding research directions. First, the paucity of recent studies indicates that too few researchers are interested in senior center research. Second, funding opportunities are limited in general for gerontological research and in particular for senior center research, perhaps because of the general reputation of senior centers for serving the "well elderly." However, because of the growing numbers of senior centers, the frail elderly populations that are being served, and policymakers' high expectations for these organizations, there is a need for funding and more involvement from a variety of researchers. The future of senior centers may depend on gerontology researchers joining practitioners and policymakers in continuing to explore what these organizations do with and for older people.

References

ABBOTT, S. D. and R. B. NOSBAUM (1982) Comprehensive Service Delivery Through Senior Centers and Other Community Focal Points: A Resource Manual. Washington, DC: National Council on Aging.

CAIN, L. D. (1977) "Evaluative research and nutrition programs for the elderly," in Evaluative Research on Social Programs for the Elderly. Washington, DC: DHEW Publication NO. (OHD) 77-20120.

CARP, F. M. (1976) "A senior center in public housing for the elderly." The Gerontologist 16: 243-249.

CHEN, H. and P. H. ROSSI (1980) "The multi-goal, theory-driven approach to evaluation: a model linking basic and applied social science." Social Forces 59: 106-122.

COBB, C. C and K. F. FERRARO (1984) "Participation at a multipurpose senior center." Presented at the annual meeting of the Gerontological Society, San Antonio.

DAUM, M, (1982) "Preference for age-homogeneous versus age-heterogeneous social integration." Journal of Gerontological Social Work 4: 41-54.

DAUM, M. and R. DOBROF (1983) "Seasonal vulnerability of the old and cold: the role of the senior citizen center." Journal of Gerontological Social Work 5: 81-106.

DEMKO, D. (1979) "Utilization, attrition and the senior center." Journal of Gerontological Social Work 2: 87-93.

DOWNING, R. and E. COPELAND (1980) "Services for the black elderly: national or local problems?" Journal of Gerontological Social Work, 2: 239-303.

FRANKEL, G. (1966) "The multipurpose senior citizens' center: a new comprehensive agency." The Gerontologist 6: 23-27.

GUTTMANN, D and P. R. MILLER (1972) "Perspective on the provision of social services in senior centers." The Gerontologist 12: 403-406.

HANSSEN, A. M., N. J. MEIMA, L. M. BUCKSPAN, B. E. HENDERSON, T. L. HELBIG, and S. H. ZARIT (1978) "Correlates of senior center participation." The Gerontologist 18: 193-199.

Louis Harris & Associates, Inc. (1975) The Myth and Reality of Aging in America. Washington, DC: National Council on Aging.

HIRSCH, C. S. (1977) "Integrating the nursing home resident into a senior center." The Gerontologist 17: 227-234.

HOPPA, M. and G. ROBERTS (1974) "Implications of the activity factor." The Gerontologist 14: 331-335.

JACOBS, B. (1975) Options and Actions for Senior Centers. Proceedings of the Ninth National Conference of Senior Centers. Washington, DC: National Council on Aging.

JACOBS, B. (1976) Projections for Tomorrow. Proceedings of the Tenth National Conference of Senior Centers. Washington, DC: National Council on Aging.

JACOBS, B. (1982) "Educational goals for senior centers: a study of perceptions of reality and aspirations." Dissertation Abstracts International 42: 4253-A.

JACOBS, B and R. PFLAUM (1982) Senior Centers: Helping Communities Serve Older Persons. Selected papers from the Twelfth and Thirteenth National Conferences of Senior Centers. Washington, DC: National Council on Aging.

JONES, E. E. (1976) "An analysis of adult education programs in selected senior citizen centers in Rhode Island." Dissertation Abstracts International 37: 5529-A.

JORDAN, J. J. (1978) Senior Center Design: An Architect's Discussion of Facility Planning. Washington, DC: National Council on Aging.

KROUT, J. A. (1983a) "Correlates of senior center utilization." Research on Aging 5: 339-352.

KROUT, J. A. (1983b) "The organization, operation, and programming of senior centers: a national survey." Fredonia, NY. (unpublished)

KROUT, J. A. (1984) "Senior center activities and services: findings from a national survey." Presented at the annual meeting of the Gerontological Society, San Antonio.

LAWTON, M. P. (1977) "Evaluation research in fluid systems," in Evaluative Research on Social Programs for the Elderly. Washington DC: DHEW Publication No. (OHD) 77-20120.

LEANSE, J. and S. WAGNER (1975) Senior Centers: Report of Senior Group Programs in America. Washington, DC: National Council on Aging.

LEANSE, J., M. TIVEN, and T. ROBB (1977) Senior Center Operation. A Guide to Organization and Management. Washington, DC: National Council on Aging.

MATTHEWS, S. (1979) The Social World of Old Women: Management of Self-Identity. Newbury Park, CA: Sage.

MAXWELL, J. (1962) Centers for Older People: Guide for Programs and Facilities. Washington, DC: National Council on Aging.

MEREDITH, G. M and C. W. AMOR (1976) "Indexing the polarization of social groups in a multipurpose senior center." Psychological Reports 39: 88-90.

National Institute of Senior Centers. (1978) Senior Center Standards: Guidelines for Practice. Washington, DC: National Council on Aging.

RALSTON, P. A. (1981) "Educational needs and activities of older adults: their relationship to senior center programs." Educational Gerontology 7: 231-244.

RALSTON, P. A. (1982) "Levels of senior centers: a broadened view of group-based programs for the elderly." Activities, Adaptation, and Aging 3: 79-91.

RALSTON, P. A. (1983) "Senior centers in rural communities: a qualitative study." Presented at Annual Meeting of Gerontological Society, San Francisco.

RALSTON, P. A. (1984) "Senior center utilization by black elderly adults: social attitudinal and knowledge correlates." Journal of Gerontology 39: 224-229.

ROSEN, C., R. J. VANDENBERG, and S. ROSEN (1981) "The fate of senior center dropouts," in P. King and C. Wilson (eds.) Toward Mental Health of the Rural Elderly. Washington, DC: University Press of America.

ROSENZWEIG, N. (1975) "Some differences between elderly people who use community resources and those who do not." Journal of the American Geriatrics Society 23: 224-233.

SADOWSKI, B. S. and W. J. SCHILL (1979) "Educational implications of affiliation factors existent among members of senior centers." Educational Gerontology 4: 67-75.

SCHNEIDER, M. J., D. D. CHAPMAN, and D. E. VOTH. (1985) "Senior center participation: a two-stage approach to impact evaluation." The Gerontologist 25: 194-200.

SCRIVEN, M. (1972) "Pros and cons about goal-free evaluation: evaluation comment." Journal of Educational Evaluation 3:1-4.

STOREY, R. (1962) "Who attends a senior activity center? A comparison of Little House members with non-members of senior centers." The Gerontologist 2: 216-222.

TAIETZ, P. (1976) "Two conceptual models of the senior center." Journal of Gerontology 31: 219-222.

TISSUE, T. (1971) "Social class and the senior citizen center." The Gerontologist 11: 196-200.

TOSELAND, R. and J. SYKES (1977) "Senior citizens center participation and other correlates of life satisfaction." The Gerontologist 17: 235-241.

TRELA, J. E. (1971) "Some political consequences of senior center and other old age group membership." The Gerontologist 11: 118-123.

TRELA, J. E. (1976) "Social class and association membership: an analysis of age-graded and non-age graded voluntary participation." Journal of Gerontology 31: 198-203.

TRELA, J E. and L. W. SIMMONS (1971) "Health and other factors affecting membership and attrition in a senior center." Journal of Gerontology 26: 46-51.

TUCKMAN, J. (1967) "Factors related to attendance in a center for older people." Journal of American Geriatrics Society 15: 474-479.

VICKERY, F. E. (1972) Creative Programming for Older Adults. New York: Association Press.

Introduction to Chapter 9

Health care for the elderly is a central issue for gerontologists and policymakers. Perhaps in no other area of public policy has the growth of the elderly population more directly affected decisions nor have policy decisions more directly affected the welfare of the elderly. Major changes in life expectancy have corresponded with increases in expenditures for health care and prompted concern for the future. Yet health care needs in the future are not as readily predictable as many assume. The next chapter identifies a number of factors that must be considered, but about which information is not yet available. More important, attention is drawn to cultural values that are likely to have major impacts on health care policy.

To date, analyses of health care policy have primarily been limited to the fine-tuning of the existing system. As a result, most presentations of the issues discuss cost-saving measures and the distribution of responsibility for care. In this discussion of health care policy, the analysis is broadened by focusing on current values and potential changes in societal values. As a result, a number of questions emerge that are not always viewed as appropriate or comfortable issues for debate. In particular, it becomes clear that health care policy is intricately tied to values about life and death and the ways in which we prevent or facilitate life and death.

9

Values, Costs, and Health Care Policy

RHONDA J. V. MONTGOMERY and EDGAR F. BORGATTA

Perhaps more than any other issue in aging, health care has attracted attention of policy analysts and policymakers. Interest in the health care of the elderly has developed as a consequence of the rising costs of health care and a growing awareness that the elderly experience health-related problems more often than younger adults.

Improved standards of living and medical advances in the prevention and control of infectious diseases have enabled increasing proportions of the population to live longer, and older persons are more vulnerable to chronic illnesses. It is estimated that 86 percent of the population 65 years and older have some chronic condition and almost half (47 percent) of the elderly report some degree of limitation in activity (U.S. House of Representatives, 1985). In contrast, less than 14 percent of the general population reports any limitation due to chronic disease (NCHS, 1983, Tab. 27). As a group the elderly report their health to be poorer, they experience more days of restricted activity, and they spend more days in bed than does any other age group (NCHS, 1983, Tabs. 27 and 28; Feller, 1983a).

Service Utilization and Costs

As a consequence of the higher rates of chronic illness and disability among the elderly, this group also uses proportionately more medical services. Although the elderly constituted 11 percent of the population in 1980, they accounted for 31 percent of the expenditures for personal health care (Hodgson and Kopstein, 1983). Data obtained through the National Health Interview Survey indicate that in 1981 persons aged 65 and over averaged 6.3 visits with physicians compared to 4.6 for the general population (NCHS, 1983, Tab. 36). This elderly segment of the population is also hospitalized more frequently and for longer stays. The elderly accounted for 27 percent of hospital discharges in 1981 and for 39 percent of all hospital days (NCHS, 1983). The average length of stay for the elderly was 10.6 days, which was considerably higher than the 6.9 day average for the total population. The elderly are also the primary users of nursing home services. At any one time about 5 percent of the elderly reside in nursing homes, and this increases with age to almost 22 percent of those 85 years and older (NCHS, 1981a).

It should be emphasized that while the elderly as a group use large amounts of medical services, the pattern is not uniform across this population segment. The 46 percent of the elderly population that reports limitations due to chronic disabilities accounts for 63 percent of physician contacts, 71 percent of hospitalization, and 82 percent of all days spent in bed (NCHS, 1981b).

The high use of medical services among the elderly has combined with an unprecedented rise in the cost of medical services to create extreme pressure on both public and private resources. The total national expenditure for health services and supplies has risen dramatically over the past two decades. In 1960, health expenditures accounted for 5 percent of the gross national product (GNP). By 1982 this percentage had doubled to 10 percent of the GNP (Schrimper and Clark, 1985). The rapid rise in medical care costs has outstripped all other components of the consumer price index, increasing 158 percent between 1973 and 1983 compared to a 123 percent increase for the average overall index (U.S. Department of Labor, 1984).

Not only has the amount and proportion of medical costs risen, but the proportion of total health expenditures paid by public funds has risen dramatically over the past two decades. Since the introduction of Medicare and Medicaid in 1965, the proportion of health expenditures paid by public funds has risen from 25.9 percent to 42.0 percent in 1982 (Gibson et al., 1983). Much of this increase in public expenditures can be attributed to growth in Medicare expenditures, which increased from $4.5 billion in 1967 to $50.9 billion in 1982, and to growth in Medicaid expenditures, which increased from $2.9

billion in 1967 to $32.4 billion in 1982. This represents a tenfold increase in expenditures from both programs over a 15-year period (Gibson et al., 1983).

Despite this increase in public expenditures, many elderly face serious personal financial burdens in meeting their health care expenses. In 1981, Medicare met only 45 percent of all health expenditures of the aged. Medicaid filled in another 14 percent, covering 3.5 million aged or 14 percent of all aged (U.S. Senate, 1983). Even with Medicare's increasing share of the costs, the per capita out-of-pocket expenditure of elderly persons for health care has continued to grow faster than increases in the average income of the elderly. Older persons now pay a larger portion of their income for health care than they did before the introduction of Medicare (U.S. House of Representatives, 1985). The situation is particularly burdensome for the poor and near poor among the elderly who pay 25 percent of their annual incomes for health care in contrast to the 2.5 percent paid by elderly persons with incomes three times that of the poverty level (Blumenthal et al., 1986).

Future Trends

Projected Growth

While the current situation has caused considerable distress and concern among policymakers, as well as the elderly, predictions for the future are even more disconcerting. Relief from the rapid growth in costs of medical care is not predicted in the immediate future and, in fact, the U.S. House of Representatives' Select Committee on Aging anticipates that the elderly will use almost 19 percent of their income for health care by the year 1990.

As medical costs continue to rise, the growth in the elderly population will also continue, due to past fertility patterns and decreases in mortality rates across the entire life span. By the year 2000 the elderly are expected to constitute 13 percent of the total population, rising to 21 percent by the year 2030 (U.S. House of Representatives, 1985). Perhaps more important is the expected expansion of the size of the population 75 years of age and older. This group has the highest proportion of persons with chronic disabilities who, in turn, use extensive medical resources.

Determinants of Dependency

Several factors must be considered before conclusions can be drawn about the implications *of this projected growth* for the system. In particular, attention must be given to likely changes in life expectancy, longevity, and the prevalence and duration of chronic disabilities. Together these factors will define the level of dependency among the elderly, which in turn will determine the consequences for the system.

First, it is appropriate to at least speculate on some of the factors that often are ignored in considering the impact of disease control and the conditions of life on life expectancy and on dependency. For example, life tables are computed on the basis of current age-specific death rates, and thus tend to be conservative in the sense that the usual expectation is that age-specific death rates will continue to improve. Thus future estimates of life expectancy are likely to be for longer lives. There are, however, limitations to how much change can occur, since age-specific death rates in the more industrialized nations are already very low in most categories until one gets to the advanced ages. The shift to extended life expectancy may continue, thus, but there are vaguely stated hypotheses about how much this extension is to be.

The maximum limit of life expectancy is determined by longevity. While we have witnessed improvement of life expectancy, there is relatively firm evidence that to this point we have not done much to change longevity, the theoretical expectation of how long one can live. This is debated in a number of contexts, but the fact is that there is no evidence that the biological basis has changed for human longevity, although improvements of the gross environment including diet, exposure to the elements, and so forth have affected life expectancy. The implicit question that is raised is whether, with the changes that have occurred in biological sciences, the actual longevity has been affected. The conservative view of this is that we may have underestimated longevity, but there is little evidence of any change. It has to be remembered that there is no single figure for longevity, since people vary with regard to biological makeup, and the figure that is usually advanced is an estimated average for the population considered. Currently, in the vague terms in which such estimates are usually made, a common figure mentioned is 85 years of age, but that is conservative according to some observers. On the other hand, despite the common attention given to the fact that we have an increasing proportion and number of cases that are living to be 100 years of age, there are very few persons recorded to be very old. So, for example, when the oldest man on record died in Japan in 1986, the age of the oldest person dropped to under 110 years of age. Persons who have been this old have been noted before, but we are not hearing of persons living to be 120 or 130 years of age. In a statistical sense, we may have some such persons in the future, but this is not expected on the basis of changes of longevity.

While changes in life expectancy and longevity together determine the actual numbers of persons living to old age, the impact of these numbers on the system will be a consequence of the condition of the population and the extent of dependency. Because we have only poor measures of the physical well-being of persons, we really have not accomplished examinations of relative well-being of age groups of the population over time. Yet we have an intuitive consensus that persons 70 years of age today look much better in terms of health and physical well-being than a comparable group would have in 1950. This implies more than a simple comparison, however, because even if they looked the same, it would be an improvement as the proportion of persons who will have reached the age of 70 has increased. Phrased another way, it has been observed that persons who are 70 years of age now look like persons who were 60 years of age did in 1950. So, within bounds, we may have a population that is in better condition than was expected, and dependency that might have been expected among 60-year-olds in 1950 is not expected today.

The impact of the improvement of the condition of the older population, thus, may have some impact on policy changes. In considerations of social security, the question of delaying benefits has already been considered on the assumption that persons will be in the labor force for a longer period, presumably with a modal expectation eventually for retirement at 70 years of age rather than 65 years of age. However, such changes do not necessarily have impact on health costs, if all that is occurring is that the costs are being delayed. If nothing else is changing, then the expectation will simply be that the amount of health care that was required earlier will be experienced by persons at a later age, but individuals will still need that health care. Thus emphasis on research and information on the changes in health status that occur in the shifting age structure are of vital interest for policy formation. Of particular importance is research on the onset and duration of chronic illness.

There is considerable controversy about the future morbidity patterns for chronic diseases among the elderly. If factors that have led to reductions in mortality, such as improvement in lifestyle, also influence the prevalence of chronic diseases, then some scholars foresee a shortened period of dependence due to disease prior to dying (Fries, 1980; Fries and Crapo, 1981). Fries refers to this as the rectangularization of the survival curves, with a notion that in the absence or control of disease, people will survive to the genetically determined time of death and then will expire more quickly than has been the case in the past. In contrast, other scholars believe that the prevalence of chronic diseases and disability will increase as life expectancy increases, as will the corresponding need for medical care in later life (Kramer, 1980; Gruenberg, 1977; Schneider and Brody, 1982).

The issue that has been raised by Fries on the length of the period of dependency is not totally unambiguous in formulation. One way of describing the issue is to compare the theoretical distribution of the period of dependency for a population that lives to its biological natural end to that of a population that lives in the presence of the diseases and environment/accident circumstances of the real world. It should be noted that because the environment/accident deaths would not be eliminated in the former population, even the theoretical figures would be somewhat difficult to consider alone. In any case, the issue boils down to the question of whether the biological natural end is something that typically comes on fast or slow in comparison to dying by disease and disorders. There is obviously little hard evidence on these issues, but contrary to the Fries thesis, it may be that as the organism gets close to its end, disability may arise in many ways and slowly, so that people appear to linger in a slow decline to the point that the total organism is no longer viable. If this is the case, and if disease tends to lead to more precipitous death, then the expectation would be that there would be longer periods of dependency associated with living to the natural biological end.

As noted, there is little that can be mustered in the way of well-designed studies that can substantiate either the Fries thesis or the counter suggestion as we have formulated it above. However, at least one review accumulates and aligns a number of materials to suggest that in a view of association of chronic disease and disorder with older age, and with tendencies to keep persons with such conditions alive longer, at least in the foreseeable future the period of dependency can be expected to be longer (Grundy, 1984). Considerable work needs to be done to gain an understanding of the precise mechanism underlying mortality reductions at advanced ages. As Manton (1986: 283) notes, "Knowing how mortality reductions are achieved will help us to understand how the health status of survivors to advanced ages is likely to be changed by improvements in life expectancy and derivatively, how the demand for health services is likely to change."

Another aspect of the dependency issue that is associated with the demographic basis of population change is a consideration of a general "dependency index" that looks at what is occurring to the proportion of the population that is both young and old, these being identified as the at-risk dependent classes. The reader should be reminded that changes that occur in the demographics of population change are of two types—the long secular trends as are described by a theoretical description such as the demographic transition, and the more episodic shifts, such as the "baby boom" that was experienced in the United States in the period following World War II. It is the baby boom projections that have been so alarming to policymakers, and of course the consequences of the baby boom are real and must be considered. But if the question is one of what is expected to occur in the future, the long-term secular trends should also be kept in mind.

As the U.S. baby boom will emphasize the proportions in the older ages in the year 2025, the general situation for more developed regions of the world will be similar. The international data thus represent a broader and more stable basis for examination of what will happen to the dependency ratio. It should be remembered that the long-term trends are for both decreased fertility, leading to smaller numbers of births, and for decreased age-specific death rates, reflecting the increased life expectancy or prolongation of life in the later years.

In the more developed regions of the world, in 1950 about 28 percent of all persons were under 15 years of age, and about 11 percent were over 60 years of age—a total of 39 percent. Projections to the year 2025 in parallel are 20 percent for the young group and 23 percent for the old group, or a total of 43 percent. This is not a trivial change, obviously, because 3 percent of, say, 330 million people is about 10 million people. However, as we have noted, with the apparent improved physical status of the population the definition of the class may be advanced, and thus the shift in percentage in the total dependent class might be negligible. This does not alter the fact, however, of the potential increase in the dependent period for older persons prior to death.

Policy Issues

Cost Containment and Shifting Responsibility

The dual pressures of rapid growth in the numbers of elderly in need of health care and of rapid growth in the cost of health care have prompted numerous analyses of health care policies for the elderly and calls for reform. The majority of these recommendations have sought cost containment through a variety of changes in Medicare or Medicaid. These have included recommendations for additional restrictions on eligibility criteria for Medicaid, reductions in both Medicaid and Medicare benefits, increases in copayments for Medicare beneficiaries, and increases in premiums (U.S. Senate, 1983; Congressional Budget Office, 1981; Blumenthal et al., 1986). Some of these recommendations have been implemented in the past two years and, in part, have contributed to increasing the proportion of income that the elderly now spend on health care (U.S. House of Representatives, 1985; Blumenthal et al., 1986). Suggestions have also been made to shift the costs of Medicare and Medicaid to different groups including families, middle- and high-income elderly, state governments, and the federal government (Congressional Budget Office, 1981; Blumenthal et al., 1986; Burwell, 1986).

Cost containment was the primary intent of the Professional Standard Review Organizations (PSRO), which were charged with the responsibility to review utilization of services. The Tax Equity and Fiscal Responsibility Act (TEFRA) in 1983 was also aimed at cost containment. The act changed hospital reimbursement methods and led to the development of a prospective payment system that reimburses hospitals according to the diagnostic related group (DRG) in which the patient is classified. Recommendations have also been made to further reform the payment procedures for both physicians and hospitals and to simplify the administration of Medicare (Estes and Harrington, 1985; Blumenthal et al., 1986).

Although the focus of previous analyses has most often been on eligibility criteria and financing issues, a number of analyses have drawn attention to the schism between acute care and long-term needs and have noted the bias of the system toward acute needs. Some analysts have advocated the use of Medicare funds for long-term care (Blumenthal et al., 1986), a recommendation that certainly is not a cost-saving measure. Still other analysts have noted the higher costs of care in acute settings where costly technologies tend to be used for the chronically ill and dying. There has been some advocacy of shifting the care of the dying to the lower-cost nursing home setting or the hospice. At the same time, there has been considerable debate about the relative costs of caring for the chronically ill in an institution versus a community setting (U.S. General Accounting Office, 1982). It is widely acknowledged that as long as families are willing to provide care and assume the costs of many community services, such care is less expensive. It is not clear, however, that care can be provided in the community at lower rates if all services must be purchased.

Finally, there have been calls for system-wide changes including a national long-term care policy and a national health care system that would subsume the special programs for the elderly (Estes and Harrington, 1985). Similar proposals have, however, been debated over the last half of the century and have been continually met with powerful opposition.

It is noteworthy that all of these proposals for change focus on the financing mechanism, the source of payment, or the source of services. The majority of recommendations are concerned with shifting the responsibility for payment in some manner. The issues that are not being addressed are the amount and type of services that are to be made available. It is an implicit and sometimes explicit assumption (Blumenthal et al., 1986) that the elderly must have the best care possible. The exact meaning of "best care possible" has not, however, been defined nor has it been raised as an important question for debate.

One interpretation of "best care possible" has been to provide intensive services to extend life to the maximum length possible. This interpretation is reflected in the fact that among those with disabilities, expenditures for medical care are not uniform. In particular, elderly persons approaching death have very high expenditures for medical care. In an analysis of Medicare expenditures for the year 1978, Lubitz and Prihoda (1983) found that 5.2 percent of enrollees who were in their last year of life accounted for 28.2 percent of Medicare expenditures. On the average, the Medicare program spent four times the amount of money on enrollees who died in 1978 than on those who survived. Furthermore, the use of services became more intense as death approached. Almost 30 percent of all expenses in the last year of life were spent in the last 30 days of life, with another 16 percent being spent in the previous 30-day period. As Lubitz and Prihoda (1983: 76) note, these findings clearly "demonstrate the reality that Medicare, by its nature, is a program involved with the dying.'' These findings should prompt policy analysts to address the values that lie behind the figures. In particular, attention is directed toward values around preserving life.

Value Dilemmas

The values around preserving life have been debated in great detail, and in the United States there have been major complications concerning policy not merely because of differences in values but also because legal issues have been raised both in the courts and through legislation. The value of life is expressed, for example, with the extraordinary effort that is put into keeping people alive at various points. For example, in some contexts there have been attempts to keep fetuses alive when they have been less than fully formed and where the attempt could be described more accurately as a contest to see just how premature an organism could be made to survive.

The issue is no less troublesome with regard to definition at other levels. It has become a matter of policy debate as to what constitutes extraordinary effort to keep a person alive because once the extraordinary effort has been put into effect, by some definitions withdrawal of the effort has been defined as essentially killing the person. The question has been phrased as, Who should have the right to determine whether a person should live or die?

These issues of maintaining life are important not merely for the moral values that are expressed but for the fact that, as has been noted, the intensive care that is required in such cases accounts for a substantial part of the effort and cost of health services. What is likely to happen in this area of values is a vital consideration for policymakers who must be responsive at the level of allocating resources.

In the current era, it is clear that competing values can be found within society that, in turn, translate into opposing policies. It is not a universally accepted value that if a person requests that extraordinary life-sustaining efforts should not be used to maintain life, the request should be honored. In fact, the ''right to die'' has generated much debate in medical journals (e.g., Hickie, 1984; Lander, 1984; *Nursing Life,* 1984; Poulschock and Stitz, 1984), the mass media, and the courts. A fairly substantial social movement may be seen in the development of laws to permit living wills, which essentially permit specification of the limits of life sustaining procedures to be used for a person on his or her own request. The Society for the Right to Die, for example, has as a major purpose the review and encouragement of legislative consideration of living wills, and of related issues such as legal definitions of death. The notion that one should not be permitted to elect to die when, in the absence of the life supports that are available, death would be natural, is viewed by some as a major restriction on personal liberty.

Given the opposing values that coexist in the society, policy formation on issues around life and death can be highly political and responsive to pressure groups representing quite different values. These will have massive consequences on health service provisions and costs. One example that is commonly noted is the issue of abortion, which is debated and constantly intrudes as a part of the political and legislative arena. Persons who assert women's rights in matters of pregnancy point to one set of values and those who are against choice for women point to another. The argument can be seen at two levels, however. One is on the matter of values and the second is on the more mundane level of consequences for the society—what might be described by some as the more rational basis. In politics, however, the latter does not always count, and there is no rule that says that the majority, even in a democratic system, makes all the right decisions. This is difficult in any event because there are strategies for the short and the long run, and these do not necessarily lead to the same policies. Policymaking for government is not simple, so anticipating appropriate policy with regard to the health and welfare of the population will not be simple.

How government is to intrude in such matters of life and death is not clear, and so the debates will continue into the future. Over history, however, the opposing tendencies can be noted. In an English law tradition, there has been a shift from not protecting people against themselves to doing so in great detail. As examples, requiring people to wear helmets while on motorcycles or to wear seatbelts while driving automobiles are laws to protect people against themselves; and as a class of laws they are recent in history. Similarly, there has been a legal tradition associated with the caution, Let the buyer beware! This tradition has also shifted to the acceptance of a responsibility for the government, and the courts, in support of this in what has become known as "our litigious society", have also moved in this direction. Additionally, of course, in what has become a tradition of attempting to solve all societal problems by passing laws, there has been a profusion of regulation into the major institutional areas of family, education, business, and so on. These historical trends sometimes have pressures in the opposite directions, but the global shift in control of behavior from the individual to the government is hard to disclaim.

If there is a secular trend that resists the above mentioned long-term trends it is the movement toward respect for alternate belief systems that is associated with greater communication, travel, and diffusion of the knowledge of other cultures, some of which is associated with the presence of many subcultures in a nation such as the United States. It is this trend that should prompt attention to be given to possible options and possible changes. We have noted the importance of the limits on resources that may at some point have major consequences for policy, especially as the contrast between the more modern and the less developed nations becomes more dramatic. But in other cultures there are notable shifts that should be considered as possible precursors of policy change here. It is pure delusion not to note that many modern nations have been involved in alternate and sometimes more effective programs of health support, and have made different decisions about how resources are to be used, particularly in areas of welfare and health. For example, the more or less automatic provision of kidney dialysis is not as available in other nations, and this decision affects older persons who may be excluded from the procedure unless they have personal wealth to invest in maintaining their lives. In the balance of costs that the society is to bear, the decision is not that all persons should be kept alive. There is implicit in some of the consideration that the persons kept alive should be able to make some contribution back to the society. This, obviously, is a Pandora's box no one likes to consider. By what standards should services be withheld in the health area?

This digression is important because it underlies consideration of the policy that is likely to develop. We have noted that there has been one view that life must be preserved at all costs. There are historical examples like the Karen Quinlan case of maintaining life at a level that has been described as "maintaining the tissue alive" at enormous costs in resources. And there have been many more less publicized cases, of course. One action that may have consequences for policy was the approval by the American Medical Association in March 1986 of a new ethics policy that *allows* the withholding of food and water from patients in irreversible comas. When this was presented in an urban paper Sunday edition as a feature for debate (*Seattle Times*, March 19, 1986), the editorial position approved the statement but then went on to express the concern of possible abuse, and to express a common position: "Of course we must always protect the weak and the sick so that their last possession, life itself, cannot be stolen from them. And we must never condone euthanasia." It should be noted that one of the featured articles was entitled "No One Has a Right to End a Human Life."

Two essential points are critical here. First, the debate above is, for some, a peculiar one, since if definitions of "brain dead" are accepted, as they are in many states and nations, then the issue is whether one is trying to keep tissue alive, not whether the medical resources are being used in a productive way for the society. When consideration is given to the fact that major costs of medical care are associated with the terminal periods for patients, this is not a trivial issue. Second, such considerations do not touch on issues that raise an almost equally vigorous debate: Should one be able to control death more directly in answer to a quality of life question, Is life worth living? In general, American society has been negative on the taking of one's own life, and it has been made difficult by some. Indeed, there are hotlines and other resources made available in a definition that suicide is never the right choice. This is seen dramatically, for example, in the Elizabeth Bouvia case, a quadriplegic, who was force-fed to keep her from starving herself, and the issue of self-determination was not settled in her favor until recently (*Seattle Times,* 1986).

An alternate side of the policy of keeping people alive at all costs is a view that some express about "checking out" with dignity. What is pointed out is that quality of life is not often good from the point of view of the individual, and to force people to continue is a cruelty. The cases that result from such a position can lead to ugly situations. The analogy is sometimes made to the antiabortion laws that do not stop abortions but do create a situation in which abortions are carried out in dangerous and unhealthy circumstances. In the absence of less dramatic techniques, persons seeking suicide may resort to firearms and other procedures. These circumstances are not exactly what the proponents of checking out with dignity support. The situation becomes even more complicated when the individual involved loses the ability to carry out a suicide, and others are implicated. This can occur because of lowered physical capacity and mobility, or because of mental and other failure leading to essential loss of intellectual control. The dramatic cases of spouses shooting their incapacitated spouses out of love and compassion have been frequent, and the policy response to such events has not always been forgiving.

Issues of assisting persons to check out have not been clearly debated in this country yet, although there has been attention to the issue in some ways. For example, the hospice movement may be seen as attempting to at least give comfort to those who are locked into a terminal trajectory, but it does not necessarily shorten the period. In general, persons who are on a terminal trajectory, whether long or short, are in a holding pattern that is inevitable in its consequences. The issues of what is being imposed on these people by not providing alternatives for checking out have not been considered in this country as they have been in some other nations.

In a section of *60 Minutes* entitled "The Last Right?" on CBS Television (January 5, 1986) the medical situation in Holland was reviewed. A government commission in Holland had "recommended that euthanasia be legalized as long as it's carried out by a doctor at the request of a patient who is suffering from a terminal illness." Among the facts considered in the report are the facts that even while illegal, one-sixth of persons dying in Holland had died by euthanasia, essentially killed by doctors, and that *NO* doctor had gone to jail. The point is that the presentation considered many cases and circumstances in cases of euthanasia, and, for that culture, it has been defined as humane and reasonable not merely to make the option of checking out feasible without having to resort to difficult solutions like firearms or hanging, but even to provide professional assistance. The discussion of issues deals not only with consideration of the patient who wants to check out with dignity, but also with the benefits available to the society as a whole. From the point of view of external observers, it is possible to view such a situation objectively in its consequences, or as is more likely, as a matter of fixed values from which one approaches that rational situation judgmentally.

What is clear is that in the United States the pressures on resources have not become as important to considerations of policy as in some other nations, and many of the policy decisions are made without consideration of unintended consequences on costs. It is not likely, however, that policymakers will be able to continue in this pattern of decision making. As the realities of both national and worldwide demographic trends come to bear on the system, greater attention must be directed toward both values and costs.

One of the costs that must be considered is the cost of caretaking. Who will be the caretakers? It has been pointed out that caretaking is essentially associated with disease and disability, and these are generally considered health issues. Major policy considerations have not yet given attention to the question of who is to provide medical services. As the population has grown more educated, medical resources have diffused and have come to be understood by many more persons. Technically, more persons can become effective caretakers, but this does not mean that they will be (or should be). There is a countering value of individual freedom, and the issue is debated as to how much responsibility should be thrust upon relatives and spouses in such matters. On the one side, there is the dictum that families should care for their own, but, on the other, there are questions that are equally pointed: Should a wife be locked into a life of being a caretaker simply because of the misfortune of her husband's early case of Alzheimer's disease? Should a 60-year-old great-grandmother have to take care of her 80-year-old mother? And by extension, should a 20-year-old woman have to take care of her 80-year-old great-grandmother? If not, who is to care for these persons? These questions indicate that the issues of care, which also show up as health care costs, are policy issues that are major and not yet well considered.

Conclusion

Much of the attention that health care policy has gotten has been, as we noted before, fine-tuning of existing programs without paying attention to the big picture. This is a dangerous practice if we truly want to prepare for the future. If the projections are accurate about a rise in numbers of older persons and the level of dependency of this population on society, policymakers will find that the issues are larger than cost containment and shifting responsibility. The dilemmas of health policy are value dilemmas.

References

BLUMENTHAL, D., M. SCHLESINGER, P. B. DRUMHELLER, and the Harvard Medicare Project (1986) "The future of Medicare." New England Journal of Medicine 314: 722-728.
BURWELL, B. O. (1986) "Shared Obligations: Public Policy Influences on Family Care for the Elderly." Medicaid Program Evaluation. New York: SysteMetrics/ McGraw-Hill.

CBS Television Network (1986) "The Last Right?" 60 Minutes, Vol. 18, No. 17.

Congressional Budget Office (CBO). (1981) Medicaid: Choices for 1982 and Beyond. Washington, DC: Government Printing Office.

ESTES, C. L. and C. HARRINGTON (1985) "Future directions in long term care," pp. 251-271 in C. Harrington et al. (eds.) Long Term Care of the Elderly. Newbury Park, CA: Sage.

FELLER, B. A. (1983a) "Americans needing help to function at home," in National Center for Health Statistics: Advanced Data. DHHS Pub. No. (PHS) 83-1250. Hyattsville, MD: National Center for Health Statistics.

FELLER, B. A. (1983b) "Need for care among the noninstitutionalized elderly," pp. 67-70 in National Center for Health Statistics. Health: United States, 1983. DHHS Pub. No. (PHS) 84-1232. Washington, DC: Government Printing Office.

FRIES, J. F. (1980) "Aging, natural death, and the compression of morbidity." New England Journal of Medicine 303: 130-135.

FRIES, J. F. and CRAPO, C. M. (1981) Vitality and Aging: Implications of the Rectangular Curve. San Francisco, CA: W. H. Freeman.

GIBSON, R. M., D. R. WALDO, and K. R. LEVIT (1983) "National health expenditures, 1982." Health Care Financing Review 5: 1-31.

GRUENBERG, E. M. (1977) "The failures of success." Milbank Memorial Fund Quarterly/Health and Society 55: 3-24.

GRUNDY, E. (1984) "Mortality and morbidity among the old." British Medical Journal 228: 663-664.

HARRINGTON, C. (1983) "Social security and Medicare: policy shifts in the 1980's," pp. 83-111 in C. L. Estes and R. Newcomer (eds.) Fiscal Austerity and Aging. Newbury Park, CA: Sage.

HICKIE, J. B. (1984) "Euthanasia 1984." The Medical Journal of Australia 141: 140-141.

HODGSON, T. A. and A. KOPSTEIN (1983) "Health care expenditures for major diseases," pp. 79-85 in National Center for Health Statistics. Health: United States, 1983. DHHS Pub. No. (PHS) 84-1232. Washington, DC: Government Printing Office.

KRAMER, M. (1980) "The rising pandemic of mental disorders and associated chronic diseases and disorders." Acta Psychiatrica Scandinavica 62: 382-396.

LANDER, H. (1984) "Some medical aspects of euthanasia." The Medical Journal of Australia 141: 173-177.

LUBITZ, J. and R. PRIHODA (1983) "Use and costs of medicare services in the last years of life," pp. 71-77 in National Center for Health Statistics: Health, United States, 1983. DHHS Pub. No. (PHS) 84-1232. Washington, DC: Government Printing Office.

MANTON, K. (1986) "Cause specific mortality patterns among the oldest old: multiple cause of death trends, 1968 to 1980." Journal of Gerontology 41: 282-289.

Nursing Life (1984) "When death is inevitable." P 3 of a special Nursing Life poll report on "the right to die." (May/June): 47-53.

POULSCHOCK, B. Z. and K. STITZ (1984) "Allowing the debilitated to die." The Journal of Family Practice 18: 945-946.

RICE, D. (1985) "Health care needs of the elderly," pp. 41-66 in C. Harrington et al. (eds.) Long Term Care of the Elderly. Newbury Park, CA: Sage.

SCHNEIDER, E. L. and J. A. BRODY (1983) "Aging, natural death, and the compression of morbidity: another view." New England Journal of Medicine 309: 854-856.

SCHRIMPER, R. A. and R. L. CLARK (1985) "Health expenditures and elderly adults." Journal of Gerontology 40: 235-243.

The Seattle Times (1986) "Feeding tube removed from woman." April 17, p. A16.

U.S. Bureau of the Census (1983) "America in transition: an aging society." Current Population Reports, Series P-23, No. 128. Washington, DC: Government Printing Office.

U.S. Department of Labor (1984) Monthly Labor Review. Washington, DC: Government Printing Office.

U.S. General Accounting Office (GAO) (1982) "The elderly should benefit from expanded home health care but increasing these services will not insure cost reductions." Report to the Chairman of the Committee on Labor and Human Resources, United States Senate. GAO/IPE-83-1.

U.S. House of Representatives, Select Committee on Aging (1985) America's Elderly at Risk. Washington, DC: Government Printing Office.

U.S. National Center for Health Statistics (NCHS) (1981a) "Characteristics of nursing home residents, health status, and care received: national nursing home survey, United States, May-December 1977." Vital and Health Statistics. DHHS Pub. No. (PHS) 81-1712. Washington, DC: Government Printing Office.

U.S. National Center for Health Statistics (NCHS) and Jack, S. S. (1981b) "Current estimates from the national health interview survey: United States, 1979." Vital and Health Statistics. DHHS Pub. No. (PHS) 81-1564. Washington, DC: Government Printing office.

U.S. National Center for Health Statistics (NCHS) (1983) Health: United States, 1983. DHHS Pub. No. (PHS) 84-1232. Washington, DC: Government Printing Office.

U.S. Senate, Special Committee on Aging (1982) "Health care expenditures for the elderly: how much protection does Medicare provide?" Information paper. Washington, DC: Government Printing Office.

U.S. Senate, Special Committee on Aging (1983) Hearing: The Future of Medicare. Washington, DC: Government Printing Office.

Introduction to Chapter 10

The control of deviant behavior is a major issue in the formulation of policy. With regard to the aging population, the most common issues considered are with regard to the protection of old people from criminals and other deviants. "Granny bopping" or abuse of the elders has been a popular topic in the tabloids as well as a popular issue for legislators who can be quite sure that few will disagree with laws designed to protect elders. Such an area has received and is receiving study, but policy issues have not involved much debate because of how they have been defined. What will be needed in this area is more attention to research on exactly how much victimization of elders there is, how and when it occurs, and how rates compare to those for other age groups.

The other side of the issue is the question of how elders are involved in crime and other deviant behavior. If there are to be more elders, what will this mean with regard to trends in crime and deviant behavior, and what may be the consequences on policy issues? Kercher's chapter gives attention to the causes of crime, particularly as they apply to elders. Systematic knowledge of the causes of crime may provide some information on what can be expected. Common knowledge of elders indicates that they do not commit crimes of particular types. In spite of improvements in health and condition, elders simply could not be as physically agile as robbers, burglars, and the like. But in what ways may they be criminal or deviant, and what does this augur for the future? Kercher's chapter provides a basis for analyzing what is known and what may be anticipated with regard to criminality among elders.

10

Causes and Correlates of Crime Committed by the Elderly
A Review of the Literature

KYLE KERCHER

As a consequence of the increasing numbers of older persons in society, researchers have rushed to fill in the gaps in our knowledge about the elderly. One area that has received little attention, however, is crime committed by elderly (Feinberg, 1984b: 35; Wilbanks and Murphy, 1984: 79). Important questions require further study: How much crime do older persons engage in relative to younger members of the population? Is the number of elderly criminals so low, as stereotypes would suggest, that it's importance as a social problem can be dismissed? What are the factors that influence and predict the prevalence and incidence of illegal behavior among older persons? For example, as some criminologists have hypothesized, do larger concentrations of aged populations (such as found in Florida) induce a "subculture" that legitimizes and thus increases the rate of crimes committed by the elderly? How do the correlates and causes of lawbreaking by the elderly differ from the factors that predict and influence more youthful criminals? In other words, in attempts to prevent and control criminality, is it necessary to use different strategies for older persons?

Limited empirical research provides only partial answers to the above questions. The following review of the literature indicates the methodological problems encountered in this research, and then points to future studies needed to address more fully the questions that remain concerning the illegal behavior of older persons. More specifically, the chapter presents, in turn, a brief discussion of types of crime and their relationship to each other and to other forms of deviance, an analysis of the kinds of lawbreaking that persons are most likely to continue into older age, and an attempt to identify through previous theory and empirical research likely causes and correlates of crimes committed by the elderly.

Dimensions of Crime

Crime encompasses diverse behaviors. A partial list of types would include murder, rape, robbery, assault, burglary, theft, illegal gambling, driving while intoxicated, disorderly conduct, public drunkenness, and vagrancy. Do these illegal behaviors form a unidimensional concept? If so, then one type of crime should display a strong tendency to predict another. Furthermore, the causes and correlates of one kind of lawbreaking should indicate a similar influence on other forms of illegal behavior.

Hindelang et al. (1981: 45-73) have reviewed research that assesses the dimensionality of crime through Guttman scaling and factor and cluster analysis. They conclude, "The consistent cluster-analytic findings of distinct yet correlated subsets of homogeneous delinquents acts reinforce the conclusion that one kind of delinquency is predictive of other kinds of delinquency, but that at least some specialization appears to take place" (1981: 70; see also pp. 216-218).

Furthermore, other empirical evidence would also indicate that illegal behavior is not an entirely unidimensional concept. Based on findings that variables differ in their ability to predict one type of crime compared to another, researchers have suggested distinguishing between "intentional" (property) and "impulsive" (violent) crimes (Stark et al., 1983: 14-16), and between serious and nonserious lawbreaking (Elliott & Ageton, 1980; Elliot and Huizinga, 1983).

Additional tests of the dimensions of crime have been advanced. The perception of crime as a form of *deviant* behavior has led investigators to attempt to predict *legal* kinds of rulebreaking with the same variables used to explain *illegal* deviance. The evidence indicates separate but related dimensions. Using a sample of adults (elderly and younger), Tittle (1977) finds that the ability of eight factors to predict deviant behavior varied widely, depending on the type of rulebreaking analyzed. Tittle had the most success in accounting for "moralistic" deviance—e.g., smoking marijuana, 46 percent of variance explained; failure to stand for the national anthem, 37 percent. He had less success predicting deviance that reflected more legal harm—e.g., felonious theft, 10 percent of variance explained; assault, 20 percent. Nevertheless, the same factors predicting one type of deviance tended also to account for the other kinds of rulebreaking, albeit at differing levels of explanatory power.

The evidence indicating distinctive but related dimensions of deviance has implications for research on the causes and correlates of crime and other forms of rulebreaking by the elderly. The evidence suggests that a set of factors predicting particular types of deviance will not necessarily explain other forms of rulebreaking as accurately. However, though the factors may not predict as well for certain kinds of deviance, they are still likely to show some influence.

Crime Rates of the Young and Old

Studies comparing the crime rate of various age groups typically define the elderly as those 55 and older (Newman, 1984; Golden, 1984: 154). This age classification is not arbitrary. Research finds a sharply lower rate of criminal activity starting after age 30 (Cline, 1980; Glueck and Glueck, 1940). However, the most striking age differences appear when comparing those 18 to 54 years old with those age 55 and older (Shichor and Kobrin, 1978).

Predicted Variations in Crime Rates
by Age and Type

The evidence showing an inverse relationship between age and lawbreaking is consistent with stereotypes of the elderly. With a decline in physiological abilities, one would expect older persons to engage in less illegal behavior, including other deviant and nondeviant activities in general, even if their motivation to commit crimes remains high. However, certain types of law violations require greater physical strength, dexterity, and mobility than do other kinds. Thus the elderly should display the largest decrease in activity level for serious (FBI Index) crimes—murder, rape, robbery, burglary, and theft. Conversely, older persons should more closely approximate their activity level at a younger age for such illegal and legal deviance as public drunkenness, gambling, driving while intoxicated, use of banned drugs, vagrancy, lying to one's spouse, sitting during the national anthem, and so on.

Age-related physiological factors also allow predictions concerning which of the Index crimes should show the greatest rate discrepancies between young and old. The physiological limitations of the elderly are likely to severely restrict their rates of rape, robbery, and burglary. However, the relative rate at which serious crimes should decrease with age is less certain for such illegal acts as murder, assault, and theft. Although murder and assault require some level of physical competence, the target of these violent acts is most likely to be another person of similar age (see Hindelang and McDermott, 1981) and, therefore, similar strength. Then, too, assaults and murders are more likely than property crimes to occur at home or within the immediate neighborhood (Brantingham and Brantingham, 1981: 30; Rhodes and Conley, 1981: 168-169; Sampson, 1983: 286-287); consequently, the likelihood of reduced mobility with age should not prevent the elderly from participating in their share of assaults and murders. Conversely, the elderly would seem to require greater strength and mobility than they typically possess to engage effectively in such personal kinds of theft as purse snatching or pocket picking. However, only the elderly's relative lack of mobility should operate against their participating in theft that involves shoplifting.

A summary of the above predictions suggests the elderly should come close to matching the rates of the young for *legal* forms of deviance (e.g., lying to spouse) and the *less serious* illegal behaviors (e.g., public intoxication); should show intermediate levels of matching for the more serious (FBI Index) crimes of murder, assault, and thefts involving shoplifting; and should display the lowest level of matching for felonies involving personal theft (e.g., purse snatching). What does the empirical evidence indicate?

Crime Statistics by Age and Type

The majority (over 60 percent) of arrests among older persons in 1979 were for public drunkenness and driving while intoxicated, with larceny or theft—primarily shoplifting—comprising the major (over 10 percent of all arrests) serious, FBI Index crime (Shichor, 1984; Wilbanks, 1984a; Feinberg, 1984b). These three offenses are likewise the most commonly occurring among younger age groups (Shichor, 1984; Wilbanks, 1984a; Feinberg, 1984b). Some researchers (e.g., Wilbanks, 1984a: 7) have interpreted these statistics to imply that the real differences between young and old lawbreakers lie not so much in the *types* of crimes they commit but in the relative frequency with which they engage in lawbreaking in general. An analysis of age rates by type of crime does reveal, however, some significant differences.

Although in 1979 persons age 55 and older constituted 21 percent of the U.S. population, they accounted for only about 4 percent of all reported arrests. However, consistent with earlier predictions, older persons participated in even a smaller proportion (2 percent) of reported arrests for FBI Index crimes (Shichor, 1984). Furthermore, when FBI Index crimes are broken down by more specific offense categories, the results remain consistent with expectations: The elderly have the highest share of arrests for murder, aggravated assault, and larceny (respectively, 5.0, 3.5, and 3.1 percent) and the lowest share of arrests for burglary, robbery, motor vehicle theft, and forcible rape (respectively, 0.4, 0.5, 0.5, and 1.6 percent).

Greenberg (1985: 7) provides additional support for the physiological explanation of the age-crime relation. He notes that familial homicides (i.e., those occurring around the home) decline more slowly than non-familial homicides. Furthermore, the latter decline more slowly than property crimes.

When less serious crimes are broken down by specific offense categories, predictions that older persons will account for a greater proportion of the arrests receive mixed support. The elderly's share of gambling, public drunkenness, and driving under the influence (respectively, 15.3, 11.3, and 7.4 percent) is higher than any of the FBI Index crimes. However, contrary to expectations, the elderly's share in such other minor offenses as vagrancy, disorderly conduct, and violation of liquor laws (respectively, 4.4, 3.5, and 1.9 percent) is lower than some of the FBI Index crimes (Shichor, 1984). These results are apparently not influenced by time of measure. The proportion of elderly criminals within both serious and minor offense categories has remained relatively stable over time. News media reports notwithstanding, there is no solid empirical evidence of a current geriatric crime wave (Sunderland, 1982; Burnett and Ortega, 1984; Meyers, 1984; Shichor, 1984; Wilbanks, 1984a).

Unlike official crime statistics, self-report data provide only weak support for the physiological explanation of the relationship between age and type of crime. In a random sample of 1,973 subjects age 15 and older (see Tittle, 1980: 188), those persons 44 years and over (representing 46 percent of the respondents) committed the following percentage of deviant acts (within the past five years) for each of nine response categories, from lowest to highest: smoking marijuana, 5 percent; assault, 12 percent; theft of approximately $5 value, 15 percent; sitting during the national anthem, 15 percent, theft of $50 value, 16 percent; occupationally specific deviance, 22 percent; income tax cheating, 23 percent; illegal gambling, 29 percent; and lying to an intimate, 30 percent.

One may wish to discount the results for marijuana smoking as representing "cohort" rather than true life-cycle (age) effects. Likewise, one might also exclude theft of $50 value as an unreliable measure due to the excessively small number of incidents reported for the sample as a whole (138 incidents) and for the older age group in particular (22 incidents). Of the remaining crime categories, the two most serious law violations, assault and $5 theft, show the least participation by older persons, as previously predicated. However, the less serious illegal and legal deviant acts indicate rates of participation that are not much higher, particularly in the case of sitting during the national anthem (though here again one might attribute this last finding to a generational effect.)

On balance, then, there does seem to be some support for a physiological explanation of why the relationship between age and illicit activities varies by type of crime or deviant behavior. Questions remain, however, regarding what social conditions (e.g., cohort effects) are responsible for those instances where physiological explanations do not offer an adequate account of the variations in the age distribution for different types of deviant behavior. (See also the debate between Hirschi and Gottfredson, 1983: 557-561, and Greenberg, 1985: 6-8.)

Accuracy of Statistics on the Age-Crime Relationship

How accurate is this profile of the elderly as participants in ordinary crime? (For a discussion of the role of older persons in professional, organized, and white collar crime, see Newman, 1984.) Researchers who have attempted to estimate the absolute number and rate of crime committed by various age groups have relied almost exclusively on national arrest data from the FBI's Uniform Crime Reports (UCR).

(Tittle's research based on self-reports is a notable exception.) Criticisms of these official crime statistics are plentiful (e.g., Biderman and Reiss, 1967; Black, 1970; Maltz, 1977; Nettler, 1978: 54-64; Silberman, 1978). Clearly, UCR arrest data underestimate the amount of lawbreaking. Many crimes are not reported to the police, and of those reported, many do not result in arrest (the degree of underestimation of law violation varying by type of offense).

However, despite this and other criticisms of the UCR, recent evidence indicates arrest statistics paint a reasonably accurate picture of the *relative* frequency with which people engage in different kinds of criminal activities—even when rates are broken down by demographic characteristics such as adult/juvenile, race, sex, neighborhood socioeconomic status, urban/rural regions, and intercity rates (Hindelang, 1974, 1976, 1978, 1979, 1981; Hindelang et al., 1981; Hindelang and McDermott, 1981; Laub and Hindelang, 1979, 1981, Danser and Laub, 1981; Sampson et al., 1981; Canter, 1982a; Savitz, 1978; Sampson, 1985a; but see also O'Brien et al., 1980; Cohen and Land, 1984).

Less certain, however, is the accuracy with which the official arrest statistics measure the relative rates at which the young and old commit crimes. Some studies suggest that the police and other agents of the criminal justice system treat the aged more leniently (Wilson, 1968; Bergman and Amir, 1973; Amir and Bergman, 1975; for a more theoretical discussion, see Cressey, 1966; Schafer, 1976; Reid, 1979).

Other and generally more recent evidence, however, would question whether there is much if any bias in favor of the elderly. Studies of postarrest decisions of criminal justice officials do not find a negative age-sanction association for adult offenders in general (e.g., Hagan, 1974; Eisenstein and Jacob, 1977; Curran, 1983; Pruitt and Wilson, 1983; Zatz, 1984; Petersilia, 1985) and for elderly/younger comparisons in particular (Wilbanks, 1985). Most important, investigations of police *arrest* decisions (the usual source of crime statistics that compare different age groups) also indicate insubstantial effects for age (Visher, 1983; Krohn et al., 1983; Smith, 1984; Smith et al., 1984; Petersilia, 1985).

Arrest data appear, then, to represent the *relative* rate of crime committed by younger compared to older age groups with reasonable accuracy. However, it would be inappropriate to conclude that age is, therefore, the only factor responsible for the differential rates of lawbreaking between age groups. The age-crime relationship suggested by official crime statistics may be partly spurious.

Longevity factors associated with crime are one potential source of spurious age effects. For example, being male, black, poor, and/or undereducated is associated with a shorter life span. These characteristics, with the possible exception of poverty, are also associated with committing crimes most likely to appear in official arrest statistics—a relationship that is particularly strong for the most serious types of lawbreaking (Moberg, 1953; Hindelang, 1976, 1978, 1979, 1981; Hindelang et al., 1981; Hindelang and McDermott, 1981; Sampson et al., 1981; Canter, 1982a; Elliott and Ageton, 1980; Thornberry and Farnworth, 1982; Elliott and Huizinga, 1983). Thus without appropriate controls for factors associated with longevity, crime statistics are likely to overestimate the decrease with age in illegal activities, particularly for FBI Index crimes.

Conversely, white-collar crime (such as income tax cheating and computer theft) is *less* likely to occur among those persons (excepting males) who tend to die at younger ages. Thus even if one were able to compile reliable data on the incidence of white-collar crime by age, uncontrolled longevity factors might introduce a bias resulting in an *underestimation* of the rate of decrease with age in white-collar crime.

The potential bias in crime statistics created by longevity factors can be at least partially overcome through appropriate controls for race and sex (official arrest data do not include a measure of socioeconomic status). Less easily overcome, however, is the potential bias introduced by cohort effects that may be present in the cross-sectional data upon which official statistics and many self-report studies are based (e.g., Greenberg, 1985: 4). For example, in his cross-sectional self-report study, Tittle (1980: 93-95; see also, Rowe and Tittle, 1977; Greenberg, 1985: 5) found evidence that the age-crime relationship can be partially explained by differences between generations in their propensity to violate the law. The elderly were much less likely than the younger cohorts in the study to have had criminal friends (a strong indicator of the respondent's own lawbreaking) when growing up.

Unfortunately, due to the absence of any longitudinal, life-span studies of crime, the amount of bias introduced by cohort effects remains unknown. Caution is therefore required in using cross-sectional crime statistics to estimate true life-cycle changes in the propensity to violate the law.

Volume of Crime Committed by the Elderly

So what may be concluded regarding the amount of crime for which older persons are responsible? Clearly the elderly display very low rates of arrests relative to other age groups. In 1980, their rate for total offences was only one-fifth that found for all age groups combined (Feinberg, 1984b). And the disparity among age groups is even more dramatic when comparing the elderly's rate of offending to that of juveniles. For example, the Index arrest rate for ages 15 to 19 is 45 times that of persons 60 and older. For the specific offenses of burglary and robbery, the ratio is substantially higher yet, 344:1 and 288:1, respectively. Even for non-Index crimes the ratio, 22:1, is considerable (Wilbanks, 1984a).

Focusing on the elderly's relative rate of offending may, however, foster the misimpression that the elderly criminal is not worth study- ing. A potentially better index of the extent of lawbreaking by the elderly is the absolute *number* of crimes they commit (Feinberg, 1984a: 87; Shichor, 1984: 29). In 1979, persons 55 and older accounted for nearly 400,000 arrests in the United States. Of this substantial volume of arrests, more than 48,000 were for FBI Index crimes, of which larceny (over 34,000) and aggravated assault (over 8,900) made up the vast majority (Shichor, 1984). In contrast, the contributions of the elderly to arrests for murder, robbery, and forcible rape were trivial, each numbering in the few hundreds.

These figures are even more impressive when one considers that they are based on UCR arrest data rather than UCR crimes reported to police. The latter measure shows a volume of crime roughly 5 times that which results in an arrest (Brown et al., 1983). Additionally, research suggests that only about one-half of all crimes committed are reported to the police (Ennis, 1967: 49). Consequently, the actual volume of criminal activity among older, as well as younger persons, may be as much as 10 times higher than arrest data indicate (see also Petersilia, 1985: 25). In other words, those 55 and older may have been responsible for roughly 4,000,000 cases of crime in the United States in 1979.

Furthermore, in contrast to the elderly's decreasing role in less serious offenses, the rate at which the aged commit major (i.e., Index) crimes is growing at a faster pace than it is for other age groups, primarily because of the elderly's expanding participation in larceny

(Feinberg, 1984a; Shichor, 1984). Additionally, because the proportion of the elderly in the population is steadily rising, their representation among all criminals is also likely to increase over time.

The evidence presented here suggests that older persons are responsible for a fairly substantial volume of illegal behavior. It is unfortunate, then, that we understand so little about the factors that motivate and predict lawbreaking by the elderly. Without such knowledge, attempts to prevent and control this behavior are less likely to succeed. Furthermore, given the evidence of the interrelatedness of crime and other deviant activities, factors predicting crime by the elderly should predict other forms of deviance by the elderly as well.

The next section examines general (non-age-specific) theories of crime. It lists causes and correlates of crime that major theories indicate should apply equally well across all age groups. The next section on elder-specific explanations of lawbreaking will then describe speculations on which of the causes and correlates implicated in general theories of crime should vary by age. A subsequent section will then examine the empirical support for the factors identified by general theory as potential predictors of crime, and the evidence of whether their effects do vary by age as elder-specific theory anticipates. A final section will reduce to an explicit path model what theory and research suggest are the causes and correlates of crime committed by the elderly.

General Theories of Crime

With some risk of oversimplification, theories of crime can be divided into two broad-based perspectives roughly distinguished by the importance they attach to external versus internal constraints on deviant behavior. In other words, they differ in the emphasis they place on the "calculation of personal gain" versus "committment to internalized norms" in influencing violations of the law. These two basic models of human behavior lead their proponents to focus on different aspects of the environment as the primary source of crime, and presumedly are relevant at all ages. The "external control" perspective emphasizes economic factors, and the "internal control" viewpoint concentrates on a person's integration within social networks of significant others. Details of these two models and the different types of theories found within each perspective follow.

External Control Model

Theories that attempt to explain criminal activity in terms of external constraints are of two types—the "rational choice" approach and the "blocked opportunities" variation.

Rational Choice

Rational choice theory is represented by economists (e.g., Fleisher, 1966; Becker, 1968; Ehrlich, 1973; and more broadly by Heath, 1976), who argue that persons choose between a "legitimate" and an "illegitimate" activity on the basis of a *rational assessment* of the potential rewards and costs derived from the respective behaviors. Thus, for example, as unemployment decreases and/or certainty of imprisonment increases crime rates should decline due to the relatively greater costs and rewards received for illegitimate as compared to legitimate activity.

Blocked Opportunities

As a variation on the rational choice thesis, sociologists who adhere to the external control perspective generally assume a more emotional model of humankind than do economists (i.e., a calculation of personal gain but with frustration added as an intervening variable). The blocked opportunities approach (Cohen, 1955; Cloward and Ohlin, 1960; Merton, 1968) suggests that persons who are denied legitimate means (such as a job or sufficient income) to attain the commonly held goal of affluence and status will turn to antisocial behavior as both an alternative means to gain recognition from others and as a form of cathartic release from the frustration (also described as "anomie") engendered by denial of legitimate opportunities. Thus whereas rational choice theory is primarily an explanation of property crime, the emotional component of the blocked opportunities model—frustration and aggression—would seem to offer an explanation of violent as well as property crimes (i.e., lawbreaking motivated by psychic as well as material gain).

Then, too, because material consumption is only one means to seek status, the blocked opportunities approach, as opposed to the rational choice model (with its emphasis on material consumption as an end in itself), points to noneconomic as well as economic factors as sources influencing crime. Based on the sociological concept of socioeconomic status (SES), the blocked opportunities perspective would argue that persons are more likely to engage in crime not only when they rank low on the economic status variables of income or unemployment but also when they rank low on the social status factors of educational or occupational prestige (see Braithwaite, 1981).

A summary, then, contrasting the rational choice and blocked opportunities versions of the external control model finds the latter viewpoint invoking both a broader range of work-related conditions (low occupation and education in addition to poverty and chronic unemployment) hypothesized to induce criminal behavior, and a larger number of illegal responses (violent as well as property crimes) to these purported causal agents. Additionally, rational choice theory considers the deterrent effects on crime of formal sanctions administered by the criminal justice system. However, these differences in emphasis notwithstanding, either theory provides a theoretical justification for anticipating more lawbreaking among the economically disadvantaged.

Internal Control Model

In contrast to theories that emphasize the calculation of personal gain in the generation of crime, proponents of the internal control model point to social integration and the internalization of conventional norms as the key to whether one engages in violations of the law. The focus is on the degree to which individuals are integrated within a network of social relations and the extent to which the values and behavior of that network or subculture coincide with those of the dominant culture or society (Crutchfield et al., 1982; and for a broader focus, see Scott, 1971; Naroll, 1983). Where involvement with others is low or where the values and behaviors of others a person interacts with are deviant, commitment to the social order is weakened and we may expect a corresponding increase in illegal behavior.

Theories that emphasize internal control assume either implicitly or explicitly that calculation of external sanctions in support of conventional conduct is eventually replaced by internalized standards relatively resistant to the lure of rewards for deviant behavior (Scott, 1971). Furthermore, the crucial reinforcers in moving persons from external to internal control over deviant temptations are not the "formal" sanctions of work (income and prestige) or the criminal justice system (threats of arrest, conviction, and imprisonment) but rather are the "informal" sanctions for adhering to social standards received in day-to-day interaction with family and friends. Thus the process of inter-nalization occurs primarily in interaction with *significant others,* though the degree of community or other group support for conventional behavior can also play a role (see Kornhauser, 1978; Akers et al., 1979). The more contact and attachment one has with members of one's social network, the stronger the influence their social approval of conven-tional (or unconventional) behavior will have, and the more rapidly will persons develop internal control—that is, adhere to norms even in the absence of sanctioning agents.

There are at least three related theories encompassed by the internal control model—differential association, control, and social learning. All share a concern for the relationship between social integration and antisocial behavior.

Differential Association and Control Theory

Control theory (Hirschi, 1969, 1983; Hindelang, 1973) points to a person's low attachment (bonds) to others as the primary source of criminal motivation (see Hansell and Wiatrowski, 1981). In contrast, differential association theory (Sunderland and Cressey, 1978) argues that the major influence on illegal behavior is whether a person associates with criminal or conventional others. Thus in explaining crime, control theory emphasizes the *quality* of associations, and dif-ferential association the *type* of associations a person experiences (Krohn and Massey, 1980: 530).

Furthermore, although both perspectives argue that criminal beliefs (i.e., weakened internalized conventional standards) play a role in fostering lawbreaking, differential association theory gives this factor a more central position in the explanation of crime: The effects of other variables (e.g., attachment) are all assumed to occur indirectly through the intervening variable of beliefs (see Matsueda, 1982).

Finally, control theory is frequently identified with two additional concepts—"commitment" and "involvement" (see Hirschi, 1969). Commitment represents investments or "stakes" in conventional lifestyles, and the calculation of the loss of these investments if caught in violation of the law. Thus Hirschi's concept of commitment appears closely aligned with utility propositions in rational choice theory (see Krohn and Massey, 1980: 531; Paternoster, 1983a: 461-462), and as such, represents a bridge between the external and internal control models. Unlike rational choice theory, however, Hirschi is not primarily concerned with the relationship between SES and crime. Instead, he focuses on *future-oriented* investments in conventional behavior—namely, a person's educational and occupational aspirations and expectations (see also Johnson, 1979: 6-7, 21-25, 107-108, for a discussion of how the discrepancy between aspirations and expectations becomes a measure of anomie rather than commitment). Additionally, research on teenage populations (the age group upon which Hirschi tests his theory) sometimes include academic performance as a measure of *current* investments in conventional behavior (see Krohn and Massey, 1980: 530-531; Paternoster et al., 1983a: 461-462).

Hirschi has also proposed that time-consuming *involvement* in conventional activities diverts attention from illicit behaviors. By his own admission, however, involvement is a theoretically weak variable. As a consequence, some researchers have either subsumed it under the concept of commitment (see Krohn and Massey, 1980: 531) or simply dropped it from their analysis (see Paternoster, 1983a: 471, fn. 14).

Social Learning Theory

The largely implicit notion of differential association and control theory, that the internalization of conventional norms is a product of patterns of sanctions persons encounter in their network of social relations, receives more explicit attention from social learning theory (Bandura, 1969, 1977; Scott, 1971; Akers, 1977; Akers et al., 1979; Conger, 1980; Patterson, 1980). Thus whereas differential association and control theory measure the social structures in which this sanctioning process is likely to occur (in families with high attachment, among peer groups where definitions unfavorable to law violations predominate, etc.), social learning theory attempts to analyze the reinforcement process itself (Akers et al., 1979; Hawkins and Weis, 1980; Conger, 1980). This analysis is accomplished most frequently by actively manipulating reinforcers in both experimental and naturalistic settings (see Alexander and Parsons, 1973; Klein et al., 1977; Loeber et al., 1984: 8). In contrast, differential association and control theory rely primarily on survey data to test research hypotheses.

In sum, the differential association, control, and social learning theories point to social integration within intimate groups as influencing lawbreaking. Social learning theory specifies *how* the process takes place; the other viewpoints look at *where* the process takes place. More broadly, the three versions of the internal control model all focus on informal sanctions in day-to-day interactions with others, whereas the two forms of the external control model (blocked opportunities and rational choice) concentrate on formal sanctions found in work and the criminal justice institution. The former model assumes an actor who responds according to internalized values fostered by others' expectations; the latter model assumes an unprincipled actor who calculates how best to attain society's formal rewards.

A Path Model

Model 1 (Figure 10.1) represents the basic concepts of the internal and external control perspectives and their interrelationship. Blocked opportunities theory predicts that anomie (frustration, alienation, low self-worth, etc.) is an intervening variable for SES factors; rational choice theory hypothesizes that SES has a direct path to crime. Both would seem to agree that one must control for social integration factors—attachment to significant others, criminal associations, criminal beliefs, and related variables (see Fleisher, 1966; Merton, 1968: 149-151). Thus Model 1 shows paths from SES to these intervening variables.

The internal control model (of social learning, differential association, and control theories) predicts that criminal associates will affect crime either indirectly through the intervening variable of criminal beliefs, or both directly and indirectly (differential association theory assumes only the former). Furthermore, the degree to which an individual is attached to significant others should influence illegal behavior—decreasing crime where the bond is to a conventional other and increasing crime where attachment is to a criminal associate. Model 1 represents this interaction between criminal associations and attachment with an arrow drawn from attachment intersecting the path from criminal associates to crime. Likewise, the effect of attachment on criminal beliefs should vary by whether the person bonded is criminal or conventional in behavior. Consequently, attachment intersects the path from criminal associates to criminal beliefs. Other pathways than those Model 1 depicts are, of course, possible. The ones presented here roughly approximate the path models that others have developed to represent the major theories of crime (see Johnson, 1979; Matsueda, 1982).

Model 1 identifies a set of factors that general theories of crime assume (at least implicitly) will apply equally well across all age cate-

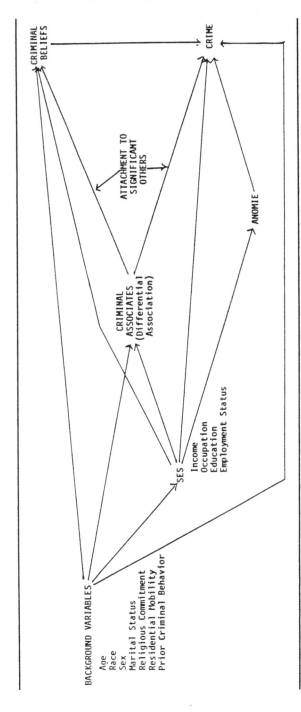

Figure 10.1 Causes and Correlates of Crime. Model 1

269

gories, including the elderly. The model leaves several questions unanswered. First, might not some of the factors implicated in general theories of crime interact with age in their effects on illegal behavior? Additionally, is the list of causes and correlates identified in Model 1 complete? Might there be some other factors not included in general theories of crime that are unique to the elderly?

The next section of this chapter examines theories of crime that focus specifically on the elderly. For the most part, these theories identify the same causes and correlates as more general theories of crime, though the list of factors they describe is not nearly as extensive or as elaborately explicated. Indeed, in most cases the explanations offered for why the elderly engage in crime might better qualify as speculations than actual theories. Nevertheless, an examination of these theories or speculations does suggest some factors that potentially may interact with age in their influence on crime. Likewise, several factors unique to the elderly are identified as potential sources of lawbreaking.

Elderly-Specific Theories of Crime

There have been few attempts to explain why the elderly violate the law. The dearth of theories probably stems in part from the relatively small numbers of older persons who engage in lawbreaking and in part because researchers face fewer obstacles in surveying the illegal behavior of youths (see Hindelang, 1981: 472).

When gerontologists do speculate on the reasons the aged might break the law, they frequently provide lists of potential causes and correlates with little attempt to justify their selection of factors through reference to an elder-specific theory, a general theory of crime, or to empirical research. For example, Abrams (1984) asserts, "Why do elderly people turn to crime? There are many factors, including loss of prestige upon retirement, boredom, feelings of helplessness as life's end draw nearer, and others (1984: xiv)." Later, he suggests research is needed to establish the relationship between crime committed by older persons and such variables as mobility (considered a measure of separation from family), religousness, inflation and unemployment, and use of prescription drugs. Again, no attempt is made to derive these hypothesized correlates from theory or previous empirical research.

Factors Shared with Other Age Groups

Feinberg (1984a, 1984b) takes a somewhat less atheoretical approach in his discussion of factors that should be associated with law violations by the elderly. He notes the many similarities between older persons and juveniles in their life situations—for example, obligations toward leisure in a society that respects work, unstructured time blocks, and a confused sense of self. In other words, juveniles and the elderly share the common experience of "marginality" or "low prestige."

As a consequence of the similarities in life situations between the aged and adolescents, Feinberg suggests theories of juvenile delinquency should at least initially guide research on elderly lawbreakers. He cautions, however, that the two age groups also differ in one important respect: Juveniles can look forward to becoming less marginal with age, while the elderly are faced with increasing marginality.

Feinberg is not very clear in specifying which factors he is selecting from theories of delinquency to explain crime by the elderly. He would seem, however, to be alluding to a blocked opportunities theory of lawbreaking, with loss of prestige as the central motivator of crime. However, the blocked opportunities perspective is not a theory of juvenile delinquency per se but of crime in general. Moreover, it would seem a poor choice for explaining how the greater marginality of juveniles and the elderly compared to other age groups generates crime. The elderly are assumed to be among the most marginal of all age groups and yet they engage in the least amount of crime. Additionally, the marginality of the elderly *increases* with age but the crime rate, even among those 55 and older, *declines* with age (Wilbanks, 1984b).

Clearly, blocked opportunities theory is an unlikely candidate to explain why the crime rate is lower for the elderly than for other age groups. Nor do other theories fare any better in their explanations (see Hirschi and Gottfredson, 1983: 553-554). However, our purpose here is not to explain differences in crime rates by age. The focus of the present chapter is to identify causes and correlates of lawbreaking and determine if these factors vary in their influence on the elderly versus other age groups. Indeed, it is conceivable, as Feinberg implies, that blocked opportunities may have a stronger effect on lawbreaking among the elderly and teenage populations than among middle age groups. But Feinberg provides no theoretical explanation of why marginality (blocked opportunities) should interact with age in its effects on lawbreaking.

Furthermore, although listed among the indices of marginality, Feinberg's concept of unstructured time blocks would seem to fit better the concept of involvement (in conventional activities) found in control theory. The distinction of how unstructured time should be conceptualized is important because in the latter case it leads one to measure amount of participation in conventional activities in general, and in the former case it leads one to measure the degree of participation in prestigious activities (primarily work). The internal control model (particularly control theory) points to the need to keep persons involved with conventional others and away from deviant others. In contrast, blocked opportunities theory emphasizes the status that may be obtained when idle time is replaced by prestigious activities.

Factors Unique to Elderly

Feinberg also discusses potential criminal factors unique to or at least much more likely to occur among the aged. Describing the uncertainty surrounding the new roles the older person must take on, he comments,

> The elderly are thus set adrift and society has provided them with neither map, itinerary, nor friendly shore. They are on their own, captain and mate, actor and agent of their own destiny. Making matters more difficult, they must often transit several roles at once: retirement, death of a spouse, physical disabilities, change in residence, and the like [1984b: 48].

Why should these four role transitions Feinberg describes influence crime by the elderly? He makes no attempt to explain. However, retirement might be conceptualized as a more permanent form of unemployment. If so, then it might constitute a more serious loss of economic and social status than does unemployment among younger age groups. On the other hand, unlike youthful joblessness, retirement is frequently voluntary and may even be eagerly awaited, and the loss of income normally experienced with unemployment is negated at least partially by retirement benefits. Thus if retirement increases crime, a reduction in income and prestige (i.e., blocked opportunities) may not be the reason for the effect. Instead, the sudden loss of law-abiding social networks encountered at work might be a more plausibie explanation.

Isolation from significant others may also occur when a spouse dies, a residence is changed (e.g., a move to the sunbelt), or health deteriorates. Although each of these situations should therefore tend to promote crime (assuming the isolation is from nondeviant others), poor health could have a negative as well as positive influence on illegality. Physical disability should make many types of illegitimate behavior (e.g., shoplifting) less easy to commit.

Because retirement, widowhood, and health problems, if not residential mobility, are much more likely to occur among the elderly, the amount of variation in lawbreaking they explain, if any, should be greater among older than younger persons. Furthermore, Feinberg would also seem to suggest an interaction effect for the four factors. In other words, the presence of all four together should have a unique influence on illegal behavior in addition to their separate effects. Note, however, that this interaction is not a true age interaction. Because three of the variables have such a low rate of occurence among the young (i.e., are unique to the elderly), one cannot reliably test whether their effect varies by age.

Interaction between Age, Race, and Sex

Hagan (1985) argues that age, race, and sex interact in their effects on crime. He notes that both females and racial minorities are restricted in their labor force participation. But minority women are much more likely than majority women to depend on labor force participation for subsistance. Consequently, Hagan predicts that males and females will be more similar in crime rate when the group is of ethnic minority rather than majority status. Furthermore, age will accentuate this discrepancy between ethnic groups in the sex ratio of criminal activity. Thus it is among the elderly that one should encounter the greatest sex ratio differences between minority and majority ethnic groups.

Interactions between Age and the Social Environment

Finally, in an analysis focusing on older persons who murder, Wilbanks and Murphy (1984: 83) hypothesize that "elderly homicide offenders will not be 'carriers' of a subculture of violence or be influenced as greatly by broader sociological conditions as people in younger age categories." What Wilbanks and Murphy seem to be implying, then, is that aging leads to less sensitivity to the social environment—that is, less sensitivity to those social factors (criminal subcultures, criminal associates, economic conditions, formal deterrence, etc.) that general theories of crime identify as influencing illegal behavior.

Why Wilbanks and Murphy predict this interaction effect between age and the social environment is unclear. They do make some reference to an analogous hypothesis based on sex (females are less influenced than males by crime correlates) rather than age, but offer no further explanation. However, if it is true that the elderly are more inflexible in their behavior and/or less responsive to external stimuli than are younger persons, then we might anticipate that older age groups would be less affected than the young by variations in environmental factors associated with murder. Indeed, there would seem to be no reason to restrict Wilbanks and Murphy's hypothesis to homicide crimes. The interaction between age and social environment should occur for crime in general.

Conversely, Hirschi and Gottfredson (1983) have argued that sociological variables do *not* interact with age in their influence on crime. "Therefore, identification of the causes of crime at one age suffices to identify them at other ages as well" (1983: 580). Hirschi and Gottfredson offer no explicit explanation for their empirically based observation. However, their proposition does offer a direct challenge to age-specific theories of crime in general, including those of Wilbanks and Murphy and others reviewed in this section.

Summary of Elder-Specific Theories

In seeking causes and correlates of crime committed by older persons, most elder-specific theories do not suggest the need to substantially alter the list of factors provided by general theories of crime.

Among those few modifications that elder-specific theories do suggest are the addition of four factors "unique" to the elderly, and several interactions involving age: Because retirement, widowhood, and health problems show much more variation among the elderly than other age groups, it is anticipated that these factors might become important determinants of crime as persons grow into old age. Additionally, because retirement, widowhood, and health problems (as well as residential mobility) may all affect the aged in close succession, one explanation for the existence of elderly lawbreakers has suggested that this set of variables contributes to an interaction effect. That is, the combined influence of these variables on crime by the elderly is greater than the sum of their individual effects.

Use of prescription drugs is a fourth factor that may have special significance for crimes committed by the elderly. It is also likely to display little variation among other than elderly populations. Though use of prescription drugs does not receive much attention as a potential predictor of crime even by elder-specific theories, it does not seem unreasonable that overuse of certain medications might cause the elderly to make misjudgments leading to illegal behavior.

Elder-specific theory also suggests several potential age interactions: age by sex by race, and age by social environment. The former interaction predicts that certain sex and race categories (specifically, female minorities) will show a less severe decrease in crime with age than other race-sex combinations. The latter age interaction is more global, suggesting that those social factors identified as causes and correlates of crime for younger age groups will have less influence on crime by the elderly. Thus support for this hypothesis requires that empirical research find numerous instances in which the causes and correlates of crime vary by age, and that the results be consistent in showing that it is the elderly for which a given factor (e.g., criminal associates) has the least influence.

Clearly, one can derive *theoretical* support for the variables that general and elder-specific theories of crime implicate as likely sources of criminal motivation among the elderly. But how much *empirical* support exists for the influence of these factors?

Empirical Research on Causes and Correlates of Crime by the Elderly

Although there is a considerable volume of empirical research on factors that predict illegal behavior, almost none of it concentrates on the elderly criminal. The following review of the empirical literature will necessarily, then, include much that is not elder-specific; the studies (using individual-level crime data) typically analyze lawbreaking by juveniles. Such research remains relevant, however, to establishing empirical support for causes and correlates of crime by the elderly, as long as the independent variables analyzed are perceived as operating across all age groups, as is generally the case.

In a few instances, individual level studies of crime survey the general population. These studies are particularly relevant because they allow an assessment of whether the results for youthful populations apply to populations that include older persons—that is, whether the variables might interact with age in their influence on crime.

Selected Methodological Issues

Causality

Research on causes and correlates of lawbreaking relies almost entirely on correlational (as opposed to experimental) analysis. Thus a common problem in these studies is establishing that a statistically significant association between two variables has the intended causal order (e.g., delinquent friends cause one to engage in illegal acts, rather than criminal behavior leads one to choose delinquent friends) and is not a spurious artifact of some unmeasured third variable (e.g., criminal associates influence both criminal beliefs and crime, thus making it appear that beliefs and crime are causally related). Logic (e.g., ethnicity must precede crime) and the selection of appropriate control variables can often help establish the veracity of a suggested causal correlation, but the problem of causal order and spuriousness remains a vexing one for most research on crime. (See Orsagh, 1979, for an elaboration of these points.)

Aggregate Crime Data

Another methodological issue concerns the level at which a variable is measured—individual versus aggregate. Given the problems encountered in interpreting aggregate data (see Robinson, 1950; Orsagh, 1979), the review of the empirical literature to follow will not include any findings that measure crime at the aggregate level.

Measures of Effect Size

Research on crime frequently provides estimates of effect size based on gamma coefficients. Unfortunately, gamma has the undesirable property of increasing in size the more poorly measured the independent and dependent variables are (Blalock, personal communication). Indeed, when gamma coefficients are compared to r^2 coefficients for the same data, the former generally indicate much larger estimates of effect size (see Tittle, 1977: 590-591; Paternoster et al., 1982; Elifson et al., 1983).

On balance, then, r^2 would seem a more reliable measure than gamma of the relative explanatory power of factors associated with crime. Consequently, when evaluating the relative importance of a factor in its influence on lawbreaking by the elderly, the review of the empirical literature to follow will give more weight to research that reports r^2's (or r's or beta's) rather than gamma coefficients.

Furthermore, in summarizing the effect of a variable on crime committed by a particular age group, r's or beta's approaching .30 and above are described as "substantial," values ranging from the mid-teens to mid-twenties are designated "modest," and coefficients of .10 or below (assuming they are statistically significant) are called "weak." Classifying the size of coefficients in this manner is admittedly somewhat arbitrary, and the reader is of course free to provide alternative ranges for a given strength level.

Comparing Results Across Different Age Groups

In the present study, we want to know if the factors predicting lawbreaking by the elderly are the same ones that predict illegal behavior among younger age categories. Ideally, an analysis of whether the causes of crime vary by age would include a sample of diverse age groups and explicit tests of interaction terms involving age and other independent variables in the study. Unfortunately, there are very few individual-level studies of crime that include a representative sample of the general population. Moreover, even when the investigations encompass a broad range of ages, they almost never consider age interactions. Thus the present review is forced to compare the results of analyses on youthful populations with those findings (very limited in number) for the more general population. Consistency across age groups is assumed where the magnitude of the standardized coefficients (r^2, standardized regression coefficient, gamma, etc.) for a given factor is similar across youthful and more general samples of the population.

There is some risk, however, in assuming that a similar standardized coefficient for youthful and more general population samples implies that the coefficient for elderly groups would therefore also be roughly the same. The failure to analyze elderly age groups separately from other age categories may mask real differences between older versus younger (middle-age and youthful) populations. Furthermore, the comparison of standardized coefficients across different age groups (samples) is undesirable (see Blalock, 1967, 1972; Hanushek and Jackson, 1977: 76-79). But in the absence of tests for age interactions within a study, or the reporting of unstandardized slope coefficients across studies, no alternative comparison procedure appears better.

An Overview of the Empirical Analysis

At the conclusion of each section reviewing the empirical evidence for a given factor that general and elder-specific theories suggest should be associated with crime committed by older persons, the findings are used to develop a more refined, empirically based Model 2 (see Figure 10.2). The latter model represents results of studies based on samples of the general population using self-report measures of general crimes (i.e., the mostly nonserious offenses that constitute the majority of lawbreaking, particularly for the elderly). Where there are differences in the findings for these studies when compared to research on youths, the model depicts the results for the former, older sample, and suggests the possibility that the effect of the given factor may vary by age. Likewise, where evidence indicates that the effect may be stronger for more serious crimes, Model 2 depicts the results for the more general (less serious) crimes, and notes that the effect may vary by seriousness of offense.

The Influence of Background Variables

Age, Race, and Sex

Surveys of the general population find strong inverse associations between age and self-report measures of illegal and deviant behavior (Tittle, 1980: 90-96; Meier and Johnson, 1977: 301; see also Minor, 1977: 128, 131) but weaker correlations for sex (Meier and Johnson, 1977: 301; Tittle, 1980: 81-86) and race (Meier and Johnson, 1977: 301; Tittle, 1980: 86-89, 93). Surveys of youthful populations find that self-report measures of crime have stronger but still modest correlations with sex (Jensen and Eve, 1976; Kraut, 1976: 360; Elifson et al., 1983: 520; Paternoster et al., 1983a; Farnworth, 1984: 203; Pestello, 1984) and weak relationships with race (Kraut, 1976: 360; Hindelang et al., 1981: 161).

The lack of strong effects for sex and race in both youthful and more general samples of the population is surprising. In contrast to these results for self-report measures of crime, victimization reports and UCR arrest data show race and sex to be strong predictors of lawbreaking for both younger and older age groups (see Hindelang, 1981; Wilbanks, 1984b). However, Hindelang et al. (1979, 1981; see also Elliott, 1982) cite evidence suggesting that self-report data typically express less serious crimes than do victimization and arrest data, and it is the more serious offenses with which race and sex are most strongly associated.

Furthermore, for both youthful and general samples of the population, introduction of control variables (including in many instances social integration factors) does not greatly reduce the sex-crime relation (Kraut, 1976; Tittle, 1980; Elifson et al., 1983; Paternoster et al., 1983a; Farnworth, 1984; Pestello, 1984; but see also Jensen and Eve, 1976: 443), indicating that the effect of sex is primarily direct. Conversely, studies of the general population (Meier and Johnson, 1977; Tittle, 1980) find no direct effect for race when using control factors. However, in their study of youths, Wolfgang et al. (1972: 275-279) find that race has a weak direct effect on official arrests (though the controls used are limited in scope).

Additionally, there is uncertainty as to whether the effects for age are primarily direct or indirect. Introducing controls for intervening social integration factors (criminal beliefs, friends' criminality, etc.) tend to reduce the age-crime relation (Rowe and Tittle, 1977; Meier and Johnson, 1977: 301), particularly in the latter study. These findings would seem to suggest at least some indirect effects for age. But such an interpretation of the results of Rowe and Tittle, which encompassed a much more representative sample of illegal behaviors than did Meier and Johnson (the latter study analyzing only marijuana use), remains controversial (compare Greenberg, 1985: 10-11, with Hirschi and Gottfredson, 1985: 24-25).

Furthermore, Tittle (1980: 92) provides the clearest evidence that age does not interact with sex or race in its effect on illegal behavior. Gamma coefficients for the age-crime relation vary little from .50 whether comparing blacks versus whites or males versus females.

Conversely, other research has found several interaction effects involving age, race, and sex (see Greenberg, 1985: 9-10; but see also Hirschi and Gottfredson, 1985: 23-24). Of particular interest, Hagan

(1985) finds that the influence of sex on illegal behavior (as measured by the percentage of the population incarcerated) is less for minority groups (Canadian Native Americans) than for whites, and this discrepancy between ethnic groups becomes larger with age (a range that encompasses 16- to 51-year-olds). Whether this three-way interaction occurs in other countries with different minority groups is unknown, but bears study. Likewise, it would be of interest to establish, through formal tests of the interaction term, how substantial the effect is, and whether the effect also occurs using self-report measures of (less serious) crime.

Applying the Findings for Age, Race, and Sex to Model 2

The majority of the evidence suggests the effects of race and sex do not vary substantially by age groups. At least for self-report measures of (less serious) crime, the two variables exhibit relatively weak coefficients regardless of whether the sample is strictly juveniles or also contains adults, including the elderly. However, although there does not appear to be any two-way interactions involving age and either race or sex, one study does find a three-way interaction, at least when official measures of crime are used. Consequently, Model 2 assigns an asterisk next to the interaction term for age, race, and sex to designate tentative support. But how strong this interaction effect is, and whether it also occurs for less serious crimes and for other minority groups than Native Canadians remains to be determined.

Marital Status

Unfortunately, although there have been a number of investigations suggesting that divorced or single parents have little effect on either juvenile delinquency (Nye, 1958: 47; Rosen and Neilson, 1978; Hawkins and Weis, 1979: 7; Matsueda, 1982:499; Loeber and Dishion, 1983: 82, 87; but see also, Wilkinson, 1980; Canter, 1982b: 161, 164; Rankin, 1983) or subsequent adult criminality (Tittle, 1980: 154), few studies have examined the relationship between a person's own marital status and lawbreaking.

An investigation of youths (18 to 21 years old) indicates that marriage and crime are not associated (Farrington, 1979: 314). Likewise, using a sample of the general population, Tittle (1980: 124) finds that marital status has no effect on lawbreaking. Indeed, before he con-

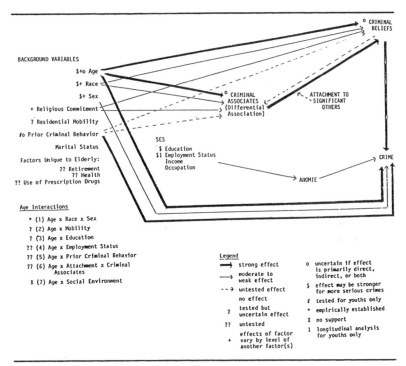

Figure 10.2 Causes and Correlates of Crime by the Elderly. Model 2

trols for age, widows appear to engage in *less* crime than married persons—a result inconsistent with the argument that widowhood places a special burden on the elderly conducive to lawbreaking.

Moreover, when Tittle tests the age-crime relation by categories of marital status (1980: 92), he reports reasonably consistent gammas (ranging from − .43 to − .63) for each category. Given these coefficients, it seems unlikely that an explicit test for an interaction between age and marital status would be statistically significant and, if significant, that the added explained variance would be substantial.

Applying the Findings for Marital Status to Model 2

Though the evidence is based on only two studies, there is little support for the proposition that the effects of marital status vary by age categories. Marital status appears to have no effect on crime for any age group, including the elderly, and Model 2 so reflects these findings.

Religious Commitment

Stark et al. (1982) have reviewed research on *juvenile* populations indicating an interaction between community and individual religiousness in their effect on crime. In communities that are highly religious, variations in the religious commitment of individuals have a substantial effect on crime. But in highly secularized communities, an individual's religious convictions have essentially no influence on lawbreaking (but see also Tittle and Welch, 1983).

However, a subsequent study of the effects of religiousness on delinquency in a religious community suggests that the gamma coefficients Stark et al. cite in support of a strong effect ($-.30$ to $-.48$) are misleading. Whereas Elifson et al. (1983: 519) obtain a zero-order gamma coefficient of $-.31$, they also report a pearson r of $-.14$, indicating a relatively weak association. Furthermore, their multivariate analysis indicates that whatever effect religiousness has on crime is probably indirect: Social integration factors appear to serve as intervening variables.

Based on a sample of the general population, Tittle (1980: 148) finds an average gamma for religious participation of $-.21$. Interestingly, the mean gamma Tittle reports represents a value intermediate to that found for youths in religious versus nonreligious areas of the country. Significantly, Tittle's sample of a broad range of age groups is drawn from a mixture of "churched" and "unchurched" regions of the United States (specifically, New Jersey, Iowa, and Oregon). Thus his results would appear consistent with the findings of research on teenagers. Furthermore, Tittle (1980: 92) finds fairly consistent gamma coefficients ($-.47$ to $-.57$) for the age-crime correlation within various categories of religious denominations, which he indicates are strongly associated with religious commitment. Therefore, there appears to be no basis for assuming that the effects of religious commitment vary by age category.

Applying the Findings for Religious Commitment to Model 2

The evidence suggests that religiousness has no effect on crime in secular communities, and has a weak to modest influence on lawbreaking in religious communities. Furthermore, this effect appears consistent across different age groups. That is, the influence of religiosity on lawbreaking appears to be approximately the same for the elderly as for younger age groups.

Residential Mobility

The findings for research on teenage populations are not consistent. Some studies show the expected positive association between mobility and illegal behavior (Reiss, 1951; Nye, 1958; Wolfgang et al., 1972: 275-279; see also Guttentag, 1968: 113); other research indicates that migrant youths are not more criminal than native adolescents and, in some instances, are possibly even less inclined to violate the law (Savitz, 1960; Simpson and Van Arsdol, 1967).

In an attempt to reconcile the discrepant results, Kornhauser (1978: 109-110) argues that residential mobility increases crime when the migration is within or between metropolitan areas, and decreases illegal behavior when moves are from rural to urban areas. Additionally, Wolfgang et al. (1972: 279) indicate that the positive (direct) effect of interurban moves is modest. Number of *intraurban moves* explains approximately 5 percent of the variation in crimes committed, controlling for race, highest grade completed, and income.

Like the results of studies of youthful populations, research based on samples of the *general population* finds inconsistent mobility effects. Green (1970) indicates that southern migrants to a small northern town are less law abiding than the natives; Crain and Weisman (1972) find southern migrants to northern metropolitan areas are more law abiding than the natives; and Kinman and Lee (1966) show contrasting effects contingent on race: Whites born out of the state of Pennsylvania (in the South or otherwise) are more criminal than those born in state; among blacks the reverse is true. None of the studies report effect size indicators.

Finally, Tittle (1980: 140) claims to have found a "strong" positive association between mobility (number of counties lived in during the past 10 years) and crime, but only among young adults, and in a few instances youths—suggesting the possibility (apparently untested) of an age by mobility interaction. However, he does not report the strength of the association by age groups (mean gamma across age and crime categories = .31). Furthermore, it is uncertain whether his measure of mobility is primarily capturing intra- and interurban moves or rural-urban moves, though it would seem likely that the former type would predominate.

Applying the Findings for Mobility to Model 2

Given the inconsistency of results, it is difficult to apply the empirical findings for mobility to a causal model. There is, however, at least some indication of a weak to moderate positive association with crime in those studies of teenagers in which the mobility variable predominantly measures moves within and between urban areas rather than migration from rural to urban regions. (The effect of rural migration to urban areas is too uncertain to attempt even a tentative conclusion regarding its direction and strength.) However, very limited evidence would suggest that the effect of inter- and intramobility, however modest for younger persons, does not occur for elderly and middle-age persons. Consequently, Model 2 shows no path between mobility and crime by the elderly but places a "?" next to the mobility factor to indicate the uncertainty of the evidence supporting this conclusion. Likewise, Model 2 also assigns a "?" to the age of mobility interaction term to indicate its uncertain status.

Prior Criminal Behavior

Prior illegal activities are a strong predictor of current illegal behavior (see Bachman et al., 1978; Blumstein and Graddy, 1981-82; Minor and Harry, 1982; Paternoster et al., 1983a; McCarthy and Hoge, 1984; Thornberry and Christenson, 1984; Elliott et al., 1985: 109-118). (See also Loeber, 1982, and Loeber and Dishion, 1983: 78-81, for evidence that childhood antisocial behavior also has a strong association with subsequent criminality.) For example, Paternoster et al. (1983) report a standardized regression coefficient of .38, which is among the *lowest* estimates that researchers have found, regardless of type and number of control variables used. However, none of the empirical research on prior criminal behavior focuses on other than youthful populations.

Additionally, Goetting (1983: 292) reviews evidence indicating a dichotomy between first-time and multiply incarcerated elderly prisoners: The former are more likely to be violent offenders, and the latter, property offenders. This finding suggests, then, that a distinction should be made between violent and property crimes in predicting the strength of the relationship between previous and current crime, at least among elderly populations.

Applying the Findings for Prior Criminal Behavior to Model 2

Research has focused exclusively on teenagers, thus we can only assume that the strong effects indicated for prior crime apply equally well to older populations. Our uncertainty in this regard results in Model 2's designation of the interaction between age and prior illegal behavior as untested.

Other background variables

Elder-specific theories suggest that retirement, health, and use of prescription drugs should become more important determinants of crime as persons grow old. These factors "unique to the elderly" remain untested, however. Model 2 therefore assigns them untested status.

Socioeconomic Status

Analysis of Youthful Populations

There are a large number of sociological studies that examine the relationship between socioeconomic factors and crime committed by youths. These studies typically use no control variables (with the frequent exception of race and sex). They are concerned with establishing whether a *zero-order* relationship between socioeconomic status and crime even exists, rather than with whether the effect is direct or indirect (through social integration factors). Contrary to the predictions of blocked opportunities and rational choice theory, these studies generally do not find substantial negative correlations (Tittle et al., 1978; Johnson, 1979; 19, 99-100, 1980; Hindelang et al., 1981: 185-187; Wiatrowski et al., 1981; Matsueda, 1982; Thornberry and Farnworth, 1982: 506; Loeber and Dishion, 1983: 82).

The conclusion that there is at best only a weak SES-crime correlation is not, however, without controversy (see, Clelland and Carter, 1980; Elliott and Ageton, 1980; Braithwaite, 1981; Kleck, 1982; Elliot and Huizinga, 1983; Nettler, 1985; but see also the rebuttals by Hirschi et al., 1982; Tittle et al., 1982; Tittle, 1985). But when critics of the "no substantial effect" conclusion cite empirical evidence showing an SES-crime relation, they consistently fail to report estimates of the *magnitude* of the SES effect. For example, Elliott and Huizinga (1983; see also Elliot and Ageton, 1980) obtain a statistically significant SES effect when they use measures of self-reported delinquency that are sensitive to frequency and seriousness. But, as noted above, we are left without an estimate of strength. Where researchers (or reviewers) do provide such estimates, the relationship is nearly always weak and, indeed, parallels that indicated for studies of official arrests (see especially, Hindelang et al, 1981: 185-197).

However, two recent studies of young adults (Thornberry and Farnworth, 1982; Thornberry and Christenson, 1984) indicate that prior research has failed to find an SES-crime relation for youthful populations because investigations have focused on the status of an individual's *parents* rather than *self*. Furthermore, a careful analysis of the results of Thornberry and Farnworth (1982) suggests that the SES-crime relation is much stronger when SES is measured by *education* rather than by income, occupation, or unemployment, and that this education effect is much more evident for *violent* crimes committed by *blacks*. Additionally, a follow-up study (Thornberry and Christenson, 1984) indicates that a substantial unemployment effect becomes apparent when using longitudinal rather than cross-sectional analyses, and that this effect is again strongest for blacks.

Analysis of the General Population

Unlike research on young adults, studies based on samples of the general population (Stark and McEvoy, 1970; Meier and Johnson, 1977; Minor, 1977; Tittle and Villemez, 1977; Tittle, 1980; Grasmick et al., 1983) find little evidence of a negative correlation between SES and crime, even when social status is measured by education level or unemployment status.

The absence of an effect for unemployment is not surprising, given that the studies of the general population all use cross-sectional data. However, the failure to obtain an effect for education is not as easily dismissed. Several studies have considered the possibility (at least indirectly) that the education-crime relation might vary by race (black/white) or type of crime (property/violent). But Stark and McEvoy (1970) find little association between education and violent crime (punched, kicked, threatened, or cut with a knife). And Tittle (1980) indicates there is a statistically significant *positive* correlation (gamma = .54) between SES (a composite index of income, occupation, and education) and violent crime (assault) by blacks.

An interaction effect between education and age is another possible explanation for the discrepancy in findings between studies of young adults and more general samples of the population. However, the results Tittle (1980: 92; see also Tittle and Villemez, 1977: 488-489) obtains would seem to indicate that the age-crime association does not vary widely when analyzed within low, medium, and high categories of SES (but see also Greenberg, 1985: 8, for an alternative interpretation of these results). However, because Tittle uses a composite measure of SES rather than one specific to education, the possibility remains that the evidence against an interaction effect is insensitive to distinctions in how SES is measured.

Then, too, Grasmick et al. (1983) argue that the discrepancy in findings occurs as a consequence of the more serious crimes analyzed in research on young adults as compared to the mostly trivial illegal behaviors considered in studies of the general population. In other words, a substantial negative correlation between SES and crime will only occur for the most serious types of lawbreaking.

In sum, extrapolating from the above findings leads to the conclusion that SES has little effect on the illegal behavior of the elderly, at least for relatively minor offenses.

Applying the Findings for SES to Model 2

Studies of young adults find that an individual's own SES has a stronger negative effect on illegal behavior than does SES of the individual's parents. The negative correlation between education and violent crimes committed by blacks is particularly strong. And longitudinal research on young adults suggests that unemployment also has a substantial influence on lawbreaking. Conversely, studies of the general population find little support for a negative SES-crime relation. The failure to obtain unemployment effects may occur as a consequence of the latter studies' exclusive use of cross-sectional data. The most plausible explanations for the lack of an education-crime relation point to an interaction effect with age (education influences older persons less than young adults), or alternatively, to the failure of studies of the general population to consider other than nonserious offenses.

Model 2 represents the absence of a zero-order relation between various indices of social class and general measures of crime by showing no paths between SES and lawbreaking by the elderly except for an indirect path through anomie. The latter effect is based on results described in the section to follow.

Anomie

Frustration, low self-worth, alienation, normlessness, and the strain between aspirations and expectations are all variations on a psychological state that Merton (1968) calls "anomie," also identified as "the discrepancy between what ought to be and what is" (Pope and Ferguson, 1982:53). From the perspective of theories based on blocked opportunities, anomie is an intervening variable between SES and crime. Limited research would seem to suggest, however, that its link to illegal behavior is not substantial.

Elliott et al. (1979: 7-8), Johnson (1979: 24-25), Bernard (1984), and Greenberg (1985: 16) review evidence indicating that the discrepancy between teenagers' aspirations and expectations for the future (i.e., perception of blocked opportunities) is related to delinquency. However, none of the reviews report measures of magnitude of effect. Where studies of youthful populations do provide estimates of effect size, the coefficients indicate a nonexistent to modest relationship (Aultman, 1979, tabs. 2 and 4; Johnson, 1979: 105-108, 115-116; Cernkovich, 1978: 348; Menard and Morse, 1984: 1373; Elliott et al., 1985: 21-30, 70-89, 109-118). Furthermore, these coefficients do not increase in size when using self-report measures that are sensitive to more serious crime (see Menard and Morse, 1984: 1368; Elliott et al., 1985: 109-118).

Likewise, Aultman (1979: tabs. 2 and 4) finds alienation (i.e., blaming the system for the discrepancy between goals and achievement) to have a weak to modest association with lawbreaking. Furthermore, his results also suggest that self-esteem (i.e., identifying the self as the source of failure to attain goals) has negligible effects on delinquency (see also McCarthy and Hoge, 1984).

All of the above studies are based on juvenile populations. However, the results of Tittle (1977), using a sample of the general population, indicate the weak to modest findings for teenagers are also applicable to older age groups. For neither of two measures of Merton's anomie factor—"alienation" and "relative deprivation"—is there a regression coefficient greater than $r = .07$, regardless of which of nine types of deviant and illegal behavior are analyzed. Unfortunately, there appears to be some multicollinearity among the control variables considered. Indeed, depending on the type of rule-breaking behavior examined, the control variables shared (as opposed to unique) explained variance ranges from 46 to 78 percent. Thus caution must be exercised in interpreting Tittle's results.

In addition to the evidence against a strong link between anomie and crime, the path from SES and anomie is also of doubtful strength. Johnson (1979: 21-24) reviews empirical evidence for adolescent populations suggesting only a "moderate" relationship (though he reports no effect size indicators). And his own study finds standardized regression coefficients of $-.13$ and lower (pp. 105, 107). Conversely, Cernkovich (1978: 348) reports a considerably stronger standardized regression coefficient of $-.27$.

Furthermore, among a sample of the general population, Richards and Tittle (1982: 340) find a weak SES-anomie correlation of $r = -.13$. Likewise, based on a sample of persons aged 40 and over, Pope and Ferguson (1982) report low correlations between SES indices and multi-item anomie scale ($r = -.15$ for education, and $-.16$ for a combined scale of education, occupation, and income).

Applying the Findings for Anomie to Model 2

Anomie appears to have only a weak to modest relationship with lawbreaking. And there is little indication that anomie interacts with age in its effect on crime. Likewise, the influence of SES is apparently insubstantial, and does not seem to vary by age group. Thus Model 2 shows the path from SES to anomie and from anomie to illegal behavior as displaying relatively weak effects for the elderly.

Criminal Associates

Criminal friends is one of the consistently strongest correlates of juvenile delinquency (Hindelang et al., 1981: 204-206; Weis et al., 1979; Elliott et al., 1985: 71-84). Hindelang et al. (1981), for example, found gammas in their Seattle study of .45 to .88 for self report and official measures of crime, analyzed by each of four race-sex combinations. And other research generally finds standardized regression coefficients of .30 and higher, either measured as a direct effect or a combination of direct and indirect effects (see Matsueda, 1982: 500; Johnson, 1979: 111, 117; Strickland, 1982: 165; Menard and Morse, 1984: 1372; Elliott et al., 1985: 109-118).

In contrast to the substantial association between criminal friends and delinquency found among samples of teenagers, Tittle (1977: 590) indicates a weak direct effect among a more representative sample of the general population. For none of nine deviance categories is he able to report a standardized regression coefficient for deviant friends (differential association) that is more than negligible (mean value = .12). It would seem, however, that his study includes so many closely related independent variables that, as noted earlier, he may be experiencing a multicollinearity problem.

Indeed, in another study of the general adult population, Dull (1983) controls *only* for demographic factors. He finds a substantial correlation between friends' drug use and one's own use consistent with research on juveniles (r varies from .36 to .49, depending on drug). In contrast, Tittle reports a regression coefficient of only .16 for friend's use-respondent's use of marijuana.

Furthermore, in yet another study of marijuana use among the general population, Meier and Johnson (1977) include a wide assortment of control variables similar to those in the Tittle investigation. But unlike Tittle they find a very strong coefficient for criminal associates (r = .78).

The weight of evidence would suggest, then, that criminal associates have a strong effect on the illegal behavior of older as well as younger populations. The contradictory findings of Tittle are most likely an artifact of multicollinear data that tend to produce weak and unstable estimates of effect size.

Questions arise, however, concerning the assumption that the predominant causal order is from criminal friends to lawbreaking rather than vice versa (see Johnson, 1979: 66-67; Conger, 1980: 138-139; Lanza-Kaduce et al., 1982: 172; Stafford and Ekland-Olson, 1982; Elliott et al., 1985: 85-89).

Equally dubious are the arguments (see Johnson, 1979: 63-65, 120-121; Matsueda, 1982: 492) that having criminal associates leads to criminal beliefs rather than vice versa. Most studies assume the former causal sequence, and find a strong association between the two variables (see Johnson, 1979: 99; Matsueda, 1982: 499; Strickland, 1982: 165).

The assumption that criminal associates determine beliefs allows criminal associates to have an indirect effect on lawbreaking through criminal beliefs. The relative strength of the direct and indirect effects remain in doubt, however. Most research finds that criminal associates has a much stronger direct than indirect effect (Johnson, 1979: 117; Strickland, 1982: 165). But using a multiple-indicators technique (LISREL) that models the measurement error in crime and predictor variables, Matsueda (1982) finds that the effect of criminal associates on lawbreaking is entirely indirect through the intervening variable of criminal beliefs.

Applying the Findings for Criminal Associates to Model 2

The majority of evidence would suggest that criminal associates should have a substantial influence on the illegal behavior of the elderly and, further, that age and type of friends do not interact in their effect on crime.

Attachment to Significant Others

Research consistently finds that *parental attachment,* where parents are assumed to be conventional, restricts delinquency (Weis et al., 1979; Johnson, 1979: 20; Hawkins and Weis, 1980; Loeber and Dishion, 1983: 82-90). However, the strength of the effect is questionable. Most researchers find relatively weak associations (Johnson, 1979: 117; Matsueda, 1982: 499; Paternoster et al., 1983a: 474; Menard and Morse, 1984: 1373-1374; Elliott et al., 1985: 109-118; but see also Liska and Reed, 1985; Wiatrowski et al., 1981: 537). Then, too, there is evidence to suggest that extending measures of attachment to encompass more microscopic analyses of parent-child interactions would result in a better prediction of delinquency (see Patterson, 1980; Loeber et al., 1984; Patterson & Dishion, 1984).

Research on *peer attachment* among juveniles shows highly inconsistent results. Some studies finding a positive correlation with delinquency, others a negative association, and still others no relation (Johnson, 1979: 26; see also Paternoster et al., 1983a: 474; Wiatrowski et al., 1981: 537). These results are hardly surprising, given that researchers routinely ignore whether the peer attachment is to conventional or criminal friends.

In a design that improves on past research, Johnson (1979: 110) does include an interaction term for "delinquent associates" by "susceptibility to peer influence." It only adds 2 percent to the explained variance. However, Johnson's susceptibility factor ("Are you ever talked into doing things by your friends that you really don't want to do?") would seem conceptually distant from more traditional measures of peer attachment (e.g., "Would you like to be the kind of person your best friends are?"). Thus, he has not provided a fair test of the interaction proposition.

Furthermore, Elliott et al. (1979: 16; 1985: 50-54) review preliminary evidence in support of the interaction proposition. But explicit tests including explained variance estimates are lacking.

Unfortunately, research has not examined the influence of attachment on illegal behavior among samples of the *general population*. Thus it is difficult to know how well the results of studies of attachment effects among juveniles generalize to the elderly. Clearly, however, any analysis of adults would need be sensitive to the potential interaction between attachment and the criminal (or conventional) behavior of the person to whom the aged are attached—spouse, siblings, friends, parents (where still living), and offspring.

Applying the Findings for Attachment to Model 2

Attachment to significant others (particularly peer attachment) has not proven to be a very strong correlate of juvenile delinquency, and thus assumedly would also not be a very good predictor of crime committed by the elderly. Researchers neglect, however, to consider whether the attachment is to law-abiding or law-violating others. Consequently, Model 2 represents the hypothesized interaction between attachment and criminal associates, and the three-way interaction involving age, attachment, and criminal associates, as untested.

Criminal Beliefs

There is considerable evidence of a relation between criminal values and juvenile lawbreaking (Johnson, 1979: 29-30, 62; Elliott et al., 1985: 43-48). Zero order r's are mostly substantial, generally ranging from .25 to .50 (Cernkovich, 1978: 344; Akers et al., 1979: 643, 644; Krohn and Massey, 1980: 535; Wiatrowski et al., 1981: 528; Paternoster et al., 1983a: 470; Bishop, 1984: 413). But adding a large number of control variables results in estimates of a modest to weak effect (Johnson 1979: 117; Strickland, 1982: 165; Krohn and Massey, 1980: 537; Wiatrowski et al., 1981: 537; Paternoster et al., 1983a: 472; Elliott et al., 1985: 109-118).

On the other hand, Matsueda (1982) also includes numerous controls in his study but finds very strong effects for criminal beliefs (standardized regression coefficient = .68). Unlike the other studies cited above, however, Matsueda models the measurement error in his set of variables. Thus he provides estimates of their effects corrected for unreliability. In contrast to previous research, Matsueda concludes that various background factors, attachment to others, and criminal friends have no direct effects on crime; their influence is entirely indirect through the intervening variable of criminal beliefs.

Matsueda's cross-sectional design unfortunately does not allow a test for the potential spurious effects created by reverse causal order. One longitudinal study claims to have preliminary evidence of a stronger effect for crime on beliefs than beliefs on crime (Paternoster et al., 1983a; 476). But the absence of a measure for criminal beliefs at time 2 (and preferably also at time 3) render dubious the causal inferences Paternoster and his associates make (see Minor and Harry, 1982: 210; but see also Paternoster et al., 1983a: 467, fn. 12).

Do estimates of the criminal beliefs-crime relation for the general population parallel those results indicated for younger age groups? The findings of two studies would suggest there are similar effects across the age range. Grasmick et al. (1983) analyze the influence of criminal beliefs on illegal behavior, controlling only for SES. Like studies that report zero-order correlations for youthful populations, Grasmick et al. (1983) indicate a substantial effect ($r = .38$). Similarly, Minor (1977: 128) finds a zero-order coefficient of .48.

Furthermore, Tittle (1977) reports results consistent with youthful studies using numerous controls. His study includes two measures of criminal beliefs: "moral commitment" (ratings of how morally wrong were each of nine deviant acts listed), and "legitimacy" (agreement/disagreement about whether there should be a law against a particular deviant behavior). He finds that neither measure has much of an effect when a large number of controls for other correlates of crime are included (mean standardized regression coefficient $= -.16$ for "moral commitment" and $-.06$ for "legitimacy").

Applying the Findings for Criminal Beliefs to Model 2

Where research on youthful or older age groups has used a large number of controls, it generally does not indicate a strong effect for criminal beliefs. However, on the basis of Matsueda's findings of a much stronger effect when measurement error is considered, Model 2 indicates that beliefs do have a strong influence on crime committed by the elderly, though the possibility remains that a large portion of this apparent effect is due to a reverse causal order. Furthermore, Model 2 does not include an interaction term for age by criminal beliefs. The consistent findings of research across different age groups argues against the probability of such an effect.

Summary and Conclusions

As a consequence of subjecting theory to empirical scrutiny, Model 2 displays results different from those predicted. Age, prior criminal behavior, criminal associates, and criminal beliefs all display the expected strong relationship with crime by the elderly, though the effect of criminal associates apparently occurs only indirectly through the intervening variable of beliefs. Additionally, religiousness indicates a relationship with lawbreaking by older persons but the effect is relatively weak and seems to occur primarily in religious communities. Likewise, the influence of sex, race, and anomie on illegal behavior is apparently not strong, at least for less serious crimes.

Furthermore, a number of factors hypothesized to influence crime by the elderly seemingly do not. These variables include marital status, income, occupation, and, less certainly, residential mobility, education, and unemployment. There is evidence to suggest, however, that the latter two variables might display an effect if more serious crimes were analyzed (preferably by separate categories of race) and, in the case of unemployment, if longitudinal data were used. Then, too, the absence of an effect for education may simply reflect an interaction with age: Education may influence lawbreaking by young adults but not older persons. (Longitudinal analysis of the general population will be required before speculations on unemployment by age interactions are worthy of consideration.) Additionally, if residential mobility has an effect on lawbreaking, limited evidence suggests it may be stronger for youths than the elderly.

Other factors and pathways to crime represented in Model 2 remain essentially untested. Attachment to significant others (particularly friends) does not seem to have much influence on law violations of adolescents; however, researchers have failed to consider the variable's influence on older populations and its potential interaction with criminal friends. Also untested is the potential path from criminal beliefs to criminal associates, which, if present, would change estimates of the influence of significant others on moral commitment and lawbreaking. Furthermore, the absence of empirical tests leaves unresolved the question of whether prior crime influences current criminal associates and beliefs. If such an effect occurs, then researcher's estimates of the influence of the latter two variables on current crime are biased.

Among those factors singled out as unique to the elderly, researchers have found no evidence of an effect for widowhood, and have not tested the influence of retirement, health, and prescription drugs. Nor have researchers analyzed the potential four-way interaction of retirement by widowhood by health by mobility. However, given the evidence that widowhood and mobility have no relation to lawbreaking by the elderly, it seems unlikely that there would be a nonadditive effect when the elderly fall into the combined category of widowhood, high mobility, poor health, and retirement.

Indeed, Model 2 suggests that few variables interact with age in their effect on illegal behavior. That is, factors that effect crime by the youthful would appear to have a similar influence on law violations by the elderly. The only reasonably well supported interaction with age occurs in combination with sex and race. As Hagan predicted, the influence of sex on illegal behavior is less for minority groups (Canadian Native Americans) than for whites, and this discrepancy between ethnic groups becomes larger with age. Whether this three-way interaction occurs in other countries with different minority groups is unknown, but bears study. Likewise, it would be of interest to establish through explicit tests how substantial the interaction effect is, and if it also occurs for less serious crimes.

Given the evidence that the causes and correlates of crime are mostly similar for younger and older age groups, the hypothesis that the elderly would be less sensitive than younger persons to social and cultural factors is rejected. Conversely, the general absence of interactions involving age would seem to confirm the hypothesis of Hirschi and Gottfredson suggesting that factors predicting illegal behavior at one age will also predict lawbreaking at other ages.

One must exercise caution, however, in claiming that an empirical review of the literature demonstrates few interactions with age. This conclusion is based on a comparison of the results of studies of youthful populations with investigations involving the general population. In almost no instances is the effect of a suspected crime correlate given an explicit test for a possible interaction with elderly versus younger age groups. Future research on crime by the elderly should therefore include samples of the general population and explicit significance tests for interactions broken down by the appropriate age categories (a methodology that would also overcome the problems of comparing standardized coefficients across different age groups).

Future studies of law violations by the elderly might also include an analysis of several factors left out of the current review of the literature. Space did not allow consideration of the effects of informal, formal and community deterrence and criminal subcultures. The latter two variables involve ecological phenomena (see Kornhauser, 1978; Crutchfield et al., 1982; Sampson, 1983, 1985a, 1985b) that most past research has unfortunately examined using aggregate crime data. Studies will need to analyze individual-level crime data before any firm conclusions can be reached concerning the effects of community deterrence and criminal subcultures.

In contrast, because a large number of investigations of formal and informal deterrence have used individual crime data, the influence of these two factors is more firmly established. Although longitudinal research on youthful populations indicates only weak or nonexistent effects for the two variables (see Minor and Harry, 1982; Salzman et al., 1982; Paternoster et al., 1983a, 1983b; Bishop, 1984), we still do not know how well the results apply to the elderly. Limited research would indicate, however, that older persons are similar to youthful age groups in their response to deterrent factors (see Tittle, 1980: 296-299).

Future investigations will also require the greater use of longitudinal designs that incorporate tests for bidirectional causality. Both theory and empirical findings suggest a reciprocal causal relationship between crime and its predictors (see Model 2, Figure 10.2 in this chapter; Minor and Harry, 1982; Salzman et al., 1982; Paternoster et al., 1983a,b; Thornberry and Christenson, 1984; Greenberg, 1985: 2-5; Liska and Reed, 1985). Cross-sectional designs are simply inadequate to control for the spurious effects introduced by a nonrecursive causal order (Heise, 1970).

Futhermore, where possible, the longitudinal designs should include a multiple-indicators approach in which measurement error is explicitly modeled. Matsueda (1982) has demonstrated that modeling measurement error leads to substantively different conclusions than those found in research that treats indicators as if they were perfect measures of underlying concepts.

Additionally, because of the relative scarcity of lawbreaking committed by older persons, studies that focus on the elderly will have to use large sample sizes. Even among more youthful populations, reliable measurement of the most serious crimes requires samples in excess of the 1,500 that McDermott and Hindelang (1981: 5) describe as the norm for self-report crime surveys. For this younger age group,

Hindelang et al. (1979) suggest it may be necessary to use sample sizes as large as those employed in the census bureau victimization surveys (over 130,000). But of course a survey this large is not practical. Alternatively, one might oversample persons from the lower strata, particularly blacks. Or one might include a relatively large number of persons from prison populations and subsequently weight them according to their proportional representation in the general population. Clearly, however, using reasonable sample sizes, no matter how stratified, one is not likely to reliably measure the most serious crimes committed by the elderly.

As a final comment, the causal model developed in this chapter should be placed in a broader context. The model is easily adapted to analyze the nonelderly as well as the elderly. As presented here, it includes some variables and interaction terms specific to older persons, but the basic structure is one suitable for all age categories. Indeed, the model is broadly inclusive of almost all the major concepts of the dominant theories of crime. Furthermore, the model's explanatory framework would seem suitable for analyzing behavior in addition to lawbreaking. Where beliefs, attachments, and associations with others are critical to the development of a problem behavior—such as mental health, suicide,and possibly even life satisfaction—then Model 2 should have relevance.

References

ABRAMS, A. (1984) "Foreward," pp. xi-xviii in E. Newman et al. (eds.) Elderly Criminals. Cambridge: Oelgeschlager, Gunn and Hain.

AGETON, S. (1983) "The dynamics of female delinquency, 1976-1980." Criminology 21: 555-584.

AKERS, R. (1977) Deviant Behavior: A Social Learning Approach. Belmont, CA: Wadsworth.

AKERS, R., M. KROHN, L. LANZA-KADUCE, and M. RADOSEVICH (1979) "Social learning and deviant behavior: a specific test of a general theory." American Sociological Review 44: 636-655.

ALEXANDER, J. and B. PARSONS (1973) "Short-term behavioral intervention with delinquent families: impact on family process and recidivism." Journal of Abnormal Psychology 81: 219-225.

AMIR, M. and S. BERGMAN (1975) "Crime among the aged in Israel." (unpublished)

AULTMAN, M. (1979) "Delinquency causation: a typological comparison of path models." Journal of Criminal Law and Criminology 70: 152-163.

AXENROTH, J. (1983) "Social class and delinquency in cross-cultural perspective." Journal of Research in Crime and Delinquency 20: 164-182.

BACHMAN, G., P. O'MALLEY, and J. JOHNSTON (1978) Youth in Transition, Volume VI. Adolescence to Adulthood: Change and Stability in the Lives of Young Men. Ann Arbor: University of Michigan, Institute for Social Research.

BANDURA, A. (1969) Principles of Behavior Modification. New York: Holt, Rinehart & Winston.

BANDURA, A. (1977) Social Learning Theory. Englewood Cliffs, NJ: Prentice-Hall.

BECKER, G. (1968) "Crime and punishment: an economic approach." Journal of Political Economy 76: 169-217.

BERGMAN, S. and M. AMIR (1973) "Crime and delinquency among the aged in Israel." Geriatrics: 149-157.

BERNARD, T. (1984) "Control criticisms of strain theories: an assessment of theoretical and empirical adequacy." Journal of Research in Crime and Delinquency 21: 353-372.

BERRY, B. and J. KASARDA (1977) Contemporary Urban Ecology. New York: Macmillan.

BIDERMAN, A. and A. REISS (1967) "On exploring the 'dark figure' of crime." The Annals of the American Academy of Political and Social Science 374: 1-15.

BISHOP, D. (1984) "Legal and extralegal barriers to delinquency." Criminology 22: 403-419.

BLACK, D. (1970) "Production of crime rates." American Sociological Review 35: 733-748.

BLALOCK, H. (1967) "Causal inferences, closed populations, and measures of association." American Political Science Review 61: 130-136.

BLALOCK, H. (1972) Social Statistics. New York: McGraw-Hill.

BLUMSTEIN, A. and E. GRADDY (1981-82) "Prevalence and recidivism in index arrests: a feedback model." Law and Society Review 16: 265-290.

BRAITHWAITE, J. (1981) "The myth of social class and criminality reconsidered." American Sociological Review 46: 36-57.

BRANTINGHAM, P. and P. BRANTINGHAM (1981) "Notes on the geometry of crime," in P. Brantingham and P. Brantingham (eds.) Environmental Criminology. Newbury Park, CA: Sage.

BROWN, B. and C. CHIANG (1983) "Drug and alcohol abuse among the elderly: is being alone the key?" International Journal of Aging and Human Development 18: 1-12.

BROWN, E., T. FLANAGAN, and M. McLEOD (1983) Sourcebook: Criminal Justice Statistics. U.S. Department of Justice. Bureau of Justice Statistics.

BURNETT, C. and S. ORTEGA (1984) "Elderly offenders: a descriptive analysis," pp. 17-40 in W. Wilbanks and P. Kim (eds.) Elderly Criminals. New York: University Press of America.

CANTER, R. (1982a) "Sex differences in self-reporting delinquency." Criminology 20: 373-393.

CANTER, R. (1982b) "Family correlates of male and female delinquency." Criminology 20: 149-167.

CERNKOVICH, S. (1978) "Evaluating two models of delinquency causation: structural theory and control theory." Criminology 16: 335-352.

CHILTON, R. and J. GALVIN (1985) "Race, crime, and criminal justice." Crime and Delinquency 31: 3-14.

CLARK, J. and E. WENNINGER (1962) "Socio-economic class and area as correlates of illegal behavior among juveniles." American Sociological Review 27: 826-834.

CLELLAND, D. and J. CARTER (1980) "The new myth of class and crime." Criminology 18: 319-336.

CLINE, H. (1980) "Criminal behavior over the life span," in O. Brim and J. Kagan (eds.) Constancy and Change in Human Development. Cambridge, MA: Harvard University Press.

CLOWARD, R. and L. OHLIN (1960) Delinquency and Opportunity. New York: Free Press.

COHEN, A. (1955) Delinquent Boys: The Culture of the Gang. New York: Free Press.

COHEN, A. (1983) "Comparing regression coefficients across subsamples: a study of the statistical test." Sociological Methods and Research 12: 77-94.

COHEN, L. and K. LAND (1984) "Discrepancies between crime reports and crime surveys." Criminology 22: 499-530.

CONGER, R. (1980) "Juvenile delinquency: behavior restraint or behavior facilitation?" pp. 131-142 in T. Hirschi and M. Gottfredson (eds.), Understanding Crime: Current Theory and Research. Newbury Park, CA: Sage.

COSTNER, H. (1965) "Criteria for measures of association." American Sociology Review 30: 341-353.

CRAIN, R. and C. WEISMAN (1972) Discrimination, Personality, and Achievement: A Survey of Northern Blacks. New York: Seminar Press.

CRESSEY, D. (1966) "Crime." In R. Merton and R. Nesbet (eds.) Contemporary Social Problems. New York: Harcourt Brace and World.

CRUTCHFIELD, R., M. GEERKEN, and W. GOVE (1982) "Crime rate and social integration." Criminology 20: 467-478.

CURRAN, D. (1983) "Judicial discretion and defendant sex." Criminology 21: 41-58.

DANSER, K. and J. LAUB (1981) Juvenile Criminal Behavior and Its Relation to Economic Conditions. Monograph 4. National Institute for Juvenile Justice and Delinquency Prevention. Washington, DC: Government Printing Office.

DULL, R. (1983) "Friends' use and adult drug and drinking behavior: a further test of differential association theory." The Journal of Criminal Law and Criminology 74: 1608-1619.

EHRLICH, I. (1973) "Participation in illegitimate activities: a theoretical and empirical investigation." Journal of Political Economy 81: 521-565.

EISENSTEIN J. and H. JACOB (1977) Felony Justice: An Organizational Analysis of Criminal Courts. Boston: Little, Brown.

ELIFSON, K., D. PETERSEN, and C. HADAWAY (1983) "Religiosity and delinquency." Criminology 21: 505-527.

ELLIOTT, D. (1982) "Review essay: measuring delinquency." Criminology 20: 527-537.

ELLIOTT, D. and S. AGETON (1980) "Reconciling race and class differences in self-reported and official estimates of delinquency." American Sociological Review 45: 95-110.

ELLIOTT, D. and D. HUIZINGA (1983) "Social class and delinquent behavior in a national youth panel." Criminology 21: 149-177.

ELLIOTT, D. and H. VOSS (1974) Delinquency and Dropout. Lexington, MA: D.C. Heath.

ELLIOTT, D., S. AGETON, and R. CANTER (1979) "An integrated theoretical perspective on delinquent behavior." Journal of Research in Crime and Delinquency 16: 3-27.

ELLIOTT, D., D. HUIZINGA, and S. AGETON (1985) Explaining Delinquency and Drug Use. Newbury Park, CA: Sage.

ENNIS, P. (1967) Criminal Victimization in the United States: A Report of a National Survey. The President's Commission on Law Enforcement and Administration of Justice. Washington, DC: Government Printing Office.

FARNWORTH, M. (1984) "Male-female differences in delinquency in a minority-group sample." Research in Crime and Delinquency 21: 191-212.

FARRINGTON, D. (1979) "Longitudinal research on crime and delinquency," in N. Morris and M. Tonry (eds.) Crime and Justice: An Annual Review of Research, Vol. 1. Chicago: University of Chicago Press.

FEINBERG, G. (1984a) "Profile of the elderly shoplifter," pp. 35-50 in E. Newman et al. (eds.) Elderly Criminals. Cambridge, MA: Oelgeschlager, Gunn, and Hain.

FEINBERG, G. (1984b) "White haired offenders: an emergent social problem," pp. 83-108 in W. Wilbanks and P. Kim (eds.) Elderly Criminals. New York: University Press of America.

FLEISHER, B. (1966) The Economics of Delinquency. Chicago: Quadrangle Books.

GLUECK, S. and E. GLUECK (1940) Juvenile Delinquents Grown Up. New York: Commonwealth Fund.

GOETTING, A. (1983) "The elderly in prison: issues and perspectives." Journal of Research in Crime and Delinquency 20: 291-309.

GOLDEN, D. (1984) "Elderly offenders in jail," pp. 143-152 in E. Newman et al. (eds.) Elderly Criminals. Cambridge, MA: Oelgeschlager, Gunn and Hain.

GRASMICK, H., D. JACOBS, and C. McCOLLOM (1983) "Social class and social control: an application of deterrence theory." Social Forces 62: 359-374.

GREEN, E. (1970) "Race, social status and criminal arrest." American Sociological Review 35: 476-490.

GREENBERG, D. (1985) "Age, crime, and social explanation." American Journal of Sociology 91: 1-21.

GUTTENTAG, M. (1968) "The relationship of unemployment to crime and delinquency." Journal of Social Issues 24: 105-114.

HAGAN, J. (1974) "Extra-legal attributes and criminal sentencing: an assessment of a sociological viewpoint." Law and Society Review 8: 357-383.

HAGAN, J. (1985) "Toward a structural theory of crime, race, and gender: The Canadian case." Crime and Delinquency 31: 129-146.

HANSELL, S. and M. WIATROWSKI (1981) "Competing conceptions of delinquent peer relations," pp. 93-108 in G. Jensen (ed.) Sociology of Delinquency: Current Issues. Newbury Park, CA: Sage.

HANUSHEK, E. and J. JACKSON (1977) Statistical Methods for Social Scientists. New York: Academic Press.

HAWKINS, D. and J. WEIS (1980) The Social Development Model: An integrated Approach to Delinquency Prevention. National Institute for Juvenile Justice and Delinquency Prevention. Office of Juvenile Justice and Delinquency Prevention. U.S. Department of Justice. Washington, DC: Government Printing Office.

HEATH, (1976) Rational Choice and Social Exchange. New York: Cambridge University Press.

HEISE, D. (1970) "Causal inference from panel data," pp. 3-27 in E. Borgatta and G. Bohrnstedt (eds.) Sociological Methodology. San Francisco: Jossey-Bass.

HINDELANG, M. (1973) "Causes of delinquency: a partial replication and extension." Social Problems 20: 471-487.

HINDELANG, M. (1974) "The Uniform Crime Reports revisited." Journal of Criminal Justice 2: 1-17.

HINDELANG, M. (1976) Criminal Victimization in Eight American Cities. Cambridge, MA: Ballinger.

HINDELANG, M. (1978) "Race and involvement in common law personal crimes." American Sociological Review 43: 93-109.

HINDELANG, M. (1979) "Sex differences in criminal activity." Social Problems 27: 143-156.

HINDELANG, M. (1981) "Variations in sex-race-age-specific incidence rates of offending." American Sociological Review 46: 461-474.

HINDELANG, M. and M. McDERMOTT (1981) Juvenile Criminal Behavior: An Analysis of Rates and Victim Characteristics. Monograph 2. National Institute for Juvenile Justice and Delinquency Prevention. Washington, DC: Government Printing Office

HINDELANG, M., T. HIRSCHI, and J. WEIS (1979) "Correlates of delinquency." American Sociological Review 44: 995-1014.

HINDELANG, M., T. HIRSCHI, and J. WEIS (1981) Measuring Delinquency. Newbury Park, CA: Sage.

HIRSCHI, T. (1969) Causes of Delinquency. Berkeley: University of California Press.

HIRSCHI, T. (1983) "Crime and the family," in J. Q. Wilson (ed.) Crime and Public Policy. San Francisco: Institute for Contemporary Studies.

HIRSCHI, T. and M. GOTTFREDSON (1983) "Age and the explanation of crime." American Journal of Sociology 89: 552-584.

HIRSCHI, T. and R. STARK (1969) "Hellfire and delinquency." Social Problems 17: 202-213.

HIRSCHI, T., M. HINDELANG, and J. WEIS (1982) "Reply to 'On the use of self-report data to determine the class distribution of criminal and delinquent behavior.' " American Sociological Review 47: 433-435.

JENSEN, G. and R. EVE (1976) "Sex differences in delinquency: an examination of popular sociological explanations." Criminology 13: 427-448.

JOHNSON, R. (1979) Juvenile Delinquency and Its Origins. Cambridge, MA: Cambridge University Press.

JOHNSTONE, J. (1978) "Social class, social areas and delinquency." Sociology and Social Research 63: 49-72.

KINMAN, J. and E. LEE (1966) "Migration and crime." International Migration Digest 3: 7-14.

KLECK, G. (1982) "On the use of self-report data to determine the class distribution of criminal and delinquent behavior." American Sociological Review 47: 427-433.

KLEIN, N., J. ALEXANDER, and B. PARSONS (1977) "Impact of family systems intervention on recidivism and sibling delinquency: a model of primary prevention and program evaluation." Journal of Consulting and Clinical Psychology 45: 469-474.

KORNHAUSER, R. (1978) Social Sources of Delinquency: An Appraisal of Analytic Models. Chicago: University of Chicago Press.

KRAUT, R. (1976) "Deterrent and definitional influences on shoplifting." Social Problems 23: 358-368.

KROHN, M. and J. MASSEY (1980) "Social control and delinquent behavior: an examination of the elements of the social bond." Sociological Quarterly 21: 529-543.

KROHN, M., R. AKERS, M. RADOSEVICH, and L. LANZA-KADUCE (1980) "Social status and deviance: class context of school, social status, and delinquent behavior." Criminology 18: 303-318.

KROHN, M., J. CURRY, and S. NELSON-KILGER (1983) "Is chivalry dead? An analysis of changes in police practices of males and females." Criminology 21: 417-437.

LANZA-KADUCE, L., R. AKERS, M. KROHN, and M. RADOSEVICH (1982) "Conceptual and analytical models in testing social learning theory." American Sociological Review 47: 169-173.

LAUB, J. and M. HINDELANG (1981) Juvenile Criminal Behavior in Urban, Suburban, and Rural Areas. Monograph 3, National Institute for Juvenile Justice and Delinquency Prevention. Washington, DC: Government Printing Office.

LISKA, A. and M. REED (1985) "Ties to conventional institutions and delinquency: estimating reciprocal effects." American Sociological Review 50: 547-560.

LOEBER, R. (1982) "The stability of antisocial and delinquent child behavior: a review." Child Development 53: 1431-1446.

LOEBER, R. and T. DISHION (1983) "Early predictors of male delinquency: a review." Psychological Bulletin 94: 68-99.

LOEBER, R.,T. DISHION, and G. PATTERSON (1984) "Multiple gating: a multistage assessment procedure for identifying youths at risk for delinquency." Journal of Research in Crime and Delinquency 21: 7-32.

MALTZ, M. (1977) "Crime statistics: an historical perspective." Crime and Delinquency 23: 32-40.

MATSUEDA, R. (1982) "Testing control theory and differential association: a causal modeling approach." American Sociological Review 47: 489-504.

McCARTHY, J. and D. HOGE (1984) "The dynamics of self-esteem and delinquency." American Journal of Sociology 90: 396-410.

McCORD, J. and W. McCORD (1964) "The effects of parental role model on criminality," pp. 170-180 in R. Cavan (ed.) Readings in Juvenile Delinquency. Philadelphia: J. B. Lippincott.

McDERMOTT, M. and M. HINDELANG (1981) "Juvenile criminal behavior in the United States: its trends and patterns." Analysis of National Crime Victimization Survey Data to Study Serious Delinquent Behavior; Research Monograph 1. National Institute for Juvenile Justice and Delinquency Prevention, Law Enforcement Assistance Administration, U.S. Department of Justice. Washington, DC: Government Printing Office.

MEIER, R. and W. JOHNSON (1977) "Deterrence as social control: the legal and extra-legal production of conformity." American Sociological Review 42: 292-304.

MENARD, S. and B. MORSE (1984) "A structuralist critique of the IQ—delinquency hypothesis: theory and evidence." American Journal of Sociology 89: 1347-1378.

MERTON, R. (1968) Social Theory and Social Structure. New York: Free Press.

MEYERS, A. (1984) "Drinking, problem drinking, and alcohol-related crime among older people," pp. 51-65 in E. Newman et al. (eds.) Elderly Criminals. Cambridge, MA: Oelgeschlager, Gunn and Hain.

MINOR, W. (1977) "A deterrence-control theory of crime," pp. 117-137 in R. Meier (ed.) Theory in Criminology: Contemporary Views. Newbury Park, CA: Sage.

MINOR, W. and J. HARRY (1982) "Deterrent and experiential effects in perceptual deterrence research: A replication and extension." Journal of Research in Crime and Delinquency 19: 190-203.

MOBERG, D. (1953) "Old age and crime." Journal of Criminal Law and Criminology 43: 764-776.

NAROLL, R. (1983) The Moral Order: An Introduction to the Human Situation. Newbury Park, CA: Sage.

NETTLER, G. (1978) Explaining Crime. New York: McGraw-Hill.

NETTLER, G. (1985) "Social class and crime, one more time." Social Forces 63: 1076-1077.

NEWMAN, D. (1984) "Elderly offenders and American crime patterns," pp. 3-15 in E. Newman et al. (eds.) Elderly Criminals. Cambridge: Oelgeschlager, Gunn and Hain.

NYE, F. (1958) Family Relationships and Delinquent Behavior. New York: McGraw-Hill.

O'BRIEN, R., D. SHICHOR, and D. DECKER (1980) "An empirical comparison of the validity of UCR and NCS crime reports." Sociological Quarterly 21: 391-401.

ORSAGH, T. (1979) "Empirical Criminology: interpreting results derived from aggregate data." Journal of Research in Crime and Delinquency 16: 294-306.

PATERNOSTER, R., L. SALTZMAN, T. CHIRICOS, and G. WALDO (1982) "Perceived risk and deterrence: methodological artifacts in perceptual deterrence research." Journal of Criminal Law and Criminology 73: 1238-1257.

PATERNOSTER, R., L. SALTZMAN, G. WALDO, and T. CHIRICOS (1983a) "Perceived risk and social control: do sanctions really deter?" Law and Society Review 17: 457-479.

PATERNOSTER, R., L. SALTZMAN, G. WALDO, and T. CHIRICOS (1983b) "Estimating perceptual stability and deterrent effects: the role of perceived legal punishment in the inhibition of criminal involvement." The Journal of Criminal Law and Criminology 74: 270-297.

PATTERSON, G. (1980) "Children who steal," pp. 73-90 in T. Hirschi and M. Gott-fredson (eds.) Understanding Crime: Current Theory and Research. Newbury Park, CA: Sage.

PATTERSON, G. and T. DISHION (in press) "Contributions of families and peers to delinquency." Research in Criminology.

PESTELLO, H. (1984) "Deterrence: a reconceptualization." Crime and Delinquency 30: 593-609.

PETERSILIA, J. (1985) "Racial disparities in the criminal justice system: a summary." Crime and Delinquency 31: 15-34.

POPE, H., and M. FERGUSON (1982) "Age and anomia in middle and later life: a multivariate analysis of a national sample of white men." International Journal of Aging and Human Development 15: 51-73.

PRUITT, C. and J. WILSON (1983) "A longitudinal study of the effect of race on sentencing." Law and Society Review 17: 613-635.

RANKIN, J. (1983) "The famly context of delinquency." Social Problems 30: 466-479.

REID, S. (1979) Crime and Delinquency. New York: Holt, Rinehart and Winston.

REISS, A. (1951) "Delinquency as the failure of personal and social controls." American Sociological Review 16: 196-207.

REISS, A. and A. RHODES (196!) "The distribution of juvenile delinquency in the social class structure." American Sociological Review 26: 720-732.

RHODES, W. and C. CONLEY (1981) "Crime and mobility: an empirical study," in P. Brantingham and P. Brantingham (eds.) Environmental Criminology. Newbury Park, CA: Sage.

RICHARD, P. and C. TITTLE (1982) "Socioeconomic status and perceptions of personal arrest probabilities." Criminology 20: 329-346.

ROBINSON, W. (1950) "Ecological correlations and behavior of individuals." American Sociological Review 15: 351-357.

ROSEN, L. and K. NEILSON (1978) "The broken home and delinquency," pp. 406-415 in L. Savitz and N. Johnston (eds.) Crime in Society. New York: Wiley.

ROWE, A. and C. TITTLE (1977) "Life cycle changes and criminal propensity." Sociological Quarterly 18: 223-236.

SALTZMAN, L., R. PATERNOSTER, G. WALDO, and T. CHIRICOS (1982) "Deterrent and experiential effects: the problem of causal order in perceptual deterrence research." Journal of Research in Crime and Delinquency 19: 172-189.

SAMPSON, R. (1983) "Structural density and criminal victimization." Criminology 21: 276-293.

SAMPSON, R. (1985a) "Neighborhood and crime: the structural determinants of personal victimization." Journal of Research in Crime and Delinquency 22: 7-40.

SAMPSON, R. (1985b) "Race and criminal violence: a demographically disaggregated analysis of urban homicide." Crime and Delinquency 31: 47-82.

SAMPSON, R., T. CASTELLANO, and J. LAUB (1981) Juvenile Criminal Behavior and Its Relation to Neighborhood Characteristics. Monograph 5, National Institute for Juvenile Justice and Delinquency Prevention. Washington, DC: Government Printing Office.

SAVITZ, K. (1978) "Official police statistics and their limitations," pp. 69-81 in L. Savitz and N. Johnston (eds.) Crime in Society. New York: Wiley.

SAVITZ, L. (1960) Delinquency and Migration. Philadelphia: Commission on Human Relations.

SCHAFER, S. (1976) Introduction to Criminology. Reston, VA: Reston Publications.

SCHAFFER, D. (1979) Social and Personality Development. Belmont, CA: Brooks/Cole.

SCHERMAN, L. (1980) "Causes of police behavior: the current state of quantitative research." Journal of Crime and Delinquency 17: 69-100.

SCOTT, J. (1971) Internalization of Norms: A Sociological Theory of Moral Commitment. Englewood Cliffs, NJ: Prentice-Hall.

SHICHOR, D. (1984) "The extent and nature of lawbreaking by the elderly: a review of arrest statistics," pp. 17-32 in E. Newman et al. (eds.) Elderly Criminals. Cambridge: Oelgeschlager, Gunn and Hain.

SHICHOR, D. and S. KOBRIN (1978) "Note: criminal behavior among the elderly." The Gerontologist 18: 213-220.

SHORT, J. and F. NYE (1957) "Reported behavior as a criterion of deviant behavior." Social Problems 5: 207-213.

SILBERMAN, C. (1978) Criminal Violence, Criminal Justice. New York: Random House.

SIMPSON, J. and M. VAN ARSDOL (1967) "Residential history and educational status of delinquents and nondelinquents." Social Problems 15: 25-40.

SMITH, D. (1984) "The organizational context of legal control." Criminology 22: 19-38.

SMITH, D., C. VISHER, and L. DAVIDSON (1984) "Equity and discretionary justice: the influence of race on police arrest decisions." Journal of Criminal Law and Criminology 75: 234-249.

STAFFORD, M. and S. EKLAND-OLSON (1982) "On social learning and deviant behavior: a reappraisal of the findings." American Sociological Review 47: 167-169.

STARK, R. (1979) "Whose status counts? Comment on Tittle, Villemez and Smith." American Sociological Review 44: 668-669.

STARK, R. and McEVOY (1970) "Middle-class violence." Psychology Today 4: 52-54.

STARK, R., D. DOYLE, and L. KENT (1980) "Rediscovering moral communities: church membership and crime," pp. 43-52 in T. Hirschi and H. Gottfredson (eds.) Understanding Crime: Current Theory and Research. Newbury Park, CA: Sage.

STARK, R., L. KENT, and D. DOYLE (1982) "Religion and delinquency: the ecology of a 'lost' relationship," Journal of Research in Crime and Delinquency 19: 4-24.

STARK, R., W. BAINBRIDGE, R. CRUTCHFIELD, D. DOYLE, and R. FINKE (1983) "Crime and delinquency in the roaring twenties." Journal of Research in Crime and Delinquency 20: 4-23.

STRICKLAND, D. (1982) "Social learning and deviant behavior: a specific test of a general theory': A comment and critique." American Sociological Review 47: 162-167.

SUNDERLAND, E. and D. CRESSEY (1978) Criminology. Philadelphia: Lippincott.

SUNDERLAND, G. (1982) "Geriatric crime wave: the great debate." The Police Chief 49: 40-44.

THORNBERRY, T. and R. CHRISTENSON (1984) "Unemployment and criminal involvement: an investigation of reciprocal causal structures." American Sociology Review 49: 398-411.

THORNBERRY, T. and M. FARNWORTH (1982) "Social correlates of criminal involvement: further evidence on the relationship between social status and criminal behavior." American Sociological Review 47: 505-518.

TILLY, C. (1970) "Race and migration to the American city," in J. Q. Wilson (ed.) The Metropolitan Enigma. Garden City, NY: Doubleday.

TITTLE, C. (1977) "Sanction fear and the maintenance of social order." Social Forces 55: 579-596.

TITTLE, C. (1980) Sanctions and Social Deviance: The Question of Deterrence. New York: Praeger.

TITTLE, C. (1985) "A plea for open minds, one more time: response to Nettler." Social Forces 63: 1078-1080.

TITTLE, C. and W. VILLEMEZ (1977) "Social class and criminality." Social Forces 56: 474-501.

TITTLE, C. and M. WELCH (1983) "Religiosity and deviance: toward a contingency theory of constraining effects." Social Forces 61: 653-682.

TITTLE, C., W. VILLEMEZ, and D. SMITH (1978) "The myth of social class and criminality: an empirical assessment of the empirical evidence." American Sociological Review 43: 643-656.

TITTLE, C., W. VILLEMEZ, and D. SMITH (1982) "One step forward, two steps back: more on the class/criminality controversy." American Sociological Review 47: 435-438.

VISHER, C. (1983) "Gender, police arrest decisions, and notions of chivalry." Criminology 21: 5-28.

VOSS, H. (1966) "Socio-economic status and reported delinquent behavior." Social Problems 13: 314-324.

WEIS, J., J. HALL, J. HENNEY, J. SEDERSTROM, K. WORSLEY, and C. ZEISS (1979) Peer Influence and Delinquency: An Evaluation of Theory and Practice, Part I and Part II. National Institute for Juvenile Justice and Delinquency Prevention. Office of Juvenile Justice and Delinquency Prevention. U.S. Department of Justice. Washington DC: Government Printing Office.

WIATROWSKI, M., D. GRISWOLD, and M. ROBERTS (1981) "Social control theory and delinquency." American Sociological Review 46: 525-541.

WILBANKS, W. (1984a) "The elderly offender: placing the problem in perspective," pp. 1-15 in W. Wilbanks and P. Kim (eds.) Elderly Criminals. New York: University Press of America.

WILBANKS, W. (1984b) "The elderly offender: sex and race variations in frequency and pattern," pp. 41-52 in W. Wilbanks and P. Kim (eds.) Elderly Criminals. New York: University Press of America.

WILBANKS, W. (1985) "Are the elderly treated more leniently by the criminal justice system?" Presented at the Third National Conference on Elderly Offenders, Kansas City, MO, April 25-26.

WILBANKS, W. and D. MURPHY (1984) "The elderly homicide offender," pp. 79-91 in E. Newman, D. Newman, M. Gewirtz, and associates (eds.), Elderly Criminals. Cambridge: Oelgeschlager, Gunn and Hain.

WILKINSON, K. (1980) "The broken home and delinquent behavior: an alternative interpretation of contradictory findings," pp. 21-42 in T. Hirschi and M. Gottfredson (eds.) Understanding Crime: Current Theory and Research. Newbury Park, CA: Sage.

WILSON, J. (1968) Varieties of Police Behavior. Chicago: University of Chicago Press.

WOLFGANG, M., R. FIGLIO, and T. SELLIN (1972) Delinquency in a Birth Cohort. Chicago: University of Chicago Press.

ZATZ, M. (1984) "Race, ethnicity, and determinate sentencing: a new dimension to an old controversy." Criminology 22: 147-171.

About the Contributors

Edgar F. Borgatta is Professor in the Department of Sociology at the University of Washington. He is interested in research on aging with regard to the impact of demographic trends and their consequences within the nation and more generally. He specializes in methodological issues in research.

Thomas K. Burch is Professor of Sociology at the University of Western Ontario. His most recent research has been in household formation in Canada and the United States, and in the relationship between changing age-sex roles and household formation.

Susan De Vos is a Research Associate with the Center for Demography and Ecology at the University of Wisconsin-Madison. She is also affiliated with the Institute on Aging at this University. Her present research interests focus on household structure of families through the life cycle in Latin America and the United States.

Laurie Russell Hatch is Assistant Professor of Sociology at the University of Kentucky. Her areas of interest include family, aging, and social inequality. Her current research focuses on how occupational circumstances and family roles influence men's and women's retirement attitudes and timing.

Kyle Kercher is Assistant Professor of Sociology at Case Western Reserve University in Cleveland. His areas of interest include causes and correlates of crime, moral development, aging, and applied methodology.

M. Powell Lawton has been Director of Behavioral Research at the Philadelphia Geriatric Center for the past 20 years, as well as an Adjunct Professor of Human Development at the Pennsylvania State University and a Research Scientist at Norristown State Hospital. He has done research in the environmental psychology of later life, in assessment of the aged, the psychological well-being of older people, and evaluative studies of programs for the aged and for the mentally ill. He is President of the Gerontological Society of America and is the first editor of the American Psychological Association's new journal, *Psychology and Aging.*

Rhonda J. V. Montgomery is Director of the Institute of Gerontology at Wayne State University in Detroit, Michigan. Her recent work has focused on factors associated with caregiving and the causes and consequences of caregiver burden. She is also interested in health service utilization among the elderly and social policy for the elderly. Currently she is conducting a policy study concerned with the impact of interventions aimed at assisting families who are providing care for the elderly.

Miriam Moss is a Senior Research Sociologist at the Philadelphia Geriatric Center. She is currently project director on research dealing with older people living alone and in their last years of life. She is widely published in social gerontology.

Thomas Pullum is a Professor in the Department of Sociology and a Research Associate in the Population Research Center at the University of Texas at Austin. He was formerly Professor of Sociology at the University of Washington. His main research interests are in kinship and family formation, including variations and changes in fertility, in the United States and in developing countries.

Penny A. Ralston is Associate Professor of Home Economics Education and Assistant Dean of the Graduate College, Iowa State University. Dr. Ralston received her M.Ed. and Ph.D. from the University of Illinois. She is the author of several publications in journals such as *Journal of Gerontology, International Journal of Aging and Human Development, Journal of Applied Gerontology,* and *Educational Gerontology.* Her research interests include senior center utilization and participant characteristics, development and evaluation of educational programs for older adults, and youth's attitudes toward and knowledge of aging.

Donald E. Stull is Assistant Professor of Sociology at the University of Akron in Akron, Ohio. He received his Ph.D. from the University of Washington. His current research interests include family relationships through the life cycle, gender roles, and long-term care of the elderly.

Andrew V. Wister is Research Assistant Professor in the Sociology Department at the University of Waterloo in Ontario, Canada. He is currently undertaking research on living arrangement and housing issues for the elderly. His other research interests include family change, demographic processes, adjustment to widowhood, and social policy.

NOTES

NOTES

NOTES

NOTES